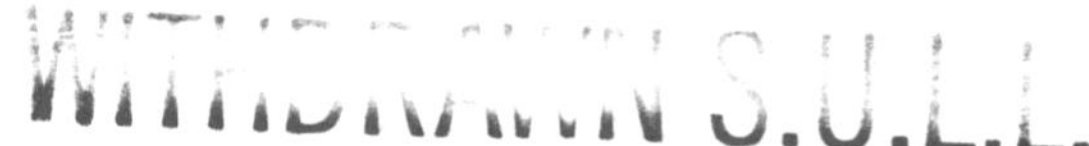

Comparative Politics

The Quest for Theory

James A. Bill
University of Texas at Austin

Robert L. Hardgrave, Jr.
University of Texas at Austin

Charles E. Merrill Publishing Company
A Bell & Howell Company
Columbus, Ohio 43216

MERRILL POLITICAL SCIENCE SERIES

Under the general editorship of

JOHN C. WAHLKE

Department of Political Science
The University of Iowa

Published by
Charles E. Merrill Publishing Company
A Bell & Howell Company
Columbus, Ohio 43216

ISBN: 0-675-09008-3

Library of Congress Catalog Card Number: 72-92139

1 2 3 4 5 6 7 8—78 77 76 75 74 73

Printed in the United States of America

To our parents

Alban and Irene Bill
Reedsburg, Wisconsin

Bob and Orlene Hardgrave
Sonora, Texas

Preface

This study constitutes a theoretical introduction to and an analytical framework for the field of comparative politics. It provides a critical guide to the literature and presents a set of criteria for evaluating works that the student will read subsequently. In particular, this volume represents an attempt to present and analyze the basic approaches to the study of comparative politics. These approaches will be pinpointed as they exist along the road to theory. Rather than offering an encyclopedia of substantive data from the literature of comparative politics, this book seeks to provide the student with a base from which he can more critically judge and evaluate the results of comparative political analysis. Thus, in the context of a course, this volume might be used as a basic text in combination with several empirical studies—cross-national comparisons or analyses of particular political systems.

A major goal of this effort is to differentiate among the various theoretical approaches to the study of comparative politics. By drawing such analytic distinctions, one is better equipped to compare and evaluate approaches. This, in turn, permits the student of politics to make more conscious and rational choices among the conceptual and theoretical tools available in the discipline. Finally, by unravelling the general web of approaches, one can more effectively discover the strengths and weaknesses that are peculiar to each approach. Such reexamination and reassessment is essential to effective theory construction.

Each approach presented in this study is analyzed separately. In actual empirical investigations, however, various approaches are employed simultaneously. In such substantive work, the strengths and weaknesses of particular approaches tend to be obscured and disguised due to the multiple nature of the orientations involved. Through analytic abstraction and differentiation, it is possible to recognize the peculiar qualities of each approach. Such analysis not only fosters an explicit recognition of the conceptual and theoretical apparatus involved, but also promotes a firmer foundation upon which the synthesis of approaches can be constructed. Since each approach is stripped to its core and presented in isolation, the critical evaluation that ensues sometimes appears overly stark in form and harsh in tone. Analysis, which is the separation of any material into its constituent parts, tends always to effect such a portrayal. The process of analyzing theoretical approaches to the study of comparative politics is no exception to this rule.

The theoretical conclusions arrived at in this volume are founded to a large extent upon the empirical experiences of non-Western societies. Although it contains little substantive discussion of Asian, African, Middle Eastern, and Latin American societies, the critique of each of the approaches implicitly incorporates an assessment of the approach vis-á-vis its utility and relevance to the study of Third World political processes. The authors have done intensive field work in South Asia and the Middle East where they have themselves adapted, discarded, and revived a number of intellectual orientations and theoretical approaches. In short, this discussion of the theory-building process consciously attempts to avoid the limitations that flow from a narrow and ethnocentric perspective.

The general goal of this study is to enable students of politics in general and students of comparative politics in particular to recognize and evaluate the basic theoretical approaches to comparative political analysis. Directly related to this general end are four specific goals which involve relating each approach to each other approach, to the theory-building process, to the discipline of political science, and to the fundamental issues of modernization and political development. Although the decision to adopt a particular approach or combination of approaches rests to a large degree upon the issue or problem that is being confronted, it is also dependent upon a clear understanding of the advantages and drawbacks of each orientation in the various approaches to comparative politics. Informed approach selection, integration, and operationalization are critical to the generation of theory and the production of explanation.

This book owes a great deal to the undergraduate and graduate students in comparative politics at the University of Texas at Austin who have struggled both to understand and to instruct. Their questions and suggestions ring through the pages of this study. The strong student support was buttressed by the aggressive but constructive comments proffered by our colleagues in the Department of Government at the University of Texas. Special appreciation is extended in this regard to Roderick Bell, Herbert Hirsch, Carl Leiden, and Joe Oppenheimer. We are also especially grateful and obligated to the following scholars who have read and criticized portions of this manuscript: David Adams of the University of Denver, Stanley J. Heginbotham of Columbia University, Alan Ryan of New College, Oxford, Kenneth Sherrill of Hunter College, John C. Wahlke of the Iowa State University, and Larry B. Hill of the University of Oklahoma. Finally, the authors owe formative intellectual debts to their own mentors in comparative politics and theory—Leonard Binder of the University of Chicago and Harry Eckstein and Manfred Halpern of Princeton University. Although these three scholars may wish to disassociate themselves from the analysis contained in the following pages, they must nonetheless bear the burden of realization that their students will forever plague them.

Contents

I THE SYSTEMATIC STUDY OF COMPARATIVE POLITICS 1

The Traditional Study of Comparative Politics 2
The Transforming Study of Comparative Politics 10
The Theoretical Mold 21
The Essence of Theory 30
The Goals of This Study 40

II MODERNIZATION AND POLITICAL DEVELOPMENT 43

Foundations of the Concept of Development 43
Dichotomous Schemes: Tradition and Modernity 50
Old Problems in the New Study of Change 57
The Challenge of Modernization 62
The Concept of Political Development 66

III POLITICAL CULTURE AND SOCIALIZATION 85

Political Culture 85
Orientation and Behavior 92
The Concept of Sentiment 96
Political Socialization 98
The Problem of Change 108
Socialization in the New Nations 110
Evaluation of the Approach 113

IV GROUP POLITICS 117

Themes and Definitions 119
The Group Approach and Comparative Analysis 121
The Group Approach Analyzed 134

V THE POLITICAL ELITE APPROACH 143

The Pioneers of Elite Analysis 144
Mosca: The Political Class 148
Pareto: The Governing Elite 151
Michels: The Oligarchy 153
Classical Elite Analysis Evaluated 156
Elite Analysis and Theory Building 159
Elite Analysis and Modernization 170

VI CLASS ANALYSIS 175

Obstacles and Objections 175
Class, Society and Politics 178
The Class Concept Defined 183
Groups, Elites, and Classes 191
Class Analysis Evaluated 195

VII FUNCTIONALISM AND SYSTEMS ANALYSIS 201

The Structural-Functional Approach 201
Systems Analysis 217
A Comparative Critique 226

VIII COMPARATIVE POLITICS AND THEORY BUILDING 229

SELECTED BIBLIOGRAPHY 239

INDEX 255

CHAPTER I

The Systematic Study of Comparative Politics

The study of comparative politics is in the midst of fundamental change. In the past quarter century, no part of the discipline of political science has witnessed a more thoroughgoing self-examination and reorientation than has the study of comparative politics. Indeed, its scope and direction have shifted so dramatically that interested students have increasingly felt trapped in a seemingly impenetrable maze of shifting theoretical emphases, unfamiliar methodology, and abstruse terminology. The deprecation and dismantling of traditional approaches to the study of politics have been accompanied by sharp controversy and extended debate. This, in turn, has fostered as much blind dogmatism as it has promoted constructive empirical and theoretical progress.

The transitional nature of comparative political analysis is illustrated by the adamant refusal of many to adopt new perspectives and to move in newly charted directions, while others enthusiastically and uncritically embrace new approaches and methods at first sight. Intense controversy continues to swirl about the following kinds of issues: the definition of politics and the scope of its study; the nature and role of theory; the normative and empirical dichotomy; the value and role of measurement and quantification; the techniques of research in cross-cultural settings; the difference between configurative and comparative study; the relation of interdisciplinary concerns to the study of politics; the need for policy oriented political analysis; and the persisting debates for and against the various theoretical approaches to the study of politics. This list, which contains the perennial issues as well as queries more recently developed, reflects the concern for the very core of political analysis. Confrontation concerning such central issues in fact documents the dynamism that infuses the contemporary study of comparative politics.

The Traditional Study of Comparative Politics

The patterns of the traditional study of comparative politics in American political science were established most firmly during the late nineteenth and early twentieth centuries. During these years, political science developed an identity that resulted in its recognition as a legitimate and fruitful focus of inquiry. At the same time, the important relationship that political analysis maintained with the study of history, philosophy, and law was appreciated and preserved. Traditional comparative political studies reflected a significant concern for both historical perspective and the norms of political behavior. A further contribution of the traditional approach was its role in educating large numbers of American citizens about their own political institutions. Finally, traditional comparative government produced a host of studies that carefully and minutely described political structures and institutions. These studies remain a valuable source of data for comparative political analysis.

Despite contributions such as these, other characteristics infused the traditional study of comparative politics, severely impeding the development of systematic comparative inquiry and comparative political explanation. This may be described in terms of six major characteristics that marked the traditional approach: configurative description, formal-legalism, parochialism, conservatism, nontheoretical emphases, and methodological insensitivity.[1] These characteristics have strongly marked the study of politics in the past and they continue to persist today in varying form and degree.[2]

---

[1]A number of these characteristics were first presented by Roy C. Macridis in *The Study of Comparative Government* (Garden City, N.Y.: Doubleday, 1955). See also Gunnar Heckscher, *The Study of Comparative Government and Politics* (New York: Macmillan, 1957); Bernard E. Brown, *New Directions in Comparative Politics* (London: Asia Publishing House, 1962); Gabriel A. Almond and G. Bingham Powell, Jr., *Comparative Politics: A Developmental Approach* (Boston: Little, Brown, 1966); and David Easton, *The Political System* (New York: Knopf, 1953).

[2]For the best available analytic study of the historical and intellectual patterns that have influenced the development of the study of comparative politics, see Harry Eckstein, "A Perspective on Comparative Politics, Past and Present," in Harry Eckstein and David Apter, eds., *Comparative Politics: A Reader* (New York: Free Press, 1963), pp. 3–32.

Configurative Description Traditional comparative politics emphasized detailed description of particular political systems or particular aspects of these systems. Such procedure was, in fact, not *comparative* politics at all, but was more accurately *configurative* government. The scholar drew configurations of governmental institutions, describing them in varying degrees of intricacy. Characteristic studies included discussions and checklists of important names, dates, relevant historical events, sections of legal and constitutional documents, and committee and cabinet organization.

Most ordinarily, one scholar would present configurative descriptions of four or five European governments within one volume, each described according to its peculiar genius. Following World War II, a trend was established in which different scholars would describe different governments, and these would then be bound together in one volume and presented as a textbook in comparative government. Occasionally, introductions, essays, or monographs would appear, attempting to compare selected aspects of these configurations. Thus, in the introduction of his widely read text, Henry Russell Spencer wrote about the "far-reaching contrasts between Westminster and Paris as to the relation of voters and ministers to elective parliament; between the constitutional kingship that is an honorific badge worn by Victor Emmanuel III of Italy, and that which is a tool deftly wielded by Gustav of Sweden; between Supreme Courts in countries which do and countries which do not possess a strong tradition of constitutional law and custom, which continues and grows and binds while parliamentary measures come and go."[3] At the most, therefore, the traditional study of comparative politics involved comparative description. Most studies, however, concentrated upon configurative descriptions of governments, one by one. Very little is comparative about this kind of exercise.[4]

Formal-Legalism For years, the study of comparative politics reflected a preoccupation with formal structures and legal strictures. Emphasis was placed upon the organized and evident institutions of government, and studies concentrated almost exclusively upon constitutions, cabinets, parliaments, courts, and bureaucracies.

---

[3]Henry R. Spencer, *Government and Politics Abroad* (New York: Henry Holt, 1936), pp. 1–2.

[4]The first two major departures from the emphasis upon configurative description in the study of comparative politics were the enormously important studies of Herman Finer and Carl J. Friedrich. For recent editions of these works, see Herman Finer, *The Theory and Practice of Modern Government,* 4th ed. (London: Methuen, 1961); and Carl J. Friedrich, *Constitutional Government and Democracy,* 4th ed. (Waltham, Mass.: Blaisdell, 1968).

The study of political science as a separate discipline—from which comparative politics developed as a sub-field—evolved out of the study of public law and institutional history.[5] The title of one mid-nineteenth century government textbook reveals the strength of the formal-legal scholarly tradition: *The Citizen's Manual of Government and Law: Comprising the Elementary Principles of Civil Government; A Practical View of the State Governments, and of the Government of the United States; A Digest of Common and Statutory Law, and of the Law of Nations; and A Summary of Parliamentary Rules for the Practice of Deliberative Assemblies.*[6] Courses were frequently in the format of comparative constitutions of the world. In the mid-1920s, the political science department at the University of Michigan offered a course entitled "Charter and Ordinance Drafting." During this same period, Columbia University taught courses under the headings "Statutes" and "Problems of the Law of Taxation."

One of the earliest comprehensive American attempts to prepare a text in comparative politics was Woodrow Wilson's *The State,* first published in 1889.[7] This 686 page study contained a 36 column index that devoted 26 lines to "constitution," 25 lines to "Senate," 23 lines to "law," 19 lines to "legislation," and 12 lines to "township." There was no reference to such concepts as "power," "interest," and "group." One line was devoted to "authority" and "competition," and two lines each to "revolution" and "slavery."

A 1927 Round Table Conference of the American Political Science Association that met to discuss the field of comparative government strongly endorsed the formal-legal perspective. As one participant pointed out, comparative politics should be particularly concerned with "the problems of federalism, judicial procedure, parliamentary practice, administration, and local government." He concluded by stating that "the comparative constitutional law of Anglo-American countries is a most satisfactory field because our law libraries offer unusual facilities."[8] This deep-seated formal-legal tradition which stresses documents rather than political activities and the formal institution rather

---

[5]As late as 1914, only 38 of some 300 American colleges and universities had distinct departments of political science. See Anna Haddow, *Political Science in American Colleges and Universities, 1636–1900* (New York: D. Appleton-Century, 1939), p. 263.

[6]Andrew W. Young, *The Citizen's Manual of Government and Law,* rev. ed. (New York: H. Dayton, 1858).

[7]Woodrow Wilson, *The State: Elements of Historical and Practical Politics* (Boston: D.C. Heath, 1889).

[8]"Reports of Round Table Conferences: Comparative Government," *The American Political Science Review* 21 (May 1927):393.

than the informal processes of competition is still evident in many contemporary studies.

Parochialism Comparative political analysis in the past focused quite exclusively upon European government. But even within the study of comparative European politics, the scope was narrowed to consider again and again the same four societies: Great Britain, France, Germany, and Russia. The tenacity of this pattern is illustrated by the fact that eight different comparative texts devoted exclusively to this popular foursome consider these societies one by one in the identical country by country order.[9] Various reasons have been proposed for this constricted emphasis. John Burgess wrote at the turn of the century that Great Britain, the United States, Germany, and France were "the most important states of the world."[10] One set of authors, who also included Italy in their study, attempted to explain their five country choices as follows: "The omission of materials relating to the other governments of Europe was due entirely to the lack of space and a desire to concentrate on the countries commonly included in college and university courses."[11] In a much more recent volume, the authors stress the "big four" which they "deem most significant to Americans both as factors in international politics and as political laboratories."[12] Other reasons for this scholarly ethnocentricity derive from the knowledge gap caused by the inaccessibility of data and the inconvenience of research in much of the world. Since most non-Western societies apparently lacked formal governmental structures, many felt that little of substance was there to study anyway. Thus, one pioneering political analyst could write in 1900 that Asian nations "have created no real states."[13]

---

[9]These texts, all published in the 1960s, are the following: Robert G. Neumann, *European Government,* 4th ed. (New York: McGraw-Hill, 1968); Herman Finer, *The Major Governments of Modern Europe* (Evanston, Ill.: Row, Peterson, 1962); Fritz Nova, *Contemporary European Governments* (Baltimore: Helicon Press, 1963); Alex N. Dragnich, *Major European Governments,* rev. ed. (Homewood, Ill.: Dorsey Press, 1966); Gwendolyn M. Carter and John H. Herz, *Major Foreign Powers,* 6th ed. (New York: Harcourt Brace Jovanovich, 1972); Roy C. Macridis and Robert E. Ward, eds., *Modern Political Systems: Europe,* 2nd ed. (Englewood Cliffs, N.J.: Prentice-Hall, 1968); and James B. Christoph and Bernard E. Brown, eds., *Cases in Comparative Politics,* 2nd ed. (Boston: Little Brown, 1969); Samuel H. Beer and Adam B. Ulam, eds., *Patterns of Government: The Major Political Systems of Europe,* 3rd ed. (New York: Random House, 1973). The last three studies listed contribute sections of valuable theoretical and comparative analysis.

[10]John Burgess, *Political Science and Comparative Constitutional Law* (Boston: Ginn, 1900), Vol. 1, p. 90.

[11]Norman L. Hill and Harold W. Stoke, *The Background of European Governments,* 2nd ed. (New York: Farrar and Rinehart, 1940), pp. vii–viii.

[12]Carter and Herz, *Major Foreign Powers,* pp. v–vi.

[13]Burgess, *Political Science and Comparative Constitutional Law,* p. 4.

Concentration upon the more "advanced," "democratic," and "civilized" political systems carried a significant normative impact as well. If comparative methods were at all introduced, American and British political structures were elevated as the models. Other political systems tended to be presented as deviations from these standard cases and were thus often labelled as exotic or alien. Most discussion of African, Asian, and Middle Eastern governments was left to archaeologists, orientalists, missionaries, diplomats, and itinerant adventurers. The impact of this neglect by social scientists is still seen in the absence both of incisive studies of numerous non-Western societies as well as of cross-societal studies that are able to draw deeply upon the Afro-Asian experience for purposes of comparative analysis.

Conservatism In the past, the study of comparative government tended to stress the permanent and the unchanging. Political institutions were examined in terms of an evolutionary development which found fulfillment in the immediate present. But while these institutions had a past, they apparently had no future. The study of British politics, for example, was reduced to a description of the evolution of institutions beginning with the Magna Carta. This historical process traced the unfolding of the unique and enduring in British political experience. Hill and Stoke wrote in the preface of their volume that they placed emphasis "on the more basic and permanent phases of the European political systems."[14] Scholars consciously stressed the changeless qualities of political institutions and such phrases as "time-honored," "immutable," and "eternal" principles of government were sprinkled throughout the literature. The various texts reflected a deep feeling for tradition, precedent, order, stability, and conserving evolution.

This insensitivity to political modernization and transforming change was in large part due to the crucial period that political science spent in incubation with precedent-sensitive law and past-oriented history. In a world where the processes of political development were perceived as having "remained throughout clear and almost free from considerable irregularities" and in which "the lines of advance are seen to be singularly straight,"[15] it is not surprising that there was little concern for or study of political dynamism.

For many years, Western scholars and statesmen alike assumed that all political systems were inexorably and inevitably evolving in the

---

[14]Hill and Stoke, *Background of European Governments,* p. viii.

[15]Wilson, *The State,* p. 576.

direction of liberal democracy. In such a climate, democracy and stability were inextricably intertwined in the minds of men. Alexis de Toqueville wrote, for example, that individuals living in democratic communities "are forever varying, altering, and restoring secondary matters; but they carefully abstain from touching what is fundamental."[16]

Nontheoretical Emphases The concern for rigorous and systematic empirical theory building was foreign to most traditional scholars of comparative politics. Virtually no attempt was made to formulate tightly organized and testable generalizations relating to political processes. Although classic political thinkers such as Machiavelli, Hobbes, Montesquieu, and Madison introduced numerous perceptive and incisive general insights into political study, they were not primarily concerned with operationalizing concepts and building scientifically rigorous theory. The great nineteenth century political sociologists, including Weber, Mosca, and Pareto, were somewhat more interested in scientific theory building. Within the early modern political science discipline, however, there was little concern for generating empirical theory.

The traditional emphasis was placed heavily upon normative theorizing, a process that had deep roots in the history of American political science. Indeed, the study of politics was first smuggled into the curriculum of American colleges and universities under the cloak of such subjects as moral philosophy and ethics. William Paley, whose classic study had a profound impact upon American political science in its formative years, wrote: "Moral Philosophy, Morality, Ethics, Casuistry, Natural Law, mean all the same thing: *namely, that science which teaches men their duty and the reasons of it.*"[17]

By the turn of the twentieth century, the emphasis had come to focus on "the good citizen." Knowledge of the duties and responsibilities of citizenship and a deepening preoccupation with political philosophy became the major concerns of political science. The former emphasis has survived until contemporary times in the curriculum of many of the nation's secondary schools, while the latter continues as an important branch of political study in American universities and graduate schools. The concern with normative political theory, or political philosophy, therefore, traditionally dominated the discipline in a manner that tended to discourage the appearance of empirical theory. Subjects such

---

[16]Alexis de Tocqueville, *Democracy in America* (New York: Vintage Books, 1961), Vol. 2, p. 270.

[17]William Paley, *The Principles of Moral and Political Philosophy* (Bridgeport, Conn.: M. Sherman, 1827), p. 17.

as moral philosophy, ethics, and jurisprudence were considered and explicitly termed "science."[18]

A certain traditional bias has been formed against a science of politics since it was (and still is in many circles) argued that applying rigorous theoretical investigation in this area was impossible. The emphasis was placed upon the unique, variable, and unpredictable nature of political phenomena. Although nineteenth century thinkers sometimes termed politics a science, they tended to define the latter in broad and varying ways. Thus, Sir Frederick Pollock argued at the turn of the century that "there is a science of politics in the same sense, and to the same, or about the same, extent, as there is a science of morals."[19]

Methodological Insensitivity The field of comparative politics was from the beginning limited in the methodological and research procedures that its practitioners could utilize. Other than the classic schemes introduced by scholars such as John Stuart Mill, Auguste Comte, and Herbert Spencer, little was available in the character of refined and systematic comparative methodology.[20] Even these classic presentations of research logic, however, were seldom utilized by political scientists. Techniques for selecting, collecting, and ordering data were undeveloped and unsystematic. Dominant methods consisted of irregular observation and secondary source examination. These kinds of procedures were buttressed and reinforced by personal intuition, impression, and insight, the value of which varied greatly from scholar to scholar. An early president of the American Political Science Association once stated that "politics is an observational, and not an experimental science."[21]

Sophisticated and systematic methodology was by and large not an area of basic concern to traditional comparative government scholars. The descriptive and formal-legal study of institutions did not demand deep behavioral and scientific research techniques. The gathering and perusal of documents and the intellectual interpretation of the legal intricacies of formal government were considered relevant procedures to the tasks at hand. Not surprisingly, therefore, as late as 1933 only one American university offered a thorough course in the methods of politi-

---

[18]Witness the titles of the following studies: Laurens P. Hickok, *A System of Moral Science* (Schenectady, N.Y.: Van Debogert, 1853); and Noah Porter, *The Elements of Moral Science, Theoretical and Practical* (New York: Charles Scribner's Sons, 1885).

[19]Sir Frederick Pollock, *An Introduction to the History of the Science of Politics,* rev. ed. (London: Macmillan & Co., 1920), p. 2.

[20]See John Stuart Mill's *A System of Logic,* esp. Books III, IV, and VI; Auguste Comte's *Positive Philosophy;* and Herbert Spencer's *Essays Scientific, Political, and Speculative.*

[21]A. L. Lowell, "The Physiology of Politics," *American Political Science Review* 4 (February 1910):10.

cal research.[22] More surprisingly, a 1952 analysis of 797 research projects underway in 61 different graduate departments of political science indicated that at most 15 of these studies were at all concerned with methodology and/or the philosophy of science.[23]

These six characteristics have been presented as the predominant features that have marked the traditional study of comparative politics. Their presence and importance have varied from study to study as works occasionally appeared that were not so parochial or descriptive or static. Indeed, few studies exhibited all six characteristics in an unadulterated and unequivocal manner. However, these were the primary patterns, and their presence is still very much in evidence in current comparative political analysis. The interesting question concerns how these characteristics were able to dominate the field for so long and why they continue to persist and to exhibit such lasting endurance.

Much of the reason resides in the manner in which all six patterns interlock and intertwine. An emphasis on one tends to develop and reinforce an emphasis on another. Parochialism, for example, increases the stress placed upon configurative description and formal-legalism. An interest in political systems in general involves increased contexts of analysis, inviting more comparison and less configuration. An acquaintance with less developed and non-Western societies indicates very soon the futility of understanding politics primarily in terms of laws and formal rules. Parochialism also lends support to the static emphasis. A more serious concern with those societies that reflect the widest gaps between "tradition" and "modernity" calls attention to the critical problems of social change and political development. In its limited analytical contexts, parochialism also does little to suggest comparative theory building and it fails to stimulate thought towards the development of fundamentally new research techniques. Pronounced ethnocentric political analysis has the further effect of indiscriminately portraying one's own political system as the ideal system. In this kind of situation, normative theory clearly assumes more importance than empirical theory.

Descriptive and formal-legal emphases in turn encourage parochialism. The minute description of formal institutions does not lend itself to the study of non-Western politics, nor do descriptive and formal approaches do much to recommend the significance of the fundamental processes of political change. Thus, these traditional characteristics sup-

---

[22] Milton W. Thompson, "The Present Status of University Instruction in Political Science," *The Historical Outlook* 24 (March 1933):143.

[23] Claud E. Hawley and Lewis A. Dexter, "Research and Methodology: Recent Political Science Research in American Universities," *American Political Science Review* 46 (June 1952):484.

port one another through a persisting pattern of reciprocal reinforcement. This explains why leading scholars as late as 1944 could refer to comparative government "as a discipline in a status of suspended animation."[24]

The Transforming Study of Comparative Politics

The 1950 Hawley-Dexter study of political science research underway in American universities tallied only 7 out of 797 projects that could be clearly and definitely considered in the area of comparative politics. The entire article devoted but four sentences to comparative politics and concluded: "At best, emphasis on the field is slight."[25] Less than a decade and a half later, Somit and Tanenhaus found the profession designated comparative politics as the field in which the most significant work was being done.[26] The first issue of the new journal *Comparative Politics,* published in 1968, described the field as an "exploding culture" and in the same issue one theoretician referred to the "continuing fermentation process" of the "new comparative politics."[27]

This changing emphasis is documented in more detail in figure 1, which indicates the twentieth century development of comparative politics courses in ten leading American universities. In 1925, approximately one of ten undergraduate political science offerings was in the comparative area; in 1945, the proportion had come to be nearly one in five; and in 1965, the proportion was rapidly approaching one in three.[28]

An early reaction to the traditional study of comparative politics began to develop in the 1920s, but not until the mid-1950s did significant and systematic new trends began to appear. The formation and

[24]See Karl Loewenstein's comments challenging this assertion in "Report on the Research Panel on Comparative Government," *American Political Science Review* 38 (June 1944:540–41.

[25]Hawley and Dexter, "Research and Methodology," p. 482. This study indicates that when the meaning of the term "comparative government" is stretched to its broadest dimensions 34 research projects might be included within this area.

[26]Albert Somit and Joseph Tanenhaus, *American Political Science: A Profile of a Discipline* (New York: Atherton Press, 1964), pp. 55–57.

[27]*Comparative Politics* 1 (October 1968):52. The theorist quoted is Joseph LaPalombara.

[28]The 26 comparative courses that these ten universities (Princeton, Harvard, University of California at Berkeley, Columbia, University of Michigan, Yale, Cornell, Stanford, University of Wisconsin, and Dartmouth) offered in 1925 had expanded to 144 by 1965. The University of Wisconsin alone offered more courses in comparative politics in 1965 than had all ten universities combined in 1925. Yale University and the University of Michigan which offered one and two comparative courses respectively in 1925 each listed 16 in 1965. Figure 1 provides a university-by-university breakdown of the growing proportion of comparative courses offered in political science departments between 1925 and 1965. The trend is pronounced. The percentage of undergraduate comparative courses tripled during the 40 year period at such universities as Dartmouth, Harvard, Yale, Wisconsin, and Berkeley. By 1965, over 40 percent of undergraduate political science offerings at Yale were in the area of comparative politics.

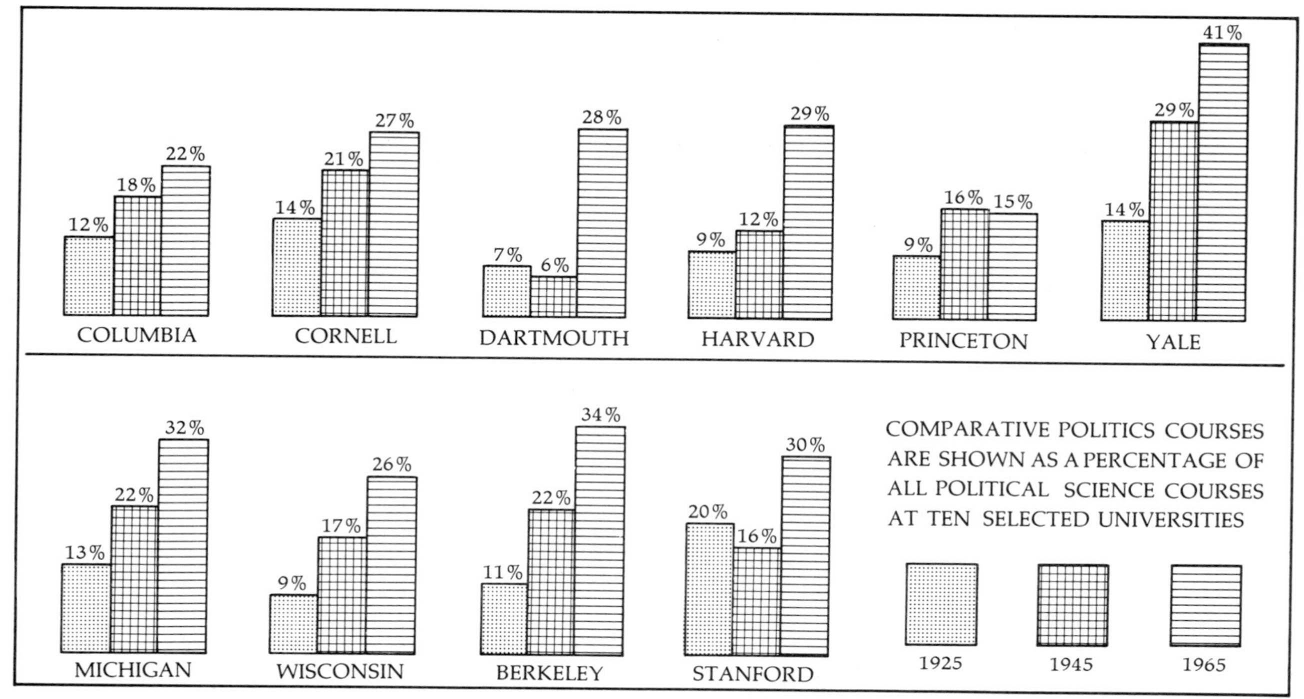

FIGURE 1 Growth of Comparative Politics Courses, 1925–1965

crystallization of these trends developed as a direct reaction to the characteristics that marked traditional comparative politics. As particular aspects of traditional comparative study were deeply attacked, the impact was felt throughout the network of mutually reinforcing emphases and methods. The behavioral revolution that occurred during this period assisted in undercutting former approaches and in unravelling the web of past procedures.

Within the social sciences in general, dissatisfaction with approaches that have stressed only configurative description has been increasing. Scholars have become preoccupied with "how" and "why" questions and are less prone to rest content with the "what" inquiry. Methods and modes of *explanation* have received growing attention in each of the major fields generally included under the term political science.[29] Although describing political configurations is an essential part of scientific political analysis, it represents only one important step in the process of theory building. It is increasingly recognized that description must be utilized to promote explanation and that configurative exercises must become an integrated part of comparative analysis. Much of the reason for the demise of the purely descriptive emphasis resides in the close relationship that existed between this focus and the prevalence of formal-legalism.[30]

The roots of reaction to formal-legalism in American political science can be traced back to the 1920s and 1930s and to the pioneering writings of scholars such as George E. G. Catlin, Charles E. Merriam, and Harold Lasswell.[31] These political scientists made similar pleas in the sense that they all cautioned against formal-legal-institutional study and called instead for the comparative analysis of power and control relationships. Not until the 1950s and 1960s, however, was the traditional emphasis upon formal-legalism replaced by a series of systematic new approaches, all of which purported to confront and explain the fundamental patterns of political behavior. A major reason for the steady decline of formal-legal study resided in the continuing discovery and increasing knowledge of political systems where formal-legal structures were obviously only of peripheral importance.

---

[29]In comparative politics, see especially Howard A. Scarrow, *Comparative Political Analysis: An Introduction* (New York: Harper & Row, 1969); in the field of international politics, see David V. Edwards, *International Political Analysis* (New York: Holt, Rinehart and Winston, 1969).

[30]For an important article that explores the relationship between comparative and configurative study in comparative research, see Sidney Verba, "Some Dilemmas in Comparative Research," *World Politics* 20 (October 1967):111–27.

[31]For a fine historical analysis stressing the contribution to political science of scholars such as these, see Richard Jensen, "History and the Political Scientist," in Seymour Martin Lipset, ed., *Politics and the Social Sciences* (New York: Oxford University Press, 1969), pp. 1–28.

The mid-twentieth century witnessed the development in the United States of a deep and real interest in African, Asian, Middle Eastern, and Latin American political processes. The era of colonialism had been shattered; the United States had established firm political and economic commitments throughout the world; sharp competition developed between rival ideologies in the struggle over the non-Western areas of the world; international and interregional organizations of varying import and impact were born; and spectacular technological advances in the fields of transportation and communications increased contact between and among all societies.

At the same time, area study programs began to appear within American universities, and students increasingly began to study the history, language, culture, and politics of societies that had been formerly considered exotic.[32] Private and public scholarship funds were made available to students and scholars interested in the sociopolitical processes of Afro-Asian and Latin American societies. Supported by a background in social science and methodology and armed with linguistic tools such as Arabic, Hindi, Swahili, Persian and Japanese, these scholars have rapidly increased the contexts necessary to successful comparative study. Table 1 reveals the tremendous growth of non-Western and Latin-American oriented courses in the political science curricula of ten major universities.

In 1925, only one course in non-Western politics was offered in all of the ten institutions of higher learning studied. This was Political Science 135 taught at the University of California and entitled "Political Development of China." Four decades later, these universities accounted for 65 different courses in non-Western and Latin-American political systems. Today, approximately every other course offered in the field of comparative politics concerns Third World systems. Many decades ago, George Catlin warned that "political studies will not be advanced by a political science of the arm-chair."[33] What Karl Loewenstein pointed out a bit prematurely in 1944 can now be reiterated more appropriately: "Supercilious aloofness from other peoples' political institutions—another facet of intellectual isolationism—has definitely come to an end."[34]

---

[32]The recent nature of the revolution of area studies can be seen by dating the first issue of each of a dozen leading area journals: *The Journal of Asian Studies* (1941); *The Middle East Journal* (1947); *Middle Eastern Affairs* (1950); *Journal of East Asian Studies* (1951); *Central Asian Review* (1953); *Asian Affairs* (1956); *African Studies Bulletin* (1958); *Journal of Inter-American Studies* (1959); *Asian Survey* (1961); *Journal of Modern African Studies* (1963); *Middle Eastern Studies* (1964); *Latin American Research Review* (1965); and *International Journal of Middle East Studies* (1970).

[33]George E. G. Catlin, *A Study of the Principles of Politics* (New York: Macmillan, 1930), p. 51.

[34]Loewenstein, "Report on the Research Panel," p. 541.

TABLE 1 Development of Comparative Politics Courses in Ten American Universities, 1925–1965[a]

Year	*Political Science Courses*	*Comparative Courses*	*Percentage of Total Offerings*	*Non-Western Courses*[b]	*Percentage of Total Offerings*	*Percentage of Comparative Offerings*
1925	232	26	11.2	1	0.4	3.8
1945	308	56	18.2	16	5.2	28.6
1965	491	144	29.3	65	13.2	45.1

SOURCES: Bulletins, catalogues, registers, and announcements for the particular years of the universities involved.

[a]The ten universities and the exact years of compilation are the following: Princeton (1923-24, 1945-46, 1965-66), Harvard (1924-25, 1944-45, 1964-65), University of California at Berkeley (1925-26, 1942-43, 1965-66), Columbia (1924-25, 1948-49, 1966-67), University of Michigan (1925-26, 1945-46, 1964-65), Yale (1924-25, 1944-45, 1965-66), Cornell (1929-30, 1943-44, 1965-66), Stanford (1925-26, 1945-46, 1966-67), University of Wisconsin (1925-26, 1942-44, 1966-68), and Dartmouth (1925-26, 1944-45, 1967-68). Only undergraduate course offerings are included in these tabulations.

[b]"Non-Western" here includes Latin America and excludes the Soviet Union.

In the 1950s, political scholars began to focus seriously and systematically upon the problems of political development and social change. Words such as "modernization," "change," "development," "revolution," "reform," "transformation," and "process" began to appear everywhere in the literature. Leading comparative specialists immediately confronted these issues and their analyses remain among the most incisive contributions to the study of political change. Scholars such as Samuel P. Huntington, Gabriel Almond, Fred W. Riggs, David E. Apter, Manfred Halpern, Lucian W. Pye, Dankwart A. Rustow and Leonard Binder continue to move the study of comparative politics in a direction that will enable it to address successfully the challenge of modernization. Not accidentally, most of these theoreticians are fundamentally concerned with non-Western societies. A deep knowledge of such societies directly reflected the existence of rapid change, great development gaps, and concomitant tension, frustration, conflict, and violence. This, in turn, occasioned a reexamination of Western political patterns in general and American politics in particular.[35] The issue of political development is presented as holding universal import.

Finally, contemporary comparative politics is marked by a deepening concern for theoretical and methodological considerations. Here the thorny issue of behavioralism becomes acutely relevant. Voices for and against a changing political science have used this term to buttress their respective stances and to vindicate their obvious dogmatism. The "behavioralists" too often have considered themselves scientific sages because of their facility in the arts of statistics and neology, while the "anti-behavioralists" have tended to sneer defensively at anything and everything that suggests scientific method and theory building. Few have bothered to define "behavioralism" cautiously, concisely, and clearly.

Behavioralism

Behavioralism can be defined as the systematic search for political patterns through the formulation of empirical theory and the technical analysis and verification thereof. Behavioralism involves two basic emphases: "the formulation of concepts, hypotheses, and explanations in systematic terms" and "empirical methods of research."[36] The essence

---

[35]See, for example, Stokely Carmichael and Charles V. Hamilton, *Black Power: The Politics of Liberation in America* (New York: Vintage Books, 1967).

[36]Samuel J. Eldersveld, Alexander Heard, Samuel P. Huntington, Morris Janowitz, Avery Leiserson, Dayton D. McKean, David B. Truman, "Research in Political Behavior," in S. Sidney Ulmer, *Introductory Readings in Political Behavior* (Chicago: Rand McNally, 1961), p. 8.

of a behavioral science is that "all hypotheses be experimentally confirmed by reference to publicly observable changes in behavior."[37]

According to David Easton, the behavioral movement within the discipline of political science has involved special concern for the following eight characteristics: regularities, verification, techniques, quantification, values, systematization, pure science, and integration.[38] There are regularities in political behavior that can be stated and tested. The discovery and validation of such uniformities can be furthered and ascertained by rigorous techniques involving the selection, collection, and ordering of data. This task can in turn be facilitated by the introduction of precision through measurement and quantification. Behavioralism does not discard values, but rather stresses the need to distinguish carefully and analytically between fact and value.[39] Systematization involves a recognition of the need to relate empirical research to theory building and to stress the symbiotic relationship between theory and data. The emphasis called "pure science" refers to the logical precedence of theory and explanation to the specific activities of political engineering. Finally, behavioralism often calls for the utilization of cross-disciplinary approaches, methods and findings.

Various scholars have stressed one or another of these characteristics of behavioralism. Indeed, intrabehavioral divisions have increasingly resulted in allegations and accusations reflected in terms such as "nonbehavioral," "prebehavioral," "pseudobehavioral," and "postbehavioral." Perhaps the major fissure in past dialogue among behavioralists has been between those seeking to confine the meaning of behavioralism to the sophisticated employment of quantitative techniques and precision of measurement and those identifying behavioralism more with the scientific methodology of conceptual rigor, hypothesis formulation, and theory building. Although controversies such as these have often generated a narrow academic dogmatism, they have also contributed to a continuing evaluation and reassessment of current trends in political analysis.

The behavioral approach as equated with technique has been challenged fundamentally by what is increasingly referred to as the "postbehavioral revolution." David Easton's "Credo of Behavioralism" is being replaced by what he terms a "Credo of Relevance."[40] The postbehavioral revolution does not displace behavioralism in its broader

---

[37] *American Behavioral Scientist* 7 (September 1963): supplement, p. 6.

[38] David Easton, "The Current Meaning of 'Behavioralism,' " in James C. Charlesworth, ed., *Contemporary Political Analysis* (New York: Free Press, 1967), pp. 16–17.

[39] "Behavioralism," therefore, is not to be confused with "behaviorism," a movement in psychology most closely associated with the work of John B. Watson. The latter school proposed to omit the subjective (e.g., values, ideas, purposes) from scientific inquiry.

[40] See David Easton, "The New Revolution in Political Science," *American Political Science Review* 63 (December 1969):1052. This is a superb analysis of the postbehavioral revolution.

dimension but sensitizes the political scientist to the role of values and the importance of policy considerations. This trend will play an important role in charting the future directions into which the study of comparative politics will move.

The major dissatisfaction with behavioral emphasis has been the preoccupation with technique rather than substance, contemplative theorizing rather than policy relevant theory, and neutral academic conservatism rather than progressive social transformation. The marked tendency to theorize about theory (metatheory) and to amass and study only that data conducive to exact measurement has occurred in a world increasingly convulsed by division, discrimination, poverty, and violence. In his 1969 presidential address to the American Political Science Association, David Easton stated that "the search for an answer as to how we as political scientists have proved so disappointingly ineffectual in anticipating the world of the 1960s has contributed significantly to the birth of the postbehavioral revolution." He pointed out that "mankind today is working under the pressure of time. Time is no longer on our side."[41] Sheldon Wolin argues that in a world that "shows increasing signs of coming apart . . . official political science exudes a complacency which almost beggars description."[42] Hans J. Morgenthau has spoken about the tendency of contemporary political scientists "to retreat from the burning political problems of the day into a kind of methodological or factual irrelevance." He argues that the "innocuous" political scientists of the past "created a respectable methodological wall between themselves and the political problems of the day and were exactly those who were irrelevant then and who are forgotten today."[43] August Heckscher has written that "research which disavows any responsibility except that of being objective and non-utilitarian may well qualify as 'pure.' But it is the kind of purity which a society—particularly a society in an age of change—can overvalue."[44]

In a world caught in the midst of fundamental change, problem selection and problem solution assume increasing importance. There is an embryonic but marked trend away from the speculative/contemplative and a movement towards the meaningful application of social and political knowledge. The methodology of behavioral science is increasingly being related directly to the sociopolitical issues of the day. Thus, David Easton foresees a "politicization of the profession," while Harold

[41]Ibid., p. 1053.

[42]Sheldon S. Wolin, "Political Theory as a Vocation," *American Political Science Review* 63 (December 1969):1081.

[43]Hans J. Morgenthau, "Conference Discussion," in James C. Charlesworth, ed., *A Design for Political Science: Scope, Objectives, and Methods* (Philadelphia: The American Academy of Political and Social Science, 1966), pp. 134, 136.

[44]August Heckscher, "A Research for Action," *Current Magazine* (July 1960):5, as quoted in Bradford B. Hudson and Howard E. Page, "The Behavioral Sciences: Challenge and Partial Response," *American Behavioral Scientist* 6 (April 1963):4.

Lasswell calls for a "problem-solving attack on political science."[45] Yet, despite the fact that the priorities and perspectives of the discipline are being increasingly reassessed as technique is measured against substantive contribution, there is little doubt that the behavioral concern for methodological rigor will long remain. The question is one of emphasis and purpose, and the movement is one that stresses the confluence of scientific methodology and problem solution. In the mainstream of this postbehavioral movement are a number of related tendencies that promise to characterize the future study of comparative politics. There are four broad categories of trends.

Interdisciplinary Cooperation and Communication

With the drive for more problem-centered inquiry, the often artificial and arbitrary lines which divide the social sciences become increasingly irrelevant and indefensible. Many of the important strides already made in the recent resurgence in the comparative study of politics owe a great deal to methods and approaches borrowed from sociology. Examples include structural-functional analysis, as well as refined group, class, and elite analysis. Future developments indicate an intellectual convergence of political science with economics, anthropology, and social psychology. In the search for truly comparative tools for the analysis of social and political behavior, for example, a growing number of political scientists have turned to economic rationality models and to supply and demand laws applied to collective goods. Others are moving in the direction of political anthropology as they seek to ferret out and compare the informal patterns of interpersonal power and authority relationships. The findings of social psychology are increasingly drawn upon by scholars seeking to apply learning theory to the study of political socialization. These represent only a few examples of an accelerating drive that is beginning gradually to break down the barriers that divide the social sciences. Departments, divisions, and institutes of social science are increasingly becoming realities. The methodologies, theoretical frameworks, and conceptual apparatus pertinent to comparative analysis are neither monopolized by nor concentrated within the discipline of political science. In this spirit leading scholars such as David Singer and David Easton have already called for the establishment of a "Federation of Social Scientists."[46]

These interdisciplinary trends, however, may carry far beyond inter-social scientific inquiry. The study of comparative political patterns, for

[45]Easton, "The New Revolution," p. 1060; and Harold Lasswell, "The Future of the Comparative Method," *Comparative Politics* 1 (October 1968):11.

[46]Easton, "The New Revolution," pp. 1060–61.

example, may gain profoundly from advances made in the biological sciences. The developing field of ethology or social biology, which concerns the analysis of animal behavior and its patterns of evolution, has already suggested numerous provocative propositions that may go far to explain the behavior of the political animal. The crucial comparative problems of conflict and cooperation closely parallel the ethologists' concern for the processes of aggression and sociability. Scholars such as Konrad Lorenz and John N. Bleibtreu provide particularly stimulating studies of animal behavioral patterns that are often explicitly related to human political behavior. Comparative political analysts are only now beginning to open their lines of communication in these less orthodox directions.[47]

Intersocietal Cooperation and Comprehension

Comparative political study has been marked by a continually widening universe of analysis that began with the narrow plethora of studies focusing almost exclusively upon Euro-American societies. This was followed by country monographs and area studies. Political analyses of particular societies that can be utilized as case studies for purposes of comparative analysis and theory building are in many cases nonexistent. Country monographs that are conceptually sound, theoretically rigorous, and problem oriented are extremely rare. Area studies which further intraregional, cross-societal investigation are only in the infancy of their development. By providing multicontextual laboratories, such studies often encourage the comparative analysis necessary to the generation of meaningful hypotheses. Future problem-oriented comparative study will draw upon the experiences of societies and cultures anywhere and everywhere in the world. Subcultures and intrasocietal structures and institutions will also serve as units for comparative study. Country and area studies will no doubt continue to develop and increase along with what Dankwart Rustow calls "cross-regional comparison."[48]

The tremendous task of confronting the multitude of varied laborato-

---

[47]See, for example, Konrad Lorenz, *On Aggression,* trans. Marjorie Kerr Wilson (New York: Harcourt, Brace and World, 1966); and John N. Bleibtreu, *The Parable of the Beast* (New York: Macmillan, 1968). For an introduction of this approach to political science, see Albert Somit, "Toward a More Biologically-Oriented Political Science: Ethology and Psycho-pharmacology," *Midwest Journal of Political Science* 12 (November 1968), 550–67; W.J.M. MacKenzie, *Politics and Social Science* (Baltimore: Penguin Books, 1967), Chapter 11; Peter A. Corning, "The Biological Bases of Behavior and Some Implications for Political Science," *World Politics* 23 (April 1971): 321–70; Jerone Stephens, "Some Questions about a More Biologically Oriented Political Science," *Midwest Journal of Political Science* 14 (November 1970): 687–707; and especially Fred H. Willhoite, Jr., "Ethology and the Tradition of Political Thought," *Journal of Politics* 33 (August 1971): 615–41.

[48]Rustow, "Modernization and Comparative Politics: Prospects in Research and Theory," *Comparative Politics* 1 (October 1968): 46–47.

ries of comparative political experience will increasingly be shared by social scientists representing nations throughout the world. African, Asian, and Latin American scholars, for example, have begun to team with Europeans and Americans for the study of political processes in the societies under investigation. Scholars native to the particular society under study carry social and cultural advantages that enable them to analyze the system from within. The outside scholars bring a differing and more detached perspective to bear upon that same political system. Cooperative efforts by such multinational research teams should improve immeasurably our understanding of comparative political processes. Scattered but serious efforts in this direction have already begun to bear fruit.

Special note might be made of the growing proclivity to treat the study of American politics as an integral part of the study of comparative politics. Surely, many of the intradisciplinary divisions are as artificial and sterile as some of the interdisciplinary distinctions referred to above. Problems such as political development, poverty, violence, and discrimination are as much a challenge to the United States as to any other society. The experiences and patterns that mark the most elaborately studied society in the world are increasingly becoming an essential part of comparative political investigation. There is no reason why an "American specialist" should not be a "comparative specialist" and vice-versa. The political and personal patterns that mark American subcultures, for example, may very well more closely approximate those of certain Afro-Asian societies than those of white middle class America.[49] This kind of comparative analysis promises to generate provocative and policy relevant hypotheses.

Academic Cooperation and Communication

Partially because of the growing demand upon the scholar of comparative politics to be a theoretician, historian, statistician, mathematician, sociologist, psychologist, linguist, and country/area specialist, and partially because of the deep need for more imaginative analyses and prognoses, increasing communication and continuing scholarly dialogue must inevitably develop. The establishment of institutes, seminars, workshops, and conferences on a more regular basis can, and in some cases has already begun to, mean a cooperative cross-fertilization of ideas. Harold Lasswell, for example, has recently called for "a nationwide and worldwide network of counterpart seminars."[50] Such semi-

---

[49]Compare, for example, the findings of the two following studies: Dean Jaros, Herbert Hirsch, Frederic J. Fleron, Jr., "The Malevolent Leader: Political Socialization in an American Sub-Culture," *American Political Science Review* 62 (June 1968): 564–75; and Marvin Zonis, "Political Elites and Political Cynicism in Iran," *Comparative Political Studies* 1 (Fall 1968), 351–71.

[50]Lasswell, "The Future of the Comparative Method," p. 17.

nars will contribute to the presentation, sharing, probing, and generation of ideas. A system of in-depth dialogue and confrontation may someday absorb students, researchers, and faculty of varied disciplines and backgrounds in a systematic effort to improve our understanding of comparative political systems.

Interprocedural Experimentation and Adaptation

The drive to refine the experimental, statistical, and mathematical techniques which were emphasized and developed during the behavioral period will continue. New quantitative procedures and measurement devices will be constantly generated to seek precision whenever and wherever possible. Social science research and experimental specialists will increasingly serve as indispensable technicians for the translation, measurement, and testing of hypotheses. The continuing advance of technology will build deeper sophistication into methods of gathering, cataloguing, storing, retrieving, and comparing data. In the search for more accurate data, methodology and techniques are beginning to be borrowed from sciences such as biology and physiology.

At the heart of the behavioral movement and the continuing transformation of the study of comparative politics has been a growing concern for theory. Much of the controversy that swirls about behavioralism and postbehavioralism concerns the role of problems, approaches, taxonomies, and data in the theory building process. The trend to theory means many things to many people, and because of this it demands explicit examination and clarification.

The Theoretical Mold

> The spirit of generalization should dominate a university . . . . During the school period the student has been mentally bending over a desk; at the university he should stand up and look around. . . . The function of the university is to enable you to shed details in favor of principles.
>
> Alfred North Whitehead[51]

During a plane trip to three societies outside of the United States, an American traveler who is interested in the question of whether there is a relationship between a society's legislative system, literacy rate, and form of government first visits country x which he knows is a Middle Eastern monarchy. During his stay there, the visitor notes an absence of any legislature and the presence of a high illiteracy rate. He then travels to country y which is a Southeast Asian monarchy where he again observes the absence of legislative politics and the existence of a

[51]Alfred North Whitehead, *Aims of Education* as quoted in Philipp Frank, *Philosophy of Science* (Englewood Cliffs, N.J.: Prentice-Hall, 1957), pp. xiii–xiv.

high rate of illiteracy. He next travels to country *z* in Africa about which he has no political knowledge. Here, the traveler notes the absence of any legislature along with high illiteracy. He concludes that this country is a monarchy.

In this situation, the traveler engaged in both inductive and deductive mental processes. In his first two experiences, the absence of a legislature and the existence of a high rate of illiteracy went together with a monarchical form of government. This was the case in the first country and it was confirmed in the second society. Although this is an obviously weak basis for conclusion, it is still enough to make a crude induction, i.e., to generalize from particular facts. The observer expected to find a monarchy if illiteracy prevailed and legislatures were nonexistent. From this, the generalization was formulated that all countries lacking legislatures and possessing high rates of illiteracy are monarchies. Upon visiting another highly illiterate and "legislatureless" society, he concluded: All "legislatureless" and highly illiterate societies are monarchies; this society is "legislatureless" and highly illiterate; therefore, this society is a monarchy. This is a logical case of deduction, i.e., formulating a specific conclusion on the basis of a general assumption. In this described reasoning process, a generalization was first established by induction and upon this generalization was founded a deduction.

The above example represents a step-by-step replication of the method of scientific investigation presented by the great nineteenth century scientist, Thomas H. Huxley.[52] Huxley once defined science as "trained and organized common sense" and told his readers that theory building is something you engage in "every day and every hour of your lives."[53] Albert Einstein has written that "the whole of science is nothing more than a refinement of everyday thinking."[54] The focus upon theory and the scientific method represents the heart of the behavioral and postbehavioral movements in contemporary political science. Nevertheless, the concept *theory* remains surrounded by tremendous confusion, and many students of comparative politics still recoil mentally when confronted with the subject. There are, of course, many reasons for this apprehensive attitude.

The concept theory has been treated in an offhand and rather cavalier manner even by leading scholars of political science. The concept has been left completely undefined;[55] it has been defined indirectly;[56] it

---

[52]Huxley, however, discusses sourness as it follows from hardness and greenness in apples. See "The Method of Scientific Investigation," in Leo E. Saidla and Warren E. Gibbs, eds., *Science and the Scientific Mind* (New York: McGraw-Hill, 1930), pp. 131–41.

[53]Ibid., p. 132.

[54]Albert Einstein, *Out of my Later Years* (London: Thames and Hudson, 1950), p. 59.

[55]See, for example, Oran Young, *Systems of Political Science* (Englewood Cliffs, N.J.: Prentice Hall, 1968); and Scarrow, *Comparative Political Analysis*.

[56]See, for example, Heinz Eulau, *The Behavioral Persuasion in Politics* (New York: Random House, 1963), pp. 24–31.

has been defined ambiguously;[57] and it has been equated with other equally confusing terms such as model and method.[58] The situation has been muddied considerably by the necessary consideration of several additional ill-defined and ambiguously-presented concepts, all of which are crucially related to theory and the process of theory building. These concepts include approach, conceptual framework, definitional system, taxonomy, classificatory scheme, typology, model, generalization, hypothesis, law, and paradigm. Philosophers of science themselves have been unclear and inconsistent in their usage of such terms. Certainly no common, agreed-upon system of definitions exists that even begins to distinguish and relate a comprehensive list of these important concepts. The political scientists' usage of these terms is considerably more confused since their views are shaped by sporadic secondhand reliance upon different philosophers of science.[59] A further cause of this confusion is the fact that a terminology generally agreed upon is as much the outcome of scientific progress as the precondition of it.

The difficulties have been compounded and continue to increase as scholars feel compelled to make perfunctory bows in the direction of these key concepts. Therefore, the literature is sprinkled with loosely presented terms that happen to be most crucial to the theorizing process. There are, for example, theoretical and conceptual approaches, theoretical and conceptual frameworks, theoretical and conceptual systems, theoretical and conceptual models, and theoretical and conceptual typologies. Approaches, taxonomies, typologies, and models are constantly presented and portrayed as theories. Taxonomies and typologies are sometimes treated as synonyms; other times they are sharply distinguished. This same kind of inconsistency marks the situation of model-paradigm and generalization-theory. Leading and theory conscious political scientists the caliber of David Easton, for example, have equated the term "conceptual framework" with "a body of theory," "a theoretical model," and "a system of working hypotheses."[60]

The following discussion represents an attempt to define, distinguish, and relate explicitly those concepts central to theory building in comparative political analysis. The uncertainty that surrounds these concepts is well recognized, but it is also relevant to note that serious

---

[57]See, for example, David Easton, ed., *Varieties of Political Theory* (Englewood Cliffs, N.J.: Prentice-Hall, 1966).

[58]See, for example, Martin Shubik, "The Uses of Game Theory" in Charlesworth, *Contemporary Political Analysis,* pp. 239–72.

[59]For an excellent analysis of the implications of the political scientists' secondhand acquaintance with this subject matter, see John G. Gunnell, "Deduction, Explanation, and Social Scientific Inquiry," *American Political Science Review* 63 (December 1969): 1233–46. In our presentation, we have attempted to take into special consideration what the physical scientists have written and said about their methodology and theory. Physics has come under closest scrutiny in this regard.

[60]Easton, *The Political System,* p. 57. In these same pages, Easton denounces "vague, ill-defined concepts" and "ambiguous terms."

dispute exists about even more fundamental matters such as the very methods presented in philosophy of science.[61] The "scientific method" itself is by no means something agreed upon and accepted.[62] The reader should not be surprised, therefore, if the definitions and distinctions presented herein do not always coincide with his own conceptions or those of a particular school of methodology. The definitions in the following list have been formulated in view of five major considerations: (1) general views on these concepts as expressed in the philosophy of science literature; (2) meanings of these terms as used in the natural and physical sciences; (3) importance of simplicity and conciseness; (4) need to relate these concepts one to another and then to the overall process of theory building; and (5) concern for the subject matter and problems of comparative politics.

Approach: A predisposition to adopt a particular conceptual framework and to explore certain types of hypotheses towards the generation of theory.

Conceptual Framework: A schema of explicitly defined and differentiated concepts necessary to the study of a particular subject.

Taxonomy: A subject divided into classes distinct from one another. A taxonomy is also referred to as a *classificatory scheme* or *classification system.*

Typology: That kind of taxonomy in which classificatory distinctions are graded or ordered.

Model: A theoretical and simplified representation of the real world.

Generalization: Statement of uniformities in the relations between two or more variables of well-defined classes.

Hypothesis: A generalization presented in tentative and conjectural terms.

Theory: A set of systematically related generalizations suggesting new observations for empirical testing.

Law: A hypothesis of universal form that has withstood intensive experimentation.

Paradigm: The worldview which legitimates the scientific community's consensus on what constitutes exemplary scientific research.

---

[61]See the debate that follows upon John Gunnell's article, "Deduction, Explanation, and Social Scientific Inquiry" in the December 1969 issue of *The American Political Science Review.*

[62]Eugene Meehan writes, therefore, that "we are in no position to assert confidently that certain roads to theory ought to be closed." See Meehan, *The Theory and Method of Political Analysis* (Homewood, Ill.: Dorsey Press, 1965), p. 42. This is one of the best and lucid discussions of social science methodology and theory.

Approach and Theory One of the most important concepts to the systematic investigation of comparative politics is reflected in the term *approach.* Basically a very simple concept, the idea of approach has in many respects become one of the most often misunderstood and distorted. The major reason for the difficulty inheres in a persisting proclivity among scholars to label and present certain approaches as theories. Such terms as "group theory," "functional theory," and "systems theory," are prime examples of this confusion. These three, for example, are approaches, and it is difficult to see how they can be termed theories since they are insufficiently articulated in terms of the systematic relationship of hypotheses.

An approach is a predisposition to adopt a particular conceptual framework and to explore certain types of hypotheses towards the generation of theory. At bottom, an approach is the particular orientation that one adopts when addressing a subject or issue. It is the line of advance that a scholar takes in initiating his investigation. This orientating framework is of crucial import to the theorizing process since it determines what sets of concepts, questions, perspectives, and procedures the researcher will adopt in pursuing his inquiry. The approach that one selects will decidedly shape the hypotheses that are generated and ultimately the theory that is formulated. An approach may be implicit or explicit; it may be crudely developed or highly refined; and it may be utilized either to describe or explain.

This volume is pre-eminently a critical survey of various theoretical *approaches* to the study of comparative politics. It is *not* a survey of theories. Rigorous, systematic, and explicit theories of politics are still in relatively embryonic stages of development. Approaches, however, provide the frameworks within which theories are constructed. This aspect and function of an approach will be strongly emphasized in the following pages. The major concern herein is for developing approaches to theory. The relation of an approach to a theory is of vital importance to this study. Thus, we use the term *theoretical approach.*

Conceptual Frameworks A conceptual framework is here considered more the equivalent of a definitional schema than of some broader system of classification or theory.[63] More accurately, it is a schema of explicitly defined and differentiated concepts that are necessary to the study of a selected subject. A conceptual framework provides a systematic arrangement of those conceptual tools that accompany a particular theoretical approach. It must not under any circumstances be considered

[63]For a discussion of this latter view of conceptual framework, see Easton, *The Political System,* pp. 57–61.

theory since it neither generalizes nor explains. A well-formulated and rigorously constructed conceptual framework, however, is an essential element in the theorizing process. If the basic concepts of an approach are ambiguous, then the resultant theory will also be ambiguous. A confusing, unclear, or contradictory conceptual schema signals confusion for any theoretical edifice that might rise around such a framework. For this reason, Arthur Stinchcombe writes that "social theorists should prefer to be wrong rather than misunderstood."[64]

The process of conceptualization is a complex one since it is directly entwined with such theory relevant exercises as classification and generalization. Concepts themselves can be classified according to the level of abstraction or stage of generality at which they are located. Karl Popper, for example, distinguishes between universal and individual concepts. According to Popper, terms such as "dictator," "planet," and "H_2O" refer to universal concepts while "Napoleon," "the earth," and "the Atlantic" are corresponding individual concepts.[65] A number of notable attempts have recently been made to confront this issue of generality with specific regard to comparative political and sociological study. One scholar writes about universal, general, and configurative conceptualizations which in turn correspond to high, medium, and low level categorizations.[66]

Another pair of theorists analyze the situation in terms of concepts dichotomously viewed as observables and constructs.[67] Observable concepts are susceptible to direct sensory observation and exist at a relatively low level of generalization. Constructs are general abstractions of persons, places, or events. The process by which one moves from the observable level of conceptualization to the more abstract constructual level has been termed abduction.[68] Observable or low level concepts are grounded more in the "real" world and tend to preserve the details and intricacies of the situation under investigation. The more abstract species of concept lends itself readily to generalization and "can transcend the limits of individual instances precisely because its terms are not completely dependent upon any one of these cases or

[64]Arthur Stinchcombe, *Constructing Social Theories* (New York: Harcourt, Brace and World, 1968), p. 6.

[65]Sir Karl R. Popper, *The Logic of Scientific Discovery* (New York: Harper Torchbook, 1965), pp. 64–68.

[66]Giovanni Sartori, "Concept Misformation in Comparative Politics," *American Political Science Review* 64 (December 1970): 1033–53. This is one of the more distinguished contributions to our knowledge of theory building in comparative politics.

[67]David Willer and Murray Webster, Jr., "Theoretical Concepts and Observables," *American Sociological Review* 35 (August 1970): 748–57.

[68]See ibid., p. 754. Abduction is a term that refers to concept formation and must therefore be distinguished from the process of induction and deduction.

a sum of them for their meaning."[69] Despite all this, both levels of conceptualization are crucial to theory construction. Also, a scholar's awareness of these kinds of conceptual distinctions is critical to successful theorizing.

One of the first requirements of scientific theory building is that the basic concepts be presented explicitly and clearly. Implicit conceptual frameworks invite imprecision and misunderstanding. This has been particularly so in comparative political analysis where the most vital concepts carry an extraordinary amount of definitional haze and ambiguity. Examples include terms such as "group," "class," "power," "authority," "structure," and "system." Despite this, scholars of comparative politics continue to leave crucial concepts undefined, and when they do indulge in definition they do so sporadically and unsystematically. The general trend seems to be that only graduate students are expected to provide rigorous conceptual schemata which must necessarily preface their term papers and theses. The point is not to support exercises in verbal hair splitting and definition bickering, but rather to stress the important theoretical role of clear and consistent conceptual presentation. Carl G. Hempel argues that the first fundamental requirement for scientific theory building is "a clear specification of the basic concepts. . . ."[70] One Nobel prize winner argues that all science "depends on its *concepts.* These are the ideas which receive names. They determine the questions one asks and so the answers one can get. They are more fundamental than the theories, which are stated in terms of them."[71]

Taxonomies, Typologies, and Models Taxonomies, typologies, and models contribute significantly to the theorizing process. Very often they are presented as theory, but like conceptual frameworks they are neither generalizing nor explanatory instruments. Richard Rudner summarizes this situation perfectly when he describes the activity of constructing taxonomies, typologies, and models as "theoretical work" but not "formulations of theory."[72]

A taxonomy (also referred to as a classificatory scheme or classification system) is a subject divided into classes distinct from one another.

---

[69]Ibid., p. 753.

[70]Carl Hempel, *Aspects of Scientific Explanation* (New York: Free Press, 1965), p. 150.

[71]Sir George Thomson, *The Inspiration of Science* (London: Oxford University Press, 1961), p. 4.

[72]Richard Rudner, *Philosophy of Social Science* (Englewood Cliffs, N.J.: Prentice-Hall, 1966), p. 28. Rudner, therefore, chooses to term these kinds of formulations as "nontheoretic"; Eugene Meehan uses the term "quasi-theory"; and Harry Eckstein refers to "pretheory."

In this kind of classification exercise, an object either falls into a defined class or it does not, depending upon whether or not it possesses the characteristics essential to inclusion in that class. Because of the shaded, graded, and changing nature of much of the subject matter central to sociopolitical affairs, however, classification is difficult. It is certainly often impossible to classify with any kind of precision. A typology carries more flexibility than a taxonomy since it permits ordered classificatory distinctions. Typologies introduce a more subtle and precise method of classification which is rendered especially so by the possibility for the introduction of quantitative techniques. Formulations that concentrate upon continua, axes, polarities, and serials are typologies, not taxonomies.[73]

A model is a theoretical and simplified representation of the real world.[74] It is an isomorphic construction of reality or anticipated reality. A model, by itself, is not an explanatory device, but it does play an important and directly suggestive role in the formulation of theory. By its very nature it suggests relationships. Whereas taxonomies and typologies divide and order, models reconstruct. The jump from a model to a theory is often made so quickly that the model is in fact believed to be the theory. A model is disguised as a theory more often than any other concept. This confusion has been complicated by the recent popularity of the term *paradigm*—a concept often confused with both model and theory.

In a general sense, the concept of paradigm is closely related to the idea of model since it is derived from the Greek term *paradeigma* meaning to set up as an example. For purposes of comparative political analysis, however, paradigm will be defined in a sense relatively akin to the meaning introduced by Thomas Kuhn, whose work has had a decided impact upon theories of scientific development.[75] The concept of paradigm refers to the fact that (1) the particular scientific community holds basic assumptions about what it is investigating; and (2) examples of recognized exemplary scientific research exist that are accounted for in terms of these assumptions. An individual who accepts this basic world view as well as the research that develops from these

---

[73]This basic distinction between taxonomy and typology has been drawn from the work of Carl Hempel. See Hempel, *Aspects of Scientific Explanation,* pp. 151–54.

[74]An unambiguous, but slightly more specialized, definition of model is presented by May Brodbeck who sees model "in terms of an isomorphism between theories." Brodbeck, "Models, Meaning, and Theories," in Llewellyn Gross, ed., *Symposium on Sociological Theory* (New York: Harper & Row, 1959), p. 379.

[75]Thomas Kuhn, *The Structure of Scientific Revolutions,* 2nd ed. (Chicago: University of Chicago Press, 1970).

assumptions is regarded as a bona fide member of the scientific community. A paradigm, then, is the worldview which legitimates the scientific community's consensus on what constitutes exemplary scientific research.[76]

Taxonomies, typologies, and models perform several positive functions in the theorizing process. They describe, order, clarify, stimulate, and compare. Typing and classifying, for example, are first methods of description. The systematic and ordered nature of such description makes it an especially valuable tool to theory building. Indeed, the ordering of data serves as a catalyst in the theorizing process because it clarifies what is usually very complex subject matter, and serves to stimulate hypotheses and generate theory. A tidy taxonomy or a refined model often reveals patterns and relations that were formerly concealed by the haphazard and jumbled arrangement of data. The very exercises of classifying, typing, and modeling also often suggest new connections and relations that can be framed as tentative generalizations. Finally, whether it is classes or types on the one hand or isomorphisms on the other, an element of implicit or explicit comparison is always involved. One class or type is, at least in some respects, compared to another class or type, and continual and reciprocal comparison is involved between models and the objects they seek to represent.

One of the major difficulties inherent in the intensive construction of taxonomies, typologies, and models involves a loss of scientific perspective. The development and refinement of these kinds of mental constructs becomes an end in itself. Taxonomies and models are developed, defended, discarded, redeveloped, and redefended in a ceaseless intellectual exercise. This kind of process can be quite fruitful if the theoretician remembers exactly what he is doing and realizes exactly what are the intellectual contributions of the exercise. If, however, the theorist presents these exercises as theory, he may in fact be impeding the theorizing process. Not only does he twist and distort the meaning of theory, but he also invests a great deal of energy in projects not related to theory-building. This "taxonomizing" or "modelmania" results, therefore, in the proliferation of sterile constructs that rest outside the process of theory building.

Despite dangers such as these, taxonomies, typologies, and models represent important steps on the road to theory. "Scientific explanation requires the systematic ordering and classification of empirical data."[77]

---

[76]We are indebted to Alan Ryan for this clarifying definition and discussion.

[77]Meehan, *The Theory and Method of Political Analysis,* p. 40.

The Essence of Theory

The analysis of comparative political theory requires that an early distinction be drawn between two types of theory, normative theory and empirical theory. Traditionally, the field of political theory within the discipline of political science concerned itself with the study of normative theory. The emphasis was placed upon norms, i.e., rules and standards, of political behavior. Investigation centered upon how man should or ought to act politically, and the history of the development of political values and goals dominated the study of political theory. Discussions concerning such fundamental values as justice, equality, freedom, and democracy have long existed at the core of normative political theory. This important area of analysis continues to contribute to political science and is now referred to as political philosophy as well as political theory. Empirical theory refers to a reliance upon experience, observation, and experiment. The basic concern is with actual and observable behavior rather than with proper or desirable behavior. Empirical theory involves the observation, generalization, and explanation of actual (empirical) behavior. In this study, theory always refers to empirical theory unless otherwise noted.[78]

A theory is a set of systematically related generalizations suggesting new observations for empirical testing. Thus defined, the concept "theory" contains three major elements: (1) theory always involves generalization, i.e., it includes statements that highlight uniformities between two or more variables; (2) theory suggests new observations, i.e., it draws relations that carry different explanations of empirical reality; and (3) theory is testable. The formulated generalizations must possess the capacity to be tested, i.e., to be falsified on the basis of evidence drawn from empirical examples. A theory is a general statement that systematically calls attention to regularities and patterns. Carl G. Hempel writes that besides a clear specification of the basic concepts, a scientific theory requires: (1) a set of general assumptions; (2) a connection between the theoretical statement and observable phenomena; and (3) "testability-in-principle" of the theory, i.e., the presence or absence of observable phenomena measured against the theory will provide confirming or disconfirming evidence concerning the theory.[79]

Various types of generalizations fall within our definition of theory. These range all the way from generalizations of probable applicability to generalizations of invariable applicability. One of the most lucid

---

[78]David Easton discusses this same distinction but uses the terms "value theory" and "causal theory." See *The Political System,* pp. 52–53.

[79]Hempel, *Aspects of Scientific Explanation,* pp. 150–51.

classifications of generalizations has been provided by Eugene Meehan who distinguishes universal generalizations, probabilistic generalizations, and tendency statements. According to Meehan, a universal generalization is phrased in terms of "All *A* is *B*" or "If *A* then *B*." An example relevant to comparative political analysis and one that at the same time preserves some modicum of credibility would be: "All military coups that result in a change in political elites are planned and engineered by middle-ranking army officers."[80] The probabilistic generalization is limited to those statements in which a particular percentage is an integral part of the generalization. An example would be: "Eighty-five percent of military coups that result in a change in political elites are planned and engineered by middle-ranking army officers." Finally, an example of a tendency statement is as follows: "Military coups that result in a change in political elites tend to be planned and engineered by middle-ranking army officers." All of these classes of statements are theoretical but only universal and probabilistic generalizations can be termed strictly theory.[81]

One of the key components of a theory is that it must carry the capacity to be falsified. If empirical evidence exists that contradicts the theoretical statement, then the latter may be refuted. Usually, it is necessary that the contradicting evidence be reproducible or recurring in order to disconfirm the theory under question.[82] It is impossible to confirm or prove a theory. This is why theory construction is a continuing and open-ended process. The distinguished physicist Richard Feynman summarizes this important point concerning the essence of theory in the following terms:

> There is always the possibility of proving any definite theory wrong; but notice that we can never prove it right. Suppose that you invent a good guess, calculate the consequences, and discover every time that the consequences you have calculated agree with experiment. The theory is then right? No, it is simply not proved wrong. In the future you could compute a wider range of consequences, there could be a wider range of experiments, and you might then discover that the theory is wrong. That is why laws like Newton's laws for the motion of planets last such a long time. He guessed the law of gravitation,

---

[80]This is a rather limited and context-bound example of a universal generalization. It indicates how restricted we are in utilizing the concept "universal generalization" in the present state of comparative political analysis.

[81]For Meehan's classification of generalizations and for his definition of theory, see *The Theory and Method of Political Analysis,* pp. 91–93, 128–32.

[82]For a sophisticated discussion of the issue of falsifiability see Popper, *The Logic of Scientific Discovery,* esp. pp. 78–92.

> calculated all kinds of consequences for the system and so on, compared them with experiment—and it took several hundred years before the slight error of the motion of Mercury was observed. During all that time the theory had not been proved wrong, and could be taken temporarily to be right. But it could never be proved right, because tomorrow's experiment might succeed in proving wrong what you thought was right. We never are definitely right, we can only be sure we are wrong.[83]

In the social sciences there is often a deceptive confidence in low level theoretical statements since they appear to resist falsification. This confidence is certainly premature for two basic reasons: (1) no theory is ever confirmed and all such statements require time to be tested; and (2) many theoretical statements are presented in forms that make falsification impossible. As such, they cannot be referred to as theory. The political science literature is laden with statements that are purported to be theory but are in fact so broad, indefinite, flexible, and ambiguous that they can indefinitely resist falsification. Feynman correctly points out that "you cannot prove a vague theory wrong."[84] And as a leading scholar of applied mathematics writes: ". . . a theory that is not rigid enough to be disproved is just a flabby bit of talk. A theory is scientific only if it can be disproved. But the moment you try to cover absolutely everything the chances are that you cover nothing."[85]

Tendency statements fall into this intellectual trap. It is extraordinarily difficult, if not impossible, to falsify such statements. For this reason, tendency statements cannot be accurately considered theory. They can, however, serve an important function in the theory building process since they can act as general orientation guides out of which theory can be fashioned. Tendency statements can be highly suggestive and intellectually provocative and, if refined, can often form the basis of theory. It is true that "a good tendency statement may be far more useful in the explanation of political phenomena than a precise statistical generalization that deals with trivia."[86] And it is also true that a continual exercise in building, connecting, and refining these kinds of generalizations leads slowly in the direction of probabilistic and universal theory. The process is one.

---

[83]Richard Feynman, *The Character of Physical Law* (Cambridge, Mass.: M.I.T. Press, 1965), pp. 157–58.

[84]Ibid., p. 158.

[85]H. Bondi, *Assumption and Myth in Physical Theory* (Cambridge: University Press, 1967), p. 12.

[86]Meehan, *The Theory and Method of Political Analysis,* p. 110.

The subject matter of comparative politics is such that theoreticians have not moved much beyond the generation of tendency statements and probabilistic generalizations. There has been an orderly retreat away from the drive for universal generalizations or high level theory and various scholars have coined various terms for the kind of theory they feel social scientists should develop. Thus, there has been a call for "singular generalizations," "narrow gauge theory," "middle range theory," "partial theories," "piecemeal theoretical insights," and "modest general propositions."[87] The changing, uncertain nature of political processes has been one major reason for the difficulty in building high level theory. (It was Albert Einstein who once pointed out that politics is more difficult than physics.) Another problem is the difficulty of gathering relevant data and the further dilemma of measuring that data or the relations that link that data.

Thus, even probabilistic theory is difficult to develop in comparative politics. Only in cases of less complex empirical issues where it is easy to collect relevant data can one build low level probabilistic theory. It has been clearly and correctly pointed out that:

> Probability can only be stated in numerical terms when the phenomena to which it relates can be measured additively. In political science, that class of measurable phenomena is quite limited and it is obvious that many significant events cannot be so measured, though they are worth explaining. We can produce precise statements about voting behavior, or population movements, or various phases of economic activity, but the range of phenomena is narrow and the boundaries of the phenomena are not easily defined.[88]

Comparative political analysis, therefore, continues to oscillate between tendency statements and probabilistic generalizations. The drive to construct theory is confined largely to the area of relatively low level empirical generalizations.

The Process of Theory Building

The actual example of theory building presented at the beginning of this section represents a crude exercise reflecting the core of the overall theorizing process sometimes referred to as the scientific method. Scientific theory building involves the interrelated processes of problemation,

---

[87]The first two terms belong to David Easton. The others have been used by Robert Merton, Charles P. Kindleberger, Arthur L. Burns, and V. O. Key respectively.

[88]Meehan, *The Theory and Method of Political Analysis,* p. 114.

observation, generalization, confirmation, and application.[89] (See figure 2.) These overlapping steps or stages are herein analytically distinguished one from the other for purposes of more detailed analysis. Despite the constant movement back and forth between and among these various processes, they are presented in the order in which they most often and logically occur.

Problem selection is one of the most important, if least discussed, exercises in theory building. This involves the determination of issues to be theorized about and the construction of patterns of questions to be raised. It is, or course, necessary to theorize *about* something, to draw relations between certain variables, to explain certain phenomena. The importance of a theory about hair styles of world political leaders is highly questionable, no matter how rigorous and refined this theory may be. Similarly, a precise and well-formulated theory about electoral patterns in the Afro-Asian world may be of little value if the votes cast in these settings reflect nothing about the actual power and authority relations in this region. The business of problem selection is that part of the theoretical process often referred to as the "context of discovery." Norwood R. Hanson stresses the crucial nature of this context when he argues that "the ingenuity, tenacity, imagination and conceptual boldness which has marked physics since Galileo shows itself more clearly in hypothesis-catching than in the deductive elaboration of caught hypotheses.[90] Barrington Moore writes that "techniques alone cannot define what is scientifically worth investigating."[91]

The process of successful theory construction relies heavily upon such considerations as intuition, imagination, insight, guesses, and hunches. Although the social and political sciences tend to play down this aspect of scientific inquiry, the more exact sciences cannot seem to stress these elements enough. The important role of chance and the unconscious is also an oft discussed topic in the literature on scientific method and theory construction in the physical and biological sciences.[92] James B. Conant has written, for example, that "the great

[89]For the equation of the last four of these processes with the scientific method, see Hugh Grayson-Smith, *The Changing Concepts of Science* (Englewood Cliffs, N.J.: Prentice-Hall, 1967), p. 5.

[90]Norwood Hanson, *Patterns of Discovery* (Cambridge: University Press, 1965), p. 72.

[91]Barrington Moore, *Political Power and Social Theory* (New York: Harper Torchbooks, 1962), pp. 93–94.

[92]For an interesting discussion of the role that chance plays in scientific inquiry, see W.I.B. Beveridge, *The Art of Scientific Investigation* (New York: Norton, 1957), pp. 27–40, 160–68. In these pages, Beveridge discusses twenty-nine important scientific discoveries that occurred by chance. Two important analyses of the relation between the unconscious and scientific discovery are: Jacques Hadamard, *The Psychology of Invention in the Mathematical Field* (Princeton: Princeton University Press, 1945), pp. 21–42: and Einstein, *Out of My Later Years,* pp. 59–65.

working hypotheses in the past have often originated in the minds of the pioneers as a result of mental processes which can be best described by such words as 'inspired guess,' 'intuitive hunch,' or 'brilliant flash of imagination.' "[93] Sharp intuitive capacities are invaluable in the selection of key problem areas and in the generation of theory.

In social and political analysis no less than in physical inquiry the ability to make the right guesses about the right issues is a crucial consideration. At any point in the theorizing process intuition can serve as the triggering mechanism that uncovers important and previously hidden patterns. New hypotheses are often generated on the basis of sensitizing hunches. One of the important keys in developing comparative political analysis is for the rigorous logicians and methodological technicists to make room for this more artistic component of science. At the same time, intuitive insights acquire more meaning when they spring up within a well organized context of theory construction. Insights, no matter how profound, must be harnessed and ordered if they are to yield fruitful explanation.

Even more dramatically illustrative of this point is the role that chance plays in scientific investigation. Chance is a significant variable and deserves recognition but its positive effects occur most readily in the correct setting. One scientist writes that "probably the majority of discoveries in biology and medicine have been come upon unexpectedly, or at least had an element of chance in them, especially the most important and revolutionary ones."[94] Two other scientists point out, however, that "chance favors the prepared mind. The great chance discoveries in science were made by people who distinguished themselves by other work as well. It is only the master of his subject who can turn to his advantage the irrational and the unsuspected."[95] The theoretical processes of problemation and discovery, in short, require a climate of informed flexibility.

Theory building requires a special kind of imagination, sensitivity, and creativity. In a limited sense, this can be stimulated by such theoretical exercises as classifying, typing, and modeling. It can also be partially developed by a broad knowledge of and deep insight into world history.

---

[93]James Conant, *Science and Common Sense* (New Haven: Yale University Press, 1951), p. 48.

[94]Beveridge, *The Art of Scientific Investigation,* p. 31. Perhaps no better example is provided of the role that chance and intuition play in scientific discovery than that of the process by which the genetic code was broken. This is vividly described in intensely personal terms in James D. Watson, *The Double Helix: A Personal Account of the Discovery of the Structure of DNA* (New York: Atheneum, 1968).

[95]Gerald Holton and Duane H. D. Roller, *Foundations of Modern Physical Science* (Reading, Mass.: Addison-Wesley, 1958), p. 249.

And finally, the kind of imagination required to sensitize one to fundamental problems can be encouraged by an ability to think in terms of continual comparison. In the end, however, there is as yet no definite information explaining why some scholars operate well and why others are uncomfortable and unproductive in the context of discovery.

Systematic observation is the next step of the theoretician. Included within this procedure are the development of conceptual frameworks, taxonomies, typologies, and models. Data is collected and classified in accord with "the scientific activity of description." [96] As there can be no explanation without description, this procedure assumes great importance. Even areas in the physical sciences including certain branches of biology are still primarily involved in the observation and classification stages of theory building. Careful and patient observation provides the basis for generalization which in turn yields explanation and understanding. When observation suggests certain uniformities and regularities, one may formulate an hypothesis or tentative generalization. This generalization is then subjected to continual testing by recourse to renewed and expanded observational procedures. No theory is ever finally and irrevocably confirmed, but the longer one survives rigorous testing the more powerful it becomes as an explanatory device.

Embedded within this brief discussion is implicit reference to a reciprocal inductive-deductive interaction. The contention that theory is essentially a deductive operation simplifies and distorts the process considerably. The idea that generalizations are somehow spun deductively and then tested misrepresents a situation which "is much more fluid than this and undoubtedly always involves an inductive effort."[97] Theories are formulated on the basis of observation, experience, and evidence. Often generalizations thus formed become the basis for deduced conclusions. There is a constant movement back and forth between research and hypothesis, observation and generalization, fact and theory. Hempel points out that the two processes are "inseparably linked," and Eulau stresses their "mutual interdependence."[98] Theories must be continually revised and modified in accord with newly observed facts and empirical evidence. At the same time, facts acquire

---

[96]Peter Caws, *The Philosophy of Science: A Systematic Account* (Princeton: D. Van Nostrand, 1965), p. 91.

[97]Hubert M. Blalock, Jr., *Theory Construction: From Verbal to Mathematical Formulations* (Englewood Cliffs, N.J.: Prentice-Hall, 1969), p. 8.

[98]Hempel, *Aspects of Scientific Explanation*, p. 243; Eulau, *Behavioral Persuasion in Politics*, p. 26.

special meaning when examined in light of generalizations suggesting new relations and interpretations.

The gap that divides those immersed in empirical research from those who spin high level formal schemes is closely related to the inductive-deductive question. In one imaginative effort, two scholars attempt to bridge the gap by calling for "grounded theory." They argue that theory is best generated by constructing it out of the data of social research.[99] Another important study addresses the issue by attempting to distinguish analytically between "general theory" and "auxiliary theory."[100] Implicit in all these attempts is the understanding that theory construction is a highly integrated process in which the various intellectual operations overlap and interlock with one another (see figure 2). Constant movement back and forth also occurs as one refines and reconsiders. Basic conceptualization, for example, is subject to change as the procedures of classification, generalization, and testing are engaged in. At any point in the process, new insights and intuitive flashes can suddenly emerge and fundamentally alter the investigation underway. The process of theory construction involves a pendulumlike movement between the specific and the general, the empirical and the formal, the climate of discovery and the exercise of testing.

The final step in the theory building process concerns the application of theory. By discovering patterns and explaining processes, theory assists in prediction. This, in turn, permits control. Theory contributes general guidelines upon which action and policy can be based. In the social sciences, the preoccupation with the construction of theories only for the sake of elegance is a luxury that we cannot afford. In a world where man limps through the darkness of uncertainty lit only by the flames of crisis, general beacons of enlightenment that serve to guide his steps are necessary. In the field of comparative politics, policy relevant theories of authority and change, for example, are among the most pressing concerns of scholars.

The Role of Theory

The advantages that theory and the theorizing process offer to the study of comparative politics are many. Eight major contributions flow from the exercise of theory building. First, theory contributes greatly in the

---

[99]Barney G. Glaser and Anselm L. Strauss, *The Discovery of Grounded Theory* (Chicago: Aldine, 1967).

[100]Hubert M. Blalock, Jr., "The Measurement Problem: A Gap Between the Languages of Theory and Research," in Hubert M. Blalock, Jr. and Ann B. Blalock, eds., *Methodology in Social Research* (New York: McGraw-Hill, 1968), pp. 5–27.

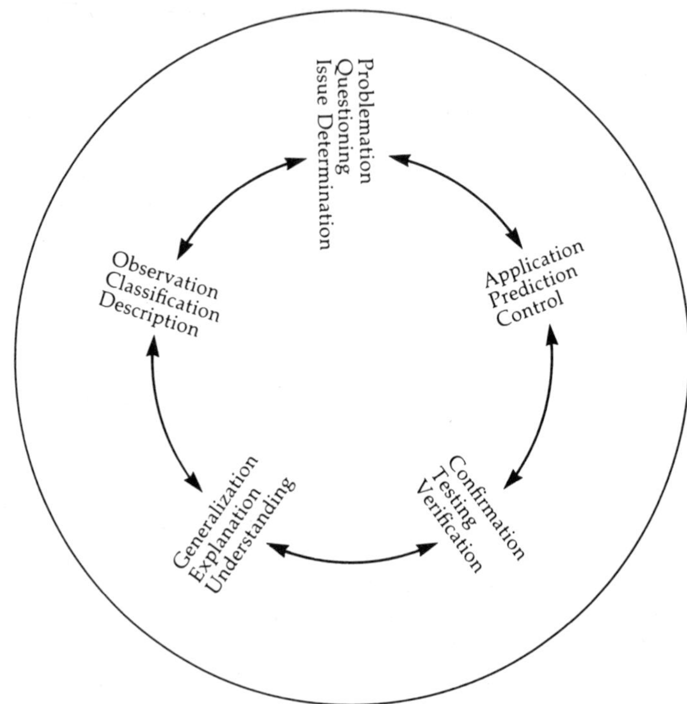

FIGURE 2 Scientific Theory Building

selection, collection, ordering, and storing of data. It exists as a thread that runs through masses of data drawing only the relevant facts to its path. Theory provides an important instrument of discrimination for selecting and collecting the relevant from the irrelevant in the sea of sociopolitical experience. This prevents the never ending process of compulsive fact accumulation that results in impressively huge but depressingly meaningless filing silos of data. Refined and rigorously developed theories also stand as repositories of ordered fact. They have been repeatedly measured against relevant data and these data then stand in at least this systematized arrangement. In this role, theory functions preeminently as a filtering device.

Second, theory building necessitates conceptual and methodological clarity. The theoretician is forced to rethink many of his basic concepts, assumptions, and hypotheses. The process of reworking and recasting verbal theories is essential for infusing rigor and precision into the theorizing process. This enterprise involves "clarifying concepts, eliminating or consolidating variables, translating existing verbal theories into common languages, searching the literature for propositions, and looking for implicit assumptions connecting the major propositions in important theoretical works."[101] This process of reexamination and clarification not only contributes to sounder theory, but also heightens communication and understanding between various theorists working with similar concepts and addressing similar problems.

The third advantage of theory is its *relational* stress which marks its special significance to *comparative* analysis. Theory always draws relations, builds connections, and states linkages. Facts and events are intertwined and interrelated. Comparative politics is fundamentally a study that relates patterns and processes that occur within two or more political contexts. The theorizing process is the most profound and systematic way of proceeding in this kind of study. Generalizations are essentially multicontextual, and their construction is what has come to transform configurative-descriptive political study into comparative political study.

Closely related to this third function of theory is the ability of theory to transcend particular time and spatial limitations. Analysis is not confined to describing and explaining one event in and of itself as it has occurred at one time and in one place. Instead, this event is viewed primarily from a very broad perspective that treats the particular happening as only one manifestation of something much larger. This question of perspective is important both for the confirmation of existing hypotheses and for the development of new hypotheses. By presenting a broader picture of relations and linkages, theory can utilize breadth to enhance depth. Theorizing is one way of transcending particularism and narrowness which stultify vision and creativity.

A fifth advantage of theory is that it is a form of explanation. In indicating that particular cases fall within certain general principles and in linking and ordering events, the theorizing process is confronting and answering key "why" questions. Whereas description is primarily concerned with the "what," the "when," and the "where," explanation concentrates upon the "why." Theory is an explanatory tool and as such it is a crucial aid towards building and furthering understanding.

Following from these last three functions is an advantage that enables man to attempt to foresee and forecast. Theory leads to prediction and enhances the ability to see ahead. By relating generalizations, theories discover and highlight patterns and trends, and it is on the basis of these

---

[101]Ibid., p. 27. For an explicit and systematic example of this process of theory building and refinement, see Harry Eckstein, "Authority Relations and Governmental Performance: A Theoretical Framework," *Comparative Political Studies* 2 (October 1969): pp. 269–325.

that man predicts. Accurate prediction in social and political life is very difficult but it can be furthered by placing more reliance upon sound theory building and often tested theoretical principles. Although prediction frequently rests on unanalyzed trends, such prediction is inevitably risky and is rarely reliable for more than very short periods of time and closely adjacent cases. Prediction over any longer term must rest on some kind of theory, for only theory provides an explanation of why we can expect the future to be as we predicted.

The seventh general contribution of theory is best described by Kurt Lewin, who once said that nothing is so practical as a good theory. Theory assists in policy-making and decision-making processes at all levels and in all systems. As a simplifying and unifying intellectual tool, it restricts the range of choices and suggests new alternatives for action. This function has been referred to above as one important form of theory application.

Finally, theory and the entire process of theory building act as a provocative force for the selection of new problems and the stimulation of new research. Discovering, clarifying, classifying, relating, explaining, and testing breed an intellectual dynamism and curiosity that continually encourage new explorations. In the field of comparative politics, for example, the leading theoreticians have been those who are constantly settling upon new problems and generating new hypotheses. This is one less recognized reason why names like Almond, Huntington, Riggs, Eckstein, and Apter have so dominated the recent study of comparative politics.

If it performs any or all of these functions, then theory has been to some degree successful. Any serious attempt to engage systematically in the theorizing process is bound to be a positive experience. It introduces a sensitivity to the importance of scientific procedure and rigor in the process of comparative analysis and explanation. The future of comparative political study rests upon effective theory building and the continuing development of a body of comparative political theory.

The Goals of This Study

A proliferation of varied approaches to the study of comparative politics has resulted in numerous and differing orientations to the construction of theory. These approaches have been traditional and modern, highly refined and hardly developed, explicit and implicit, more popular and less popular. In some cases, approaches have overlapped with one another; in other instances, they have been quite exclusive and separate. Often, concepts basic to one approach are utilized in another approach, sometimes with the same meanings, sometimes with quite different meanings. Various approaches have offered differing strengths to comparative political analysis and theory building. In terms of relevance, rigor, and researchability, for example, there are marked differences in the kinds of contributions that flow from each theoretical approach.

Perhaps the greatest difficulty in analyzing the role of a particular approach in the study of comparative politics is the absence of any clear understanding of the nature of any one approach in relation to any other approach. This intellectual fuzziness has had an impeding and retarding effect upon the study of comparative politics for several reasons. First, it has had a negative impact upon theory building. A confusing jumble of approaches prohibits one from discerning which approach contributes most to which stage in the theorizing process. The lack of clear analytic distinctions here also fosters conceptual and procedural confusion which is destructive to rigorous theory building. Second, an unclear view of existing approaches tends to blind a scholar to his own particular theoretical orientations. He lacks a clear awareness of what approach or approaches he utilizes under what circumstances and in what form. Nor is he able to distinguish lucidly the general orientations of other observers and scholars. This kind of confusion is deepened by the fact that many scholars adopt a changing and eclectic hodgepodge of approaches that defy identification and clarification. The lack of awareness of basic orientating perspectives dulls the tools of comparative political analysis from the very beginning. Finally, a clouded view of theoretical approaches prevents one from making discriminating evaluations of research results in comparative politics. Unless the projects themselves present an explicit discussion of the approaches and procedures that led to the relevant conclusions, one is often unable to judge adequately the results put forth.

Chapters 3 through 7 in this study attempt to clarify, distinguish, relate, and evaluate five major theoretical approaches to the study of comparative politics: the political culture approach, the group approach, the elite approach, the class approach, the functional and systems approaches. The presentation of these approaches will not rely upon the works of any particular practitioner, but rather will represent a distillation of relevant work through time. The major conceptual equipment of each approach will be carefully investigated and judged in terms of the tasks at hand. All approaches will be evaluated in terms of their capacity to confront, elucidate, and explain certain problems. The fundamental issue against which the approaches will be measured is the subject of the next chapter.

CHAPTER II

Modernization and Political Development

In the study of comparative politics, the developing nations of Africa and Asia have become a critical focus of concern. Traditionally, these "exotic" areas were ignored in comparative study, or, at most, were examined as colonial adjuncts to the nations of Europe. In the years following the Second World War, however, the emergent nations of the Third World became critical arenas of conflict in the cold war. Their politics and development became the objects of awakened diplomatic and intellectual concern throughout the world. At the same time, the role of theory and self-conscious methodology assumed new importance in comparative political research. The new nations became laboratories for the analysis of social and political change, and the central concepts of this analysis came to be modernization and political development.

Foundations of the Concept of Development

The concept of development is rooted in man's earliest attempt to understand change. The intellectual threads in the contemporary understanding of change extend back through twenty-five hundred years of political philosophy. What we so often assume to be the unique contributions of the modern social scientific perspective have direct ties to classical Greece. The popular view of political development as stages of growth in inevitable progress only gives modern form to an understanding of change that has dominated Western thought for centuries.

One of the central debates embedded in ancient Greek philosophy involved two diametrically opposed views concerning the basic issue of continuity and change. While Heraclitus believed that everything constantly changes and indeed that one cannot even put one's foot in the same river twice, Parmenides argued that everything is being and nothing ever changes.[1] Plato regarded change as appearance. Reality was to be known only through the form, or idea, one and unchanging, with which he identified the good and the true.

As man sought to explain change in society, he drew upon his observation of growth and development in plants and animals, of "change proceeding gradually, cumulatively, and irreversibly through a kind of unfolding of internal potentiality—the whole moving toward some end that is presumably contained in the process from the start."[2] Metaphor provided the means for affecting the fusion of the experience of change in society and the observation of growth in nature. Robert Nisbet, in his study of *Social Change and History,* argues that "of all metaphors in Western thought, the oldest and most powerful is the metaphor of growth. When we say that a culture or institution or nation 'grows' or 'develops,' . . . we are not referring to random changes, to changes induced by some external deity or other being. We are referring to change that is intrinsic to the entity, to change that is held to be as much a part of the entity's nature as any purely structural element."[3]

Growth, or development, is teleological. The origin of a thing, and the pattern of its change, is explained in terms of the end which it must, by its nature, attain if unhindered by outside forces. Development, so understood, is characterized by directionality, by genetically related stages following sequentially one necessarily out of the other, and by purpose. From the closely related analogy of social change to the life cycle of the organism, and from the metaphor of growth, the Greeks derived the concept *physis,* or "way of growth."[4] "If the nature of a

---

[1]The Parmenidean syllogism denying change was the following: Everything that comes to be must come either from being or non-being. From being, however, nothing can become for whatever is being already is and does not come to be. On the other hand, nothing comes from nothing (non-being). Therefore, nothing comes to be. There is no change.

[2]Robert A. Nisbet, *Social Change and History* (New York: Oxford University Press, 1969), p. 3. For another commentary on classical perspectives of change, see Irving Louis Horowitz, *Three Worlds of Development* (New York: Oxford University Press, 1966), pp. 47–55.

[3]Nisbet, *Social Change and History,* p. 7.

[4]Ibid., pp. 8–9. *Physis* was somewhat mistranslated by the Romans as *natura* or "nature."

thing, then, is how it grows, and if everything in the universe, physical and social alike, has a *physis* of its own, a distinctive way of growing, a life-cycle, then the task of the philosopher or scientist is clear. It is to find out what the *physis* is of each thing: to learn its original condition, its successive stages of development, the external factors . . . that affect it, and, finally, what its 'end' is; that is, its final form, the form which may be said to be the ultimate 'cause' of it all."[5]

This was the task that Aristotle set for himself in his account of the nature of the state in *Politics.* For Aristotle, empirical reality was subject to the laws of birth, growth, maturity, and decay. Such change was understood to actualize the potentiality of a thing. In growth, the potential is inherent in the origin, just as the seed has the "potentiality" of the mature plant. Development is the realization of that potential.[6]

Greek metaphysics and the metaphor of genesis and decay were fused in Christian thought with Hebrew sacred law in a conception of man's development through the will of an omnipotent God. For the Greeks, the cycle of growth in society, as among plants and animals, is repeated again and again. In the Christian view, the cycle of genesis, decay, and final destruction is unique, never to be repeated. The history of mankind and its fall was determined within the Creation. All that has happened *necessarily* happened and could not have happened differently—because it was ordained by God before man ever made his appearance. This is not the God of the Hebrews, intervening in history on behalf of the Chosen People, but a God who expresses his sovereignty in a predetermined design, a divine *physis,* from which even he does not deviate.[7]

The French Enlightenment separated God's will from the plan of creation. Over time, the idea of the design of nature gained secular footing, and God was a premise no longer required.[8] With the Enlightenment also came the first expression of the modern idea of progress. The cycle of birth, maturity, and decay gave way to the belief that "there will be no end to growth and development of human wisdom."[9] Leibniz understood nature in terms of its potentiality as well as its actuality: "The present is big with the future," he wrote, and human

---

[5]Ibid., pp. 22–23.

[6]Perhaps no one has written more extensively about change than Aristotle. The treatises *Physics* and *On Generation and Corruption* are where he lays out his basic theoretical framework concerning the issue of change. He relies on this framework explicitly in the analysis of specific problems raised in *On the Heavens, Nicomachean Ethics, On the Soul,* and *Metaphysics.*

[7]Nisbet, *Social Change and History,* pp. 63–81.

[8]Ibid., pp. 81–82.

[9]Fontenelle, quoted in ibid., p. 104. See also J. B. Bury, *The Idea of Progress* (New York: Macmillan, 1932). For an exploration of conception of modernity, see Louis Kampf, *On Modernism: The Prospects for Literature and Freedom* (Boston: M. I. T. Press, 1967).

progress proceeds according to necessary stages: "Nature never makes leaps." For Kant, human history was seen "to be steady, and progressive through slow evolution of its original endowment."[10]

All things were seen to have a "natural history" of progress if undiverted by artificial circumstances. From the laissez faire perspective of Adam Smith, man progresses only if enlightened political action could remove the underbrush of convention that hid nature and its laws. On the other hand, "if one saw the natural order so heavily overladen by convention and tradition, so reinforced by the power of government, clergy, and aristocracy, that working through any existing institution appeared futile," Rousseau's prescription for revolution, for the total destruction of the existing social order, might well appear man's only course for liberation.[11]

Out of the eighteenth century's concern for the progress of human development came an inquiry into the successive stages through which man had passed to attain his state of eminence. From the works of Comte, Hegel, Spencer, and Marx, the theory of natural history emerged as that of social evolution. Although it gained popularity following the publication of Darwin's *Origin of Species* in 1859, the theory of social evolution is built upon nothing comparable to the phenomena of variation which Darwin described in his theory of natural selection. Social evolutionary theory is built upon precisely that conception of organismic growth involved in the notion of *physis.*[12] Hegel makes this clear: "The principle of development involves . . . the existence of a latent germ of being—a capacity or potentiality striving to realize itself."[13]

Nisbet identifies six premises in the theory of social evolution:[14]

1. Change is *natural,* and the dichotomy between order and change is, as Comte declared, false: change is understood as the incessant realization of higher levels of order.

2. Change is *directional* and is characterized by a sequence of stages. Marx, for example, defined the stages of economic evolution as moving from primitive communism (the equality of scarcity) to slavery, feudalism, capitalism, socialism, and, finally, to communism (the equality of abundance). But whether it is Marx, Comte, Hegel, Maine, Spencer, or Durkheim, the direction of change in social evolution was toward the specific set of qualities possessed by Western Europe alone.

3. Change is *immanent,* the core attribute of the whole theory of social evolution. "I mean," Leibniz wrote, "that each created being is

---

[10]Quoted in Nisbet, *Social Change and History,* Leibniz, pp. 115-16, Kant, p. 118.

[11]Ibid., pp. 139–43.

[12]Ibid., p. 164.

[13]Quoted in ibid., p. 159.

[14]Ibid., pp. 166–88.

pregnant with its future state, and that it naturally follows a certain course if nothing hinders it."[15]

4. Change is *continuous,* involving a logical succession of genetically related stages which follow one after the other. Revolution, for example, in the Marxian sense, is feasible and theoretically rational only when the shape of the new society has taken form within the preceding order. "No social order ever disappears," Marx wrote, "before all the productive forces for which there is room in it have been developed, and new, higher relations of production never appear before the material conditions for their existence have matured in the womb of the old society."[16]

5. Change is *necessary,* that is, the stages of development in social evolution proceed necessarily according to a certain order—what the Greeks called *physis.* "Progress is not an accident, not a thing within human control," Herbert Spencer declared, "but a beneficient necessity."[17] Taking Marx again as an example, he refers to laws and tendencies "working with iron necessity toward inevitable results." The nation "that is more developed industrially only shows, to the less developed, the image of its own future."[18]

6. Change proceeds from *uniform causes,* fundamental sources of change in evolution. Perhaps the oldest of the concepts of uniform cause is conflict, the dialectical struggle of contrary and internal forces which proceed until a new stage of reality is achieved. It is the dynamic to be found in Heraclitus, St. Augustine, Kant, and Marx.

These six premises of social evolution summarize the dominant themes in the concept of change as it emerged in the West. The remarkable continuity in the conceptions of development, growth, and change over twenty-five hundred years, from the early Greeks to the emergence of modern social science in the nineteenth century, was not accompanied by uniformity of judgment on the value and meaning of change.

In examining the different ways by which man's original condition may be specified, Nisbet distinguishes between (1) the psychological, that is, the imagined states of mind of primitive man—his happiness or misery, security or insecurity, and (2) the cultural, the actual traits of man's earliest condition—material and immaterial, physical and social.[19]

Aeschylus and Lucretius were among those who associated primal ignorance with fear and misery. Aeschylus—especially through the

---

[15]Quoted in ibid., pp. 170–71.

[16]From Karl Marx, *A Contribution to the Critique of Political Economy,* quoted in ibid., p. 178.

[17]Quoted in Nisbet, *Social Change and History,* p. 123.

[18]In the Preface of the first edition of Karl Marx, *Capital,* quoted in ibid., p. 180.

[19]Nisbet, *Social Change and History,* p. 49.

words of Prometheus, the fire-giver, in *Prometheus Bound*—believed that only through knowledge was mankind liberated from fear. The dominant classical view, however, more nearly reflected that of Hesiod, who in the eighth century B.C., believed that man's earliest psychological condition was "golden." It was a time of innocence and felicity, accompanied by material conditions of simplicity. In man's cultural advance through knowledge and technology, Hesiod saw a decline from the simple goodness and happiness of the primordial state. Indeed, there was a causal relationship between happiness and ignorance. In knowledge lies the beginning of the fall from happiness.

The Hesiodic conception is embodied in Plato, as he writes in *The Laws* of man's loss of goodness in the gradual advance of knowledge. It is carried in Christian thought in Augustine's belief that the advancement of knowledge is accompanied by a decay of the soul. "Whether for Greek or Christian," Nisbet writes, *"the conception of moral and spiritual decline is inextricably tied up with man's possession of faculties which are crucial to his material and cultural progress on earth."*[20]

The philosophers of the Enlightenment saw in progress the infinite perfectibility of man. They were not unconscious of corruption, decay, and decline in history, but they had "a profound faith that if only, for the first time in history, the interferences to progress could be removed by wise legislation or enlightened despotism, the natural order of progressive development would take over."[21] By no means did everyone share this optimistic view of man. Along side the prophets of progress were those who viewed man's history as one of decline, of cultural and moral disintegration. Rousseau proclaimed that "our minds have been corrupted in proportion as the arts and sciences have been improved."[22] Others, like the Scottish moral philosophers, notably David Hume, had "emphatic doubts" about man's progress and regarded human history more in terms of inertia than of either progress or degeneration.[23]

The theory of social evolution in the nineteenth century represented at once the apogee of the idea of progress and at the same time a glorious justification for the ascendancy of the West in the imperial age. The successive stages of development in the West were taken "as evidence of the direction in which mankind as a whole *would* move, and, flowing from this, *should* move."[24] Western Europe provided the linear map of

---

[20]Ibid., pp. 94–95.

[21]Ibid., p. 129.

[22]Jean Jacques Rousseau, "A Discourse on the Moral Effects of the Arts and Sciences," in *The Social Contract and Discourses* (New York: Dutton, 1950), p. 150.

[23]Nisbet, *Social Change and History,* pp. 125–28.

[24]Ibid., p. 191.

man's progress from tradition to modernity. The earlier stages of the most advanced societies were embodied in the contemporary world in primitive or traditional cultures, which would, with time and encouragement from the West, attain modernity in the image of Europe. "One could categorize non-Western peoples as not simply exotic or different but as reflecting lower stages of an evolutionary advancement that was thought to be universal."[25]

Too often, "modernity becomes what we imagine ourselves to be."[26] Like the nineteenth century social evolutionists, social scientists of the past two decades generally assumed that the advanced, liberal democracies had "arrived" and that their past mapped the course for other nations in their struggle to modernity. The idea of progress was frequently taken by American social scientists and policy makers as justification for intervention in non-Western societies, while at the same time it nurtured complacency towards American society. The United States represented the fulfillment of the democratic ideal to which all nations should strive—with American assistance and military support if necessary.

If most theorists of social evolution regarded the successive stages of man's development as not only inevitable, but good, many others viewed such change with considerable ambivalence. De Tocqueville, in his study of American democracy, perceived a tragic element in man's progress—that which was potentially good was also potentially bad. Both Sir Henry Maine and Ferdinand Tönnies expressed "some anxiety over the prospects of a chillingly impersonal and ruthlessly calculating modern society."[27] Emile Durkheim saw in man's loss of traditional relationships the increasing unhappiness and insecurity of *anomie.* In our own time, the impersonality of the large city, the university, factory, or corporation is identified as a source of man's alienation—alienation not only from his fellow man, but from himself. In escape from the freedom that anonymity imposes on man, the more determinant, ascribed and prescribed relationships attributed to tradition—of the village, small town, or tribe—are viewed with lingering nostalgia. Henry Adams, in his intellectual autobiography, recounts his infinite prefer-

---

[25]Ibid., p. 201. Also see Ali A. Mazrui, "From Social Darwinism to Current Theories of Modernization: A Tradition of Analysis," *World Politics* 21 (October 1968): 69–83.

[26]Lloyd and Susanne Rudolph, *The Modernity of Tradition: Political Development in India* (Chicago: University of Chicago Press, 1967), p. 7.

[27]Lucian W. Pye, *Politics, Personality, and Nation-Building: Burma's Search for Identity* (New Haven: Yale University Press, 1962), p. 34. Also see Leonard Binder, "The Crises of Political Development," in Leonard Binder, James S. Coleman, Joseph LaPalombara, Lucian W. Pye, Sidney Verba and Myron Weiner, *Crises and Sequences in Political Development* (Princeton: Princeton University Press, 1971), pp. 41–42. (Cited hereafter as SSRC Committee, *Crises and Sequences.*)

ence for the Middle Ages over his own time, for the Virgin over the dynamo.[28] Hippies, dropouts from the affluent society, seek a form of retribalization in the commune. Many social scientists, touched by a kind of naive cultural relativism, idealize primitive or traditional societies and attribute to them virtues seemingly lost in the process of modernization.[29]

Whether exalted or decried, modernity and tradition are seen, from this perspective, as mutually exclusive polar opposites. The concept of social evolution involves the transition from one to the other in a sequence of successive stages: To be more modern is, necessarily, to be less traditional. Lloyd and Susanne Rudolph, in an imaginative study entitled *The Modernity of Tradition,* challenge this conception. "The assumption that modernity and tradition are radically contradictory rests on a misdiagnosis of tradition as it is found in traditional societies, a misunderstanding of modernity as it is found in modern societies, and a misapprehension of the relationship between them."[30] The analytic gap between tradition and modernity arises out of what has been called the "misplaced polarities" of the dichotomous schemes.[31]

Dichotomous Schemes: Tradition and Modernity

Over the past century or so, a variety of dichotomous schemes have been offered as analytical approaches to development. These have involved polarities such as the following:

rural and urban
folk and urban
agricultural and industrial

[28]Henry Adams, *The Education of Henry Adams* (New York: Random House, Modern Library, 1931).

[29]The modern nostalgia for the simplicity, intimacy, and spirituality attributed to traditional societies may represent a form of reversed ethnocentrism. In the eyes of those leaders of the Third World who seek to lift their people from poverty and ignorance and to gain access to the benefits of modernization, it is rank hypocrisy for the sons of Western affluence to bemoan the burden which prosperity has thrust upon them, while at the same time enjoying what they would deny to the rest of the world.

[30]Lloyd and Susanne Rudolph, *The Modernity of Tradition,* p. 3.

[31]Joseph R. Gusfield, "Tradition and Modernity: Misplaced Polarities in the Study of Social Change," *American Journal of Sociology* 72 (January 1967): 351–62. Also see Reinhard Bendix, "Tradition and Modernity Reconsidered," *Comparative Studies in History and Society* 9 (April 1967): 292–346. For an analysis of the structure, forms, and functions of tradition, see Edward Shils, "Tradition," *Comparative Studies in History and Society* 13 (April 1971): 122–59.

primitive and civilized
static and dynamic
sacred and secular
Gemainschaft and *Gesellschaft*
traditional and rational
traditional and modern

Sir Henry Maine, in his study of *Ancient Law* (1861), identified two types of societies, "status" and "contract," and argued that progress, or development, involved the transition from one to the other—from traditionally ascribed and status-oriented relationships to those which were secular, rationally-determined, contractually negotiated, and based on specific consideration.[32]

Ferdinand Tönnies, in *Gemainschaft und Gesellschaft* (1887), sought to refine Maine's distinction. "The Gemainschaft (community) is characterized by the social will as concord, folkways, mores, and religion; the Gesellschaft (society) by the social will as convention, legislation, and public opinion."[33] The keynote of Gemainschaft is natural will, oriented to the collectivity; for Gesellschaft, it is rational will in pursuit of individual self-interest.

Emile Durkheim, the father of modern sociology, put forth a dichotomous scheme in 1893, contrasting two forms of social solidarity, the "mechanical" and the "organic." Durkheim's polarity is a source of some confusion, because (as Pye has noted) the labels "are curiously reversed in terms of what would be expected." Where most writers have characterized traditional societies as organic, Durkheim characterized the traditional order as having "mechanical" relationships, based on the sharing of common sentiment. Modern society, on the other hand, is "organic," with a highly specialized division of labor in which interests and sentiments differ but are mutually complementary.[34]

Max Weber brought the strands of these various dichotomous schemes together in his contrast between traditional and rational-legal forms of authority. Traditional authority rests "on an established belief in the sanctity of immemorial traditions," while rational authority rests "on a belief in the 'legality' of patterns of normative rules." Weber also identified the charismatic as a transitional form of authority, resting "on devotion to the specific and exceptional sanctity, heroism or exemplary

---

[32]Sir Henry Maine, *Ancient Law* (London: Murray, 1861). Also see Pye, *Politics, Personality and Nation-Building,* pp. 33–34.

[33]Ferdinand Tönnies, *Community and Society* (New York: Harper Torchbooks, 1963), p. 231.

[34]Emile Durkheim, *The Division of Labor in Society* (Glencoe, Ill.: Free Press, 1949). Also see Pye, *Politics, Personality and Nation-Building,* pp. 34–35.

character of an individual person" and on "the normative patterns or order revealed or ordained by him."[35]

Reaching back into the work of Maine, Tönnies, Durkheim, and Weber, Talcott Parsons devised a series of polarities, termed "pattern variables," to reveal the recurrent and contrasting norms of social systems. Although the use of the pattern variables has been criticized by Gabriel Almond and others for its tendency to exaggerate differences between Western and non-Western systems, the dichotomies have been widely used for the analysis of social change. Within comparative politics, the pattern variables have been freely adapted to contrast traditional and modern societies as ideal types:

Traditional Society	*Modern Society*
Ascriptive status	Achievement status
Diffuse roles	Specific roles
Particularistic values	Universalistic values
Collectivity orientation	Self orientation
Affectivity	Affective neutrality

The pattern variables refer to mutually exclusive value orientations. Ascriptive orientations are based on such considerations as ethnicity, religion, family, and social connection. Achievement orientations are based on merit and relevant performance—past, present, or prospective. Diffuse orientations are undifferentiated, in contrast to the restricted and specialized range of specific orientations. In government, for example, this involves the contrast between the diffuse roles of a tribal chieftain, who is at once king, judge, general, and priest, and the specific roles of a differentiated social system. The particularistic-universalistic polarity involves the distinction between transcendent values and those determined by a particular situation or relationship—in other words, whether everyone is to be judged by a common standard, as of law. Collective versus self orientation is the problem of private against collective interest; and affectivity versus affective neutrality contrasts impulse gratification with restraint and discipline.[36]

[35]Max Weber, *The Theory of Social and Economic Organization* (New York: Free Press, 1947), p. 328. Also see Reinhard Bendix, *Max Weber: An Intellectual Portrait* (Garden City, N.Y.: Doubleday Anchor, 1962): and Julien Freund, *The Sociology of Max Weber* (New York: Vintage Books, 1969).

[36]Talcott Parsons and Edward Shils, eds., *Toward a General Theory of Action* (Cambridge: Harvard University Press, 1951), pp. 76–91; Parsons, *The Social System* (New York: Free Press, 1951), especially chapters II and III, pp. 24–112. Also see William C. Mitchell, *Sociological Analysis and Politics: The Theories of Talcott Parsons* (Englewood Cliffs, N.J.: Prentice-Hall, 1967). Seymour M. Lipset has offered additional distinctions in pattern variables between elitist and egalitarian relationships, corresponding to the traditional-modern dichotomy. See *The First New Nation* (New York: Basic Books, 1963), pp. 209–13.

David Apter contrasts two polar models, the secular-libertarian and the sacred-collectivity, on a continuum of authority systems. The secular-libertarian model is characterized by the instrumental values of rationality and self-interest. Empirically, it is represented by the modern reconciliation system, with the limited governmental functions of mediation and coordination. Characteristic of the liberal democracies, the reconciliation system is best suited to modern industrial societies. In the sacred-collectivity model, the stress is upon the consummatory values of community and moral purpose. Empirically, it is represented by the modern mobilization system, with a mass party of solidarity, a charismatic leader, and an ideology in the form of a political religion. It is most successful as a "conversion" system, for the establishment of a new polity or in affecting the transition from traditional to modern society.[37]

Pattern variable analysis has been used by F. X. Sutton in the distinction between two broad types of societies, the agricultural and the industrial. The essential characteristics of the "agricultural" society are:

1. Predominance of ascriptive, particularistic, diffuse patterns.
2. Stable local groups and limited spatial mobility.
3. Relatively simple and stable "occupational" differentiation.
4. A "deferential" stratification system of diffuse impact.

The essential features of the "industrial" society are:

1. Predominance of universalistic, specific, and achievement norms.
2. High degree of social mobility (in a general—not necessarily "vertical"—sense).
3. Well-developed occupational system, insulated from other social structures.
4. "Egalitarian" class system based on generalized patterns of occupational achievement.
5. Prevalence of "associations," i.e., functionally specific non-ascriptive structures.[38]

Fred Riggs extends and elaborates Sutton's models for the analysis of administrative systems using the polar images of *agraria* and *industria.*[39] The distinction provides the base for Riggs' later development

[37]David E. Apter, *The Politics of Modernization* (Chicago: University of Chicago Press, 1965). See especially pp. 22–42 and 357–90. Also see Gianfranco Pasquino, "The Politics of Modernization: An Appraisal of David Apter's Contributions," *Comparative Political Studies* 3 (October 1970): 297–322.

[38]F. X. Sutton, "Social Theory and Comparative Politics," in Harry Eckstein and David E. Apter, eds., *Comparative Politics: A Reader* (New York: Free Press, 1963), p. 71.

[39]Fred W. Riggs, "Agraria and Industria—Toward a Typology of Comparative Administration," in William J. Siffin, ed., *Toward the Comparative Study of Public Administration* (Bloomington, Ind.: Indiana University Press, 1957), pp. 23–110.

of a typology based on functional differentiation. Corresponding to *agraria,* he offers the model of the *fused* society, characterized by highly diffuse structures, each performing a number of functions. In contrast, and roughly similar to the image of *industria,* is the *diffracted* society in which structures are highly specific in function. A transitional model, that of the *prismatic* society, is characterized by heterogeneity and an overlap of incongruous system requirements.[40]

The empirical study of either "traditional" or "modern" societies reveals an often fundamental lack of congruence with the ideal type of the various dichotomous schemes. It is not simply that all systems are "mixed" (in Almond's terms), but that qualities often attributed to traditional societies may bear little relationship to the actual nature of a given traditional society—that, in fact, these qualities simply represent the logical antithesis to those defined as distinctly modern. If modern societies are characterized by achievement orientations, there is no reason to assume, automatically, that traditional societies are necessarily ascriptive. Indeed, many traditional societies may evidence high degrees of achievement, specificity, and universalism. After all, traditional society, as a category, embraces primitive tribes, feudal states, and bureaucratic empires—an incredible diversity of structures and values.

From Maine to Parsons, social scientists have characterized tradition and modernity in terms of mutually exclusive attributes. The abstract formulation of such contrasts, Bendix warns, can be seriously misleading. "The use of one or several abstract terms to characterize either tradition or modernity tends to mistake labeling for analysis."[41] The caution of Max Weber might well be taken: "*Developmental* sequences can be constructed into ideal types and these constructs can have quite considerable heuristic value. But this quite particularly gives rise to the danger that the ideal type and reality will be confused with one another."[42]

The dichotomous schemes involve numerous conceptual problems. They represent, in their polarities, a continuum between two ideal types. The model is heuristic in purpose, but the approach leaves the nature and character of the transitional process ambiguous. All systems are transitional, in that no society is wholly traditional or wholly modern. The dichotomy, however, posits a zero-sum situation, in which transition involves the movement from one pole to the other: the more modern, necessarily the less traditional; the more industrial, the less

---

[40]Fred W. Riggs, *Administration in Developing Countries: The Theory of Prismatic Society* (Boston: Houghton Mifflin, 1964).

[41]Bendix, "Tradition and Modernity Reconsidered," p. 314.

[42]Max Weber, *The Methodology of the Social Sciences* (Glencoe, Ill.: Free Press, 1949), p. 101.

agricultural; the more urban, the less rural. The neatness of the scheme has great appeal, but it may so violate empirical reality that it serves only to obscure the nature of social change.

The rural-urban continuum provides a useful example, as it is readily operationalized in statistical terms. The question is whether we are measuring what we think we are measuring. Urbanization may reflect the relative increase in the populations of cities through migration from rural areas, but it suggests nothing concerning the style of life that is distinctly urban. Indeed, migration into the cities of Asia, Africa, and Latin America has involved, in degree, a process of ruralization, in which the life style of the village is recreated in an urban context and influences the city at the same time that it is influenced by it. On the other side, through the development of modern transportation and communications facilities—particularly the mass media—urbanism as a way of life has extended out from the cities into the countryside.[43]

Tradition and modernity are seen in dichotomous terms as mutually exclusive polar opposites, but any society—even the most modern—will contain both traditional and modern elements, and each individual is characterized by both traditional and modern attitudes and behavior. These may be synthesized within the individual so that traditional and modern aspects can only be distinguished analytically. Frequently, however, particularly in those more traditional societies of the Third World which have experienced the sudden impact of modernization, individuals may operate with remarkable effectiveness in two discrete worlds of experience through a process of compartmentalization. In this adaptive process, potential conflict is minimized through the separation of spheres of conduct and norms.[44] Rather than being "marginal men," at home in neither world, they may be quite modern in one situation, traditional in another. The Japanese or Indian businessman, for example, may have all of the appropriate entrepreneurial attitudes of the modern corporation and, at the same time, in the setting of his home, operate according to the most traditional and orthodox modes of behavior. His behavior is situationally determined. Modernity, in this case, does not replace tradition, but is added to it.

Tradition and modernity are often mutually reinforcing, rather than systems in conflict. Bureaucracy, for example, would probably prove

---

[43]See Gerald Breese, *Urbanization in Newly Developing Countries* (Englewood Cliffs, N.J.: Prentice-Hall, 1966); and Joel M. Halpern, *The Changing Village Community* (Englewood Cliffs, N.J.: Prentice-Hall, 1967).

[44]See Milton Singer, "The Indian Joint Family in Modern Industry," in Milton Singer and Barnard S. Cohn, eds., *Structure and Change in Indian Society* (Chicago: Aldine, 1968); Singer, "Beyond Tradition and Modernity in Madras," *Comparative Studies in History and Society* 13 (April 1971): 160–95; and R.S. Khare, "Home and Office: Some Trends of Modernization among the Kanya-Kubja Brahmans," *Comparative Studies in History and Society* 13 (April 1971): 196–216.

ineffectual if its formal, legalistic, and functionally specific relationships were not reinforced by informal patterns of association and communication—in short, by those relationships identified as traditional. "The modern, formal superstructure of relationships," Pye has argued, "can give an organization strength only if supported by the powerful emotional forces arising from particularistic loyalties and by the cohesive powers of complex but functionally diffuse sentiments."[45]

The Rudolphs contend that modernity and tradition "infiltrate and transform each other." They react strongly against the notion that social change in the Third World arises only out of confrontation with modernity as embodied in the West. They seek the dynamic of change within the contradictions of the historical situation. "If tradition and modernity are seen as continuous rather than separated by an abyss, if they are dialectically rather than dichotomously related, and if internal variations are attended to and taken seriously, then those sectors of traditional society that contain or express potentialities for change from dominant norms and structures become critical for understanding the nature and processes of modernization."[46]

The dialectics of change involve neither wholly external nor wholly internal contradictions. Analytically, we may distinguish between internal and external contradictions within any situation.[47] A society may contain internal contradictions which provide, in the successive resolution of conflict between thesis and antithesis in new synthesis, a motive force in the process of change and modernization. It is in the confrontation between traditional society and an outside modern challenge that the external contradiction is to be found. In the new nations, the external contradiction, represented primarily by the impact of the West (both directly and indirectly, as in the structure of international trade), has been an overwhelming force for change—often obscuring the processes of internal change, but by no means displacing them. The societies of the non-Western world confront both external and internal contradictions, each deepening the other.

The relationship between tradition and modernity must begin to be analyzed in dialectical rather than dichotomous terms. The dichotomous schemes which involve end points on continua emphasize the static and mutually exclusive model so easily divorced from empirical reality. Even in the movement from one pole to the other, in successive stages, the dynamic of conflict is obscured by the fact that all change is understood from the vantage point of one or the other of the two

---

[45]Pye, *Politics, Personality and Nation-Building,* pp. 38–42.

[46]Lloyd and Susanne Rudolph, *The Modernity of Tradition,* pp. 3, 10.

[47]For an interesting discussion of this point, see Binder, in SSRC Committee, *Crises and Sequences,* pp. 50–52.

polar extremes. Dialectical analysis, on the other hand, emphasizes the tension between tradition and modernity in any situation. It focuses on the dynamic and interacting elements central to the process of change.

Old Problems in the New Study of Change

The concept of change in dichotomous terms, as movement between two poles, has been the foundation upon which the modern analysis of development has been based. During the 1950s and early 1960s, as the concepts of modernization and political development were gaining currency, social scientists sought in some way to measure whatever it was they understood as "development." Aspiring to quantitative precision, they chose to define operationally political development in terms immediately available—through a variety of socioeconomic indices. The economists had after all achieved increasing concensus on what they meant by economic development—the growth of output per head of population. Surely political scientists could do as well.

Political development came to be defined then in terms of the nonpolitical, in terms of economic and social variables. This perspective involves a fundamental disregard of politics as a factor that can decisively shape social reality. It denies politics any autonomy and engages in a form of reductionism by which political phenomena are "explained" in terms of social, economic, and psychological factors. Social scientists of this trade turn deaf ears to the emphasis of Lenin and of the leaders of the Third World on the primacy of politics. This myopic vision is related to a model of European experience in which political development is thought to be the dependent variable and modernization the independent variable. Binder contrasts this with the perspective of the Third World. In the non-Western model, modernization emerges as the dependent variable, political development as the independent variable.[48]

Seymour Martin Lipset, in an article entitled "Some Social Requisites of Democracy" (1959), argued on the basis of an analysis of correlations that the more well-do-do a nation, the greater the chances that it will sustain democracy. He found that high levels of industrialization, urbanization, wealth, and education are all so closely interrelated as to form one major factor which has the political correlate of democracy. Lipset warned, however, that an extremely high correlation in any given society between such things as income and education, on the one hand, and democracy, on the other, should not be anticipated even on theoretical grounds, because to the extent that the political system of the society is autonomous, a political form may persist under conditions

[48]Ibid., pp. 15–16.

normally adverse to the emergence of that form. Nazi Germany, high on all the indices of modernization, is the classic example.[49]

Phillips Cutright, building upon Lipset's work, sought to establish an index of national political development. "The degree of political development of a nation," according to Cutright, "can be defined by the degree of complexity and specialization of its national political institutions. . . . The principle hypothesis tested is that political institutions are interdependent with educational systems, economic institutions, communications systems, degree of urbanization, and the distribution of labor force."[50] Using an index scale by which each nation's development can be measured, Cutright posits a linear relationship between socioeconomic development and political development—that is, that political development in and of itself is a function of the social and economic characteristics of society.

The index of political development offered by Cutright, first of all, does not measure political development, but *democratic* political development. He defines political development operationally in terms of the extent to which nations institute and maintain party systems and "open elections." The use of the index is "equivalent to asserting that those nations which are characterized by the institutions of liberal democracy are those which are the most highly developed politically."[51] What emerges from Cutright's analysis is the hypothesis that the more socially and economically developed a nation is, the more democratic it is likely to be—Lipset's hypothesis, but without the note of caution. Cutright confuses correlation with causation. The direction of causality if the correlation is not accidental is in no way implied and involves, in all probability, multiple and circular interaction.[52]

Beyond the equation of democracy with development, Cutright's index does not adequately measure democratic development, for it fails

---

[49]Seymour M. Lipset, "Some Social Requisites of Democracy," *American Political Science Review* 53 (March 1959): 69–105.

[50]Phillips Cutright, "National Political Development: Its Measurement and Social Correlates," in Nelson W. Polsby *et. al.*, eds., *Politics and Social Life* (Boston: Houghton Mifflin, 1963), p. 571.

[51]Deane E. Neubauer, "Some Conditions of Democracy," *American Political Science Review* 61 (December 1967): 1004. See discussions of democracy and political development in Lucian W. Pye, *Aspects of Political Development* (Boston: Little, Brown, 1966), pp. 71–88 and Satish K. Arora, "Pre-Empted Future? Notes on Theories of Political Development," *Behavioral Sciences and Community Development* (India) 2 (September 1968): 85–120.

[52]Irma Adelman and Cynthia T. Morris reverse Cutright's argument and conclude that "the purely economic performance of a community is strongly conditioned by the social and political setting in which economic activity takes place." Specifically, they argue that participant democracy "tends to generate a capacity to adapt existing institutional frameworks to continual economic and social change. This malleability of social structure is essential both to successful entrepreneurial activity and to effective political modernization." Rather than unidirectional causality, however, they find "a systematic pattern of

to draw meaningful distinctions among the countries categorized as "most democratic." Looking at twenty-three democratic countries, Deane Neubauer constructed an index of democratic performance and found no relationship between the level of democratic performance and measures of socioeconomic development. There may be a threshold phenomenon, in that "certain levels of 'basic' socio-economic development appear necessary to elevate countries to a level at which they can begin to support complex, nation-wide patterns of political interaction, one of which may be democracy." Above this level, however, democratic performance is no longer a function of continued socioeconomic development.[53]

While Cutright's later work reflects increasing sophistication,[54] his early efforts can be criticized for two fallacies which characterize much of the literature on political development. First, he has equated political development with democracy. This democratic bias is usually more disguised, but the normative is clearly fused with the empirical. Democracy, American style, is valued and regarded as the highest form of political development. It provides the model for the rest of the world, the image for world transformation—and, as in the earlier theories of social evolution, the criteria against which all nations of the Third World are measured.

Cutright's second fallacy is of unilinear development. As countries become more "advanced" economically and socially, that is, attain higher levels of industrialization, urbanization, education, and communications, they also tend to become more "advanced" politically. Political development becomes an epiphenomenon of social and economic change—and democracy, it would appear, is the end toward which all

---

interaction among mutually interdependent economic, social and political forces, all of which combine to generate a unified complex of change in the style of life of a community." "A Factor Analysis of the Interrelationship Between Social and Political Variables and per capita Gross National Product," *Quarterly Journal of Economics* 79 (1965):555–78; reprinted in John V. Gillespie and Betty A. Nesvold, eds., *Macro-Quantitative Analysis: Conflict, Development, and Democratization* (Beverly Hills, Calif.: Sage Publications, 1971), pp. 331–52.

Donald J. McCrone and Charles F. Cnudde, focusing on democratic political development as such, have sought to go beyond simple correlation in the construction of a causal model, linking urbanization, education, communications, and democratic political development. "Toward a Communications Theory of Democratic Political Development: A Causal Model," *American Political Science Review* 61 (March 1967), 72–79. A number of articles on "the prerequisites of democracy" are reprinted in Charles F. Cnudde and Deane E. Neubauer, eds., *Empirical Democratic Theory* (Chicago: Markham, 1969).

[53]Neubauer, "Conditions of Democracy," p. 1007.

[54]Phillips Cutright, "Inequality: A Cross-National Analysis," *The American Sociological Review* 32 (August 1967): 562–78; Phillips Cutright, "Political Structure, Economic Development, and National Security Programs," *American Journal of Sociology* 70 (March 1965): 537–50.

are necessarily moving. The concept of unilinear growth provides a prescription for development. With a model of the pattern of modernization and development derived from the European experience, the social scientist can turn then to the Third World and say: "Go and do likewise."

The popularity of the concept of stages of political growth or of stages in political development is derived largely from the work of W. W. Rostow. The Marxists view development as the unfolding of five stages of economic growth: primitive communism, slavery, feudalism, capitalism, socialism, and communism. Rostow, in his *Stages of Economic Growth: A Non-Communist Manifesto,* published in 1960, likewise delineates five stages:

1. *Traditional Society*—characterized by pre-Newtonian science and technology, with a very high proportion of resources devoted to agriculture.
2. *The Preconditions for Take-Off*—characterized by the translation of scientific discovery into technological advance and, in the non-Western world, by the intrusion of the more advanced societies.
3. *The Take-Off*—the resistance to steady growth is finally overcome, with increase in investment, industrial expansion, and commercialization of agriculture.
4. *The Drive Toward Maturity*—when output regularly outstrips the increase in population.
5. *The Age of High Mass Consumption*—when the leading sectors shift toward durable consumer goods and services.[55]

Writing a decade later, in *Politics and the Stages of Growth,* Rostow suggests an additional stage, "the Search for Quality," involving the enrichment of private life in an age of abundance.[56]

Rostow's model of economic growth is based on the level of production. Although in *Politics and the Stages of Growth,* Rostow is concerned with the problems of security, welfare, and constitutional order, in his earlier work he gives little consideration to the allocation of investment and the distribution of wealth. Irving Louis Horowitz argues that Rostow's "only real model of development is the United States since it is highest on the measurements of economic growth he deems crucial." Rostow can say this, Horowitz contends, only by ignoring the imbalances in the American economy: the disproportionate ownership and control of industry, the continued gap between rich and poor, the huge ecological and economic separation of blacks, the disparity of wealth

---

[55]Walt W. Rostow, *The Stages of Economic Growth: A Non-Communist Manifesto* (Cambridge: Cambridge University Press, 1960) pp. 4–11.

[56]Walt W. Rostow, *Politics and the Stages of Growth* (Cambridge: Cambridge University Press, 1971), pp. 230–66.

between areas of the country, the growing chasm between high payments for intellectual activities and low payments for manual skills. Rostow's Mass Consumption Stage, Horowitz alleges, "is a byproduct of extreme asymmetry in the economic growth of the United States." It is a function of inequality and status disequilibrium. The model has little realistic application to the Third World. "It assumes an immense transfer of bourgeois values, which, even if possible, would tend to exacerbate rather than alleviate the pressures for social change."[57]

Rostow's stages of growth initially applied to economic development, but the idea was quickly adopted by a number of political scientists. A. F. K. Organski, in his *Stages of Political Development,* defines political development as "increasing governmental efficiency in utilizing the human and material resources of the nation for national goals." He specifies four stages, each characterized by a primary function. The first stage is that of primitive unification, in which the primary governmental function is the creation of national unity. The second stage is that of industrialization, and the main function of government is to permit and aid economic development. The third stage is that of national welfare, in which the task of government is "to protect the people from the hardships of industrial life: to keep the economy running smoothly, to provide the higher living standards so long sought, and to aid the disadvantaged." The fourth and final stage is that of abundance, in which the primary function of government is "to cushion the adjustments of social reorganization in order to make automation possible and to make an automated economy politically responsible." If it is to qualify as "developed," according to Organski, the national government must fulfill the new function at each stage as well as consolidate the gains of the past.[58]

The concept of stage development as offered to the Third World rests on the assumption that the development of the West came out of underdevelopment and that, by the same process of growth, the nations of the Third World can also achieve democracy, abundance, and mass consumption. Explicit in the stage theory of Rostow, and implicit in those who would use the pattern variables to chart unilinear growth, is the belief that traditional society is underdeveloped. As with the social evolutionists of the nineteenth century, contemporary social scientists often assume that development occurs in a succession of stages and that "today's underdeveloped countries are still in a stage, sometime depicted as an original stage, of history through which the now developed countries passed long ago." A. G. Frank contends that "underdevelop-

---

[57]Horowitz, *Three Worlds of Development,* pp. 397–401.

[58]A. F. K. Organski, *The Stages of Political Development* (New York: Knopf, 1965), pp. 3–17.

ment is not original or traditional and that neither the past nor the present of the underdeveloped countries resembles in any important respect the past of the now developed countries."[59] The now developed countries, though surely once undeveloped, were never underdeveloped in the sense of the relationships of cultural, economic, and political dependence which bind the Third World today to foreign powers.

The emphasis upon developmental stages attributes a history to the developed countries, but denies a history to underdevelopment because it is regarded as an original condition. The underdeveloped nations of the Third World, however, participated in the same historical processes as did the developed nations. Indeed, Frank argues that underdevelopment is causally related to the process of development in the West. "Underdevelopment is not due to the survival of archaic institutions and the existence of capital shortage in regions that have remained isolated from the stream of world history. On the contrary, underdevelopment was and still is generated by the very same historical process which also generated economic development: the development of capitalism itself."[60]

Whether or not one would adopt the Marxist perspective of A. G. Frank, the model of the stages of growth (as derived from the experience of the West) has little applicability as a prescriptive formula for development in the non-Western world. Increasingly, most theorists would agree with Dankwart Rustow that there is no single pattern of modernization and development, no one universal and indispensable prerequisite. "There is no reason to search for a single universal recipe," Rustow writes. "Instead, each country must start with a frank assessment of its particular liabilities and assets; and each will be able to learn most from those countries whose problems most closely resemble its own."[61]

The Challenge of Modernization

If the definition and measurement of political development has been the subject of debate, the notion of modernization has been even more of a problem. Modernity is a chimera which haunts the social sciences. Endless debates occur over the exact date or the decisive event or events

[59]A. G. Frank, "The Development of Underdevelopment," in *Latin America: Underdevelopment or Revolution* (New York: Monthly Review Press, 1969), p. 4.

[60]Ibid., p. 9.

[61]Dankwart A. Rustow, *A World of Nations: Problems of Political Modernization* (Washington: The Brookings Institution, 1967), pp. 275–76. The ethnocentric bias of the development literature is examined in the excellent article by Satish Arora, "Pre-Empted Future?" cited above.

which ushered in modernity, and in the attempt to conceptualize its elusive character, a plethora of definitions have been put forward.

Marion Levy has sought a definition of modernity in the relationship of man to technology. "The greater the ratio of inanimate to animate sources of power and the greater the multiplication of effort as the effect of application of tools, the greater the degree of modernization."[62] C. E. Black describes modernization as "the process by which historically evolved institutions are adapted to the rapidly changing functions that reflect the unprecedented increase in man's knowledge, permitting control over his environment, that accompanied the scientific revolution." It involves, he argues, "a worldwide transformation affecting all human relationships."[63] For Dankwart Rustow, modernization is a process of "rapidly widening control over nature through closer cooperation among men." It implies "an intellectual, a technological, and a social revolution."[64]

Fundamental to the concept of modernization is the increasing control man has over his natural and social environments. In this notion of modernization, at least three separate dimensions may be discerned—the technological, the organizational, and the attitudinal. The technological dimension involves preeminently industrialization and embodies the contrast between pre-industrial and industrial societies. The organizational dimension reflects the degree of differentiation and specialization and embodies the contrast between simple and complex societies. The attitudinal dimension is that of rationality and secularization and contrasts the scientific versus the religious-magical perspective.

The dimensions of modernization (technological, organizational and attitudinal) are frequently associated with a supporting complex of more specific changes—urbanization, the growth of literacy, the spread of mass communications, and political participation. While it may be argued that certain changes go together with a high incidence of correlation, it is yet to be empirically determined whether or not modernization is a package, that is, whether, or in what degree, the various elements of the complex are systemically related. Indeed, the various aspects of modernization may be discrete and have no necessary relationship one to another. Few nations of Africa or Asia, for example, are ever likely to become predominantly urban or industrial, although they may well come to be characterized by highly differentiated political structures, a rational-scientific perspective, widespread literacy, and mass communi-

---

[62]Marion J. Levy, Jr., *Modernization and the Structure of Societies* (Princeton: Princeton University Press, 1966), pp. 35–36.

[63]C. E. Black, *The Dynamics of Modernization* (New York: Harper and Row, 1966), p. 7.

[64]Rustow, *A World of Nations*, pp. 1–5.

cations. Modernity, as defined in terms of a syndrome of qualities, an all-or-nothing package deal, may simply be an ethnocentric projection of Western experience—and is, in some respects, a highly idealized self-image.

The *image* of modernity, however, is infused with a Western bias, and just "how much of modernity is Western and how much of Western society is modern" remains both a theoretical and empirical question.[65] The process of modernization is accompanied almost always by the adoption of what are peculiarly Western cultural traits. This is the excess baggage that is most accurately described as "Westernization."

Rustow suggests that the spread of modernization involves a dynamic blend of traditional and Western influences. There are those modern traits developed or adopted "by virtue of their rationality and instrumental efficiency." There are those "traditional or parochial traits retained by the original modernizers and taken over by others on the strength of the prestige of those pioneers." Finally, there are those traditional elements of the indigenous culture which survive after the modern impact. "Some of these may even be reasserted more strongly as psychological counterweights to imported modernity."[66] Aspects of traditional culture—as in the arts, for example—may be emphasized so as to provide a context of cultural continuity and of identity in the process of modernization and change.

Seeking the fulfillment of their aspirations for independence, the nationalist elites of the new states have committed themselves to rapid economic growth and social transformation. They aim to bring their countries into the modern world without loss of cultural integrity, to enable them to share what they see as a better life provided by an expanding technological-scientific world culture. The aspiration for modernity is almost universal: Few leaders are willing to relegate their nations to ethnographic museums—fewer still have the choice.

The desires for a higher standard of living, for better health and education, for the ease and efficiency of mechanical and electronic gadgetry, and for the delights of mass entertainment have given the push toward modernization compelling force. But, as Rustow warns, "the effects of modernization are morally ambiguous." Together with unprecedented benefits, modernization "brings inevitable hazards and deprivations."[67] The process of modernization is disruptive, the source of discontent and social conflict. Indeed, in those areas where modernization has proceeded most rapidly, conflict and discontent may be most

---

[65]Samuel P. Huntington, "The Change to Change: Modernization, Development, and Politics," *Comparative Politics* 3(April, 1971): 295.

[66]Rustow, *A World of Nations,* p. 10.

[67]Ibid., pp. 8–9.

evident. This arises, in part, because of differential access to the benefits of modernity and new awareness of relative group differences. Also, modernization may well bring an absolute decline in the quality of life for those least able to take advantage of it. Beyond all this, however, even for the beneficiaries of modernization, the revolution of rising expectations may set goals which are unrealistic and simply unattainable. The hopes which modernization creates may then become the frustrations which feed political unrest and revolution.

Sensitive to the problems of unilinear and evolutionary sequence, C. E. Black has sought to distinguish certain critical problems that all modernizing societies must face. He does so in terms of "phases of modernization":

> (1) *the challenge of modernity*—the initial confrontation of a society, within its traditional framework of knowledge, with modern ideas and institutions, and the emergence of advocates of modernity; (2) *the consolidation of modernizing leadership*—the transfer of power from traditional to modernizing leaders in the course of a normally bitter revolutionary struggle often lasting several generations; (3) *economic and social transformation*—the development of economic growth and social change to a point where a society is transformed from a predominantly rural and agrarian way of life to one predominantly urban and industrial; and (4) *the integration of society*—the phase in which economic and social transformation produces a fundamental reorganization of the structure throughout the society.[68]

Black examines each of these problems in terms of various criteria which determine the pattern of modernization. He is concerned with the timing of the transfer of power from traditional to modernizing elites —whether it occurred early or late relative to other societies. He wants to know whether the immediate political challenge of modernity to the traditional elite was internal or external; whether the society retained a continuity of territory and population in the process of modernization or whether it experienced a fundamental regrouping of lands and peoples; and whether or not the society experienced a prolonged period of colonial rule. Lastly, Black distinguishes between those societies which confronted the challenge of modernization with developed institutions which could to a substantial degree be adapted to the functions of modernity and those with essentially undeveloped institutions which largely gave way to those borrowed from more modern societies.[69] It is

---

[68]Black, *The Dynamics of Modernization,* pp. 67–68.

[69]Ibid., p. 96.

the *challenge of modernization* that gives fundamental importance to the problem of political development.

The Concept of Political Development

Political modernization and political development, as terms, have each been used to refer to the same process of change. Frequently, they are used interchangeably by the same person. Each writer, however, has tended to modify the definition of one or the other of the terms to suit his specific interests. Thus, virtually every definition of political modernization and of political development has been unique.

Lucian Pye has drawn from the literature ten different definitions of political development:

1. the political prerequisite of economic development;
2. the politics typical of industrial society;
3. political modernization;
4. the operation of a nation-state;
5. administrative and legal development;
6. mass mobilization and participation;
7. building of democracy;
8. stability and orderly change;
9. mobilization and power;
10. one aspect of a multi-dimensional process of social change.[70]

Referring to Pye's list, Dankwart Rustow argues that this "is obviously at least nine too many."[71] Huntington goes further to suggest that "if there are ten definitions of political development, there are ten too many, and the concept is, in all likelihood, superfluous and dysfunctional."[72] In lieu of another term altogether to describe this elusive yet important concept, most political scientists have sought to refine the notion of political development and give it more precise meaning.

We distinguish the concept of political modernization from that of political development and regard them as theoretically distinct pro-

---

[70] Pye, *Aspects of Political Development,* pp. 33–45.

[71] Dankwart Rustow, "Change as the Theme of Political Science," paper delivered at the International Political Science Association Round Table, Torino, September, 1969, quoted in Huntington, "The Change to Change," p. 303.

[72] Huntington, "The Change to Change," p. 303. Huntington backs away from his earlier use of the term and focuses on "the critical relationship between political participation and political institutionalization without worrying about the issue of which should be labeled 'political development.' " (pp. 303–305) Development, however, as we shall argue later, if it has any utility as a concept, lies not in one or the other of these two variables, but in the relationship itself.

cesses. As we shall argue later, development is most usefully understood in terms of a system's response capacity in relationship to demands. We reserve the term "modernization" to refer to those changes (not necessarily systematically related) associated with man's increasing control over his natural and social environments—changes associated most frequently with the technological and scientific revolution of the past four hundred years. The identification of development with modernization, as Huntington suggests, drastically limits the applicability of the concept of political development "in both time and space." Development would be "identified with one type of political system, rather than a quality which might characterize any type of political system."[73] If development is defined in terms of modernization, it would be impossible to speak of "political development" with regard to ancient Athens, the Roman Empire, or the Zulu kingdom before its encounter with the British—though each of these may have been fully developed in capacity to meet the limited demands made upon it. Indeed, some "traditional" societies may have been better able to meet certain types of demands than modern, technological societies.

The processes of modernization and development, if distinct, are not unrelated. Modernization has provided the thrust behind increasing demands on political systems throughout the world. To effectively respond, they must enhance their capacity to meet these demands—one way or another. The vehicle of increased capacity may itself be modernization—political modernization, involving technological, organizational, and attitudinal change. Organizationally, the process involves the emergence of differentiated and specialized political structures—of which a centralized bureaucracy and an infrastructure of political parties and interest groups are most frequently identified as critical. Attitudinally, political modernization has been associated with a broad syndrome of rational and secular orientations—and particularly with a participant orientation.[74] Robert Ward and Dankwart Rustow have described the modern polity as characterized by:

1. A highly differentiated and functionally specific system of governmental organization;
2. A high degree of integration within this governmental structure;
3. The prevalence of rational and secular procedures for the making of political decisions;

---

[73]Samuel P. Huntington, "Political Development and Political Decay," *World Politics* 17 (1965): 389.

[74]See Kenneth Sherrill, "The Attitudes of Modernity," *Comparative Politics* 1 (January 1969): 184–210; Alex Inkeles, "Participant Citizenship in Six Developing Countries," *American Political Science Review* 63 (December 1969): 1120–41; and Daniel Lerner, *The Passing of Traditional Society: Modernizing the Middle East* (Glencoe, Ill.: Free Press, 1958).

4. The large volume, wide range, and high efficiency of its political and administrative decisions;
5. A widespread and effective sense of popular identification with the history, territory, and national identity of the state;
6. Widespread popular interest and involvement in the political system, though not necessarily in the decision-making aspects thereof;
7. The allocation of political roles by achievement rather than ascription; and
8. Judicial and regulatory techniques based upon a predominantly secular and impersonal system of law.[75]

We use "political modernization" in a special and restricted sense. Political parties, for example, are a modern phenomena and are structures which may significantly enhance system capacity, but their mere existence in a system does not denote development. The qualities of Ward and Rustow's "modern polity" are no guarantee of a system's capacity to meet demands.

The term *political development* continues to be used ambiguously, but, for all the variation, something of a consensus is beginning to emerge. Some of the most important contributions to the study of political development have come out of the Committee on Comparative Politics of the Social Science Research Council (SSRC). Under the inspiration of Gabriel Almond, its chairman during the late 1950s and early 1960s, the Committee has evolved a broad conception of development.[76]

James S. Coleman contrasts the perspective of the SSRC Committee with two views of political development he describes as historical and typological. "From the *historical* perspective political development refers to the totality of changes in political culture and structure associated with the major transformative processes of social and economic modernization first unleashed in Western Europe in the sixteenth century and which subsequently have spread, unevenly and incompletely, throughout the world. The *typological* perspective envisages the process

[75]Dankwart A. Rustow and Robert E. Ward, "Introduction," in Ward and Rustow, eds., *Political Modernization in Japan and Turkey* (Princeton: Princeton University Press, 1964), pp. 6–7.

[76]Beginning with *The Politics of Developing Areas,* edited by Almond and Coleman and published in 1960, the SSRC group opened a decade of empirical research on the problems of political development. The approach, formulated in Almond's influential introduction to that volume, was modified and extended in Almond and Powell's *Comparative Politics: A Developmental Approach* (1966), but Almond's most critical role has been in his stimulus to others. From his early efforts the SSRC Committee on Comparative Politics initiated its "Studies in Political Development," published by Princeton University Press. The series culminated in 1971 in *Crises and Sequences in Political Development,* with contributions by Binder, Coleman, LaPalombara, Pye, Verba, and Weiner. While the volume exposes serious differences and yet unresolved problems (as Verba's last chapter clearly indicates), it underscores a fundamentally common perspective.

as a movement from a postulated pre-modern 'traditional' polity to a post-traditional 'modern' (or developed) polity. . . ." Each of these approaches, he suggests, are vulnerable to at least three criticisms: (1) they tend to "exaggerate the static, sacred, and undifferentiated character of 'traditional' societies and suppress the enormous diversity of 'initial institutional patterns:' " (2) they imply a unilinear and irreversible movement between the poles of tradition and modernity; and (3) they are heavily ethnocentric, with an image of the "end stage" reflecting a Western normative bias. In contrast, Coleman offers (in an unfortunate choice of terms) what he calls an "evolutionary perspective." Political development is regarded as a process involving an "open-ended increase in the capacity of political man to initiate and institutionalize new structures, and supporting cultures, to cope with or resolve problems, to absorb and adapt to continuous change, and to strive purposively and creatively for the attainment of new societal goals."[77]

In the conception of the SSRC Committee, "the political development process is a continuous interaction among the processes of structural *differentiation,* the imperatives of *equality,* and the integrative, responsive, and adaptive *capacity* of a political system."[78] These three key variables—differentiation, equality, and capacity—constitute the "development syndrome."

Looking back over the eight years' work of the Committee, Lucian Pye writes:

> What began as a pragmatic exercise in collecting statements characterizing political modernization and development led in time to the analytical observation that the strains of development involve more than just the tensions of change, for inherent within modern societies are certain fundamental and dynamic contradictions unknown to traditional society. Basic to the development syndrome are the contradictions among the rising demands for *equality,* which involves popular participation, adherence to universalistic laws, and respect for achievement performance; a greater need for *capacity* and for a more efficient and far-ranging governmental system; and an inexorable tendency toward greater *differentiation* as the division of labor and specialization of tasks becomes more widespread.[79]

In the process of modernization, all societies must come to terms with the problems and contradictions inherent within the development syndrome. These problems, or *crises,* have arisen historically and are identi-

---

[77]James S. Coleman, "The Development Syndrome: Differentiation-Equality-Capacity," in SSRC Committee, *Crises and Sequences,* pp. 73–74.

[78]Ibid., p. 74.

[79]"Forward," in SSRC Committee, *Crises and Sequences,* p. vii.

fied as those of identity, legitimacy, participation, penetration, and distribution.[80]

The Identity Crisis: Development requires that, in a process of horizontal integration, the people of a state come to recognize themselves as forming a single political community and that as individuals they feel their personal identities in part defined by their attachment to that community. This involves the process of nation building, in which a new political community is created so as to bring the nation and the state into alignment.[81]

The Legitimacy Crisis involves the problem of agreement on the legitimate nature of authority and the proper responsibilities of government.[82]

The Participation Crisis occurs when uncertainty exists over the appropriate rate of expanding participation and when the influx of new participants creates serious strains on existing institutions. In a sense, the participation crisis arises out of the emergence of interest groups and parties—catalysts to increasing demands.[83]

The Penetration Crisis involves the problem of creating a political infrastructure of formal institutions linking the rulers and the ruled for the purpose of implementing governmental policy and securing compliance. This is the process of state building and is associated with the emergence of a centralized bureaucracy and with increased regulative and extractive capacity.[84]

The Distribution Crisis fundamentally involves the question "Who gets what, when, and for what purpose?" and reflects the responsive capacity of the political system in meeting the rising demands.[85]

> Political development, in these terms, is seen as the acquisition by a political system of a consciously sought, and a qualitatively new and enhanced political capacity as manifested in the successful institution-

---

[80]An additional crisis, "integration," had appeared in earlier discussions. "This crisis covers the problems of relating popular politics to governmental performance, and thus it represents the effect and compatible solution of both the penetration and participation crises." Pye, *Aspects of Political Development,* p. 65.

[81]See Pye, "Identity and the Political Culture," in SSRC Committee, *Crises and Sequences,* pp. 101–34.

[82]See Pye, "The Legitimacy Crisis," in SSRC Committee, *Crises and Sequences* pp. 135–58.

[83]See Myron Weiner, "Political Participation: Crisis of the Political Process," in SSRC Committee, *Crises and Sequences,* pp. 159–204.

[84]See Joseph LaPalombara, "Penetration: A Crisis of Governmental Capacity," in SSRC Committee *Crises and Sequences,* pp. 205–32.

[85]See LaPalombara, "Distribution: A Crisis of Resource Management," in SSRC Committee, *Crises and Sequences,* pp. 233–82.

> alization of (1) new patterns of *integration* and *penetration* regulating and containing the tensions and conflicts produced by increased differentiation, and (2) new patterns of *participation* and resource *distribution* adequately responsive to the demands generated by the imperatives of equality. The acquisition of such a performance capacity is, in turn, a decisive factor in the resolution of the problems of *identity* and *legitimacy*.[86]

The particular pattern of political development in any society, according to Pye, will depend largely upon the sequence in which these crises arise and the ways in which they are resolved. In the new states of the Third World, they appear simultaneously and with overpowering immediacy.[87]

Sidney Verba argues that these crises "do not easily or naturally form a sequential pattern. They are problems or questions that exist at any point in time . . . They may arise, be resolved, and arise again in a different form."[88] Verba prefers to reserve the term *crisis* for the situation where a "problem" arises and some new institutionalized means of handling it is required to satisfy discontent. In this sense, crises represent "the major decisional points at which the society is redefined, and are therefore relevant to sequential changes."[89] Statements about sequential ordering must necessarily be probabilistic. Contradictions may exist among the variables of differentiation, equality, and capacity, and in the resolution of one crisis, another may be deepened. Institutionalized capacity in one area may be a major source of demands for capacity elsewhere. Balanced growth (that is, more institutionalized capacity in all five problem areas) may be a long-run phenomenon, but, as Verba points out, the short-run may be characterized by considerable imbalance.[90]

In *Comparative Politics: A Developmental Approach,* Gabriel Almond and G. Bingham Powell, Jr. examine system performance in terms of "capabilities." *Extractive capability* refers to system performance in drawing material and human resources from the domestic and international environments. "The capability to obtain such resources underlies the other capabilities, and limits or expands the possibilities of attaining various goals for the system and the society." *Regulative capability* refers to the exercise of control over the behavior of individuals and groups.

---

[86]Coleman, "The Development Syndrome," pp. 74–75.

[87]Pye, *Aspects of Political Development,* pp. 63–67.

[88]Sidney Verba, "Sequences and Development," SSRC Committee, *Crises and Sequences,* pp. 299–300.

[89]Ibid., p. 306.

[90]Ibid., p. 310.

Distributive capability refers to the allocation of values—"goods, services, honors, statuses, and opportunities of various kinds." *Symbolic capability* is "the rate of *effective* symbol flow from the political system into the society and the international environment." These symbolic outputs include affirmation of values, statements of policy, displays of flags, appeals to patriotism, etc. Through symbolic outputs, the political leaders may mobilize support in the face of low levels of extractive, regulative, and distributive capabilities or may seek "to gain acceptance of policies which they deem necessary but which are painful or unpopular." Clearly, however, symbolic capability, in drawing on the reserves of support, may be quickly exhausted unless augmented by enhanced capabilities in other areas.

Almond and Powell then turn to capabilities of an analytically different character. They identify the *responsive capability* as the relationship between inputs and outputs. Although they emphasize response in terms of meeting demands, response may be either positive or negative, that is, it may involve an attempt to satisfy demands or to repress them through coercion. "Relating system challenges to system responses," Almond and Powell state, "is the way to explanation and prediction in the field of political development."[91] Political systems interact both with their domestic and international environments, and each system may be analyzed in terms of performance capabilities with each. Thus, Almond and Powell distinguish *domestic and international capabilities*, each characterized by extractive, regulative, distributive, and symbolic capabilities.[92]

Their "developmental approach" is essentially taxonomic. They make little effort to operationalize the concept of capability in terms of which performance levels can be measured. In a later article, however, Almond recognizes that the "capacity to measure and evaluate performance is one of the principal goals of political theory." In the primitive stages of theory in comparative politics, Almond feels that he can do no more than offer "a set of coding categories preliminary to operationalizing and empirical research which might bring us closer to a reliable set of indicators of performance."[93]

Almond and Powell define political development as "the increased differentiation and specialization of political structures and the in-

---

[91]Gabriel Almond and G. Bingham Powell, Jr., *Comparative Politics: A Developmental Approach* (Boston: Little, Brown, 1966), p. 37.

[92]Ibid., pp. 190–205.

[93]Gabriel Almond, "Political Development: Analytical and Normative Perspectives," *Comparative Political Studies* 1 (January 1969): 461. See also his discussion of tentative measures, pp. 462–64.

creased secularization of political culture."[94] By secularization, they mean "the process whereby men become increasingly rational, analytic, and empirical in their political action."[95] "The significance of such development is in general," they contend, "to increase the effectiveness and efficiency of the performance of the political system: to increase its capabilities."[96] Enhanced capabilities, however, are by no means guaranteed by structural differentiation and cultural secularization. Indeed, these processes may well undermine system capabilities and exacerbate system challenges as roles and structures become so fragmented as to be unable to effectively respond to demands which may be increasing both in volume and in intensity. What they have done in focusing on differentiation and secularization is to define political development in terms of modernization. Development defined in terms of the vehicles of capability rather than in term of capability itself necessarily leads to the rather clumsy distinction between positive and negative development—negative development referring to the decline in performance capabilities which Huntington has described as "political decay."[97]

Almond and Powell's "basic theoretical statement" is that "the development of higher levels of system capabilities is dependent upon the development of greater structural differentiation and cultural secularization."[98] Their concern is fundamentally with problem solving capability—with the capacity of the political system to respond successfully to new problems and demands.

Capacity is also the critical element in the SSRC Committee's development syndrome. Differentiation may be a vehicle of enhanced system capacity, but unless differentiation involves at the same time the integration of newly differentiated structures and roles, it may reduce rather than increase a system's capacity to adapt and respond. The demands for equality—for meaningful access to the political system and for the distribution of material and symbolic benefits—impose strain on the limited resources of the system. Development demands an integrative, responsive, adaptive, and innovative capacity. Capacity involves sheer magnitude or scope in political and governmental performance; rationality in administration; and effectiveness in the implementation of public policy. "It is a capacity not only to overcome the divisions and manage the tensions created by increased differentiation, but to respond

---

[94]Almond and Powell, *Comparative Politics: A Developmental Approach,* p. 105.

[95]Ibid., p. 24.

[96]Ibid., p. 105.

[97]See ibid., pp. 34–35: Samuel P. Huntington, "Political Development and Political Decay," pp. 386–430.

[98]Almond and Powell, *Comparative Politics: A Developmental Approach,* p. 323.

to or contain the participatory and distributive demands generated by the imperatives of equality. It is also a capacity to innovate and to manage continuous change."[99]

This conception is closely related to that of Alfred Diamant. "In its most general form," Diamant writes, "political development is a process by which a political system acquires an increased capacity to sustain successfully and continuously new types of goals and demands and the creation of new types of organizations." For this process to continue over time, Diamant posits the need for differentiated and centralized political structures "to command resources from and power over wide spheres and regions of society." The notion of equality is implied in the criterion of sustaining new goals and demands as an ever increasing number of groups demand the right to participate in political life. Political development, while having common content, is unlikely to have a common outcome. It is not a unilinear process toward a given "end" or "final stage," but is a continuous process of "meeting new goals and demands in a flexible manner."[100]

S. N. Eisenstadt argues that the central problem of political development (or, as he prefers, political modernization) is the ability of a political system to adapt itself to changing demands, "to absorb them in terms of policy-making and to assure its own continuity in the face of continuous new demands and new forms of political organization. . . . The ability to deal with continuous changes in political demands is the crucial test of such sustained political . . . development. . . ."[101] Diamant and Eisenstadt, in defining development in terms of the capacity to sustain continuous change, emphasize the responsive capacity of the system.

The political system, however, is not simply reactive, a dependent variable defined in terms of a changing environment to which it is open and responsive. It possesses an autonomy which can shape and control its environment at the same time it may be affected by that environment. Recognizing this dynamic and dialectical relationship, Manfred

---

[99]Coleman, "The Development Syndrome," pp. 78–79.

[100]Alfred Diamant, "The Nature of Political Development," in Jason L. Finkle and Richard W. Gable, eds., *Political Development and Social Change,* 1st ed. (New York: John Wiley and Sons, 1966), pp. 92–93. Also see Diamant, "Political Development: Approaches to Theory and Strategy," in John D. Montgomery and William J. Siffin, eds., *Approaches to Development: Politics, Administration, and Change* (New York: McGraw-Hill, 1966), pp. 15–47.

[101]S. N. Eisenstadt, "Initial Institutional Patterns of Political Mobilization," *Civilizations* 12 (1962), reprinted in Claude E. Welch, Jr., ed., *Political Modernization* (Belmont, Calif.: Wadsworth, 1967), p. 252. Also see Eisenstadt, "Modernization: Growth & Diversity," *India Quarterly* 20 (1964): 17–42; Eisenstadt, *Modernization: Protest and Change* (Englewood Cliffs, N.J.: Prentice-Hall, 1966).

Halpern defines political development as the "enduring capacity to generate and absorb persistent transformation." "What we need to know in order to understand any political system in relationship to modernization," Halpern argues, "is the interaction among three elements: the *imbalances* existing within and among the systems of a society. . . . and the *will* and *capacity* of a society to transform these imbalances so that it may generate and absorb continuing transformation."[102] Capacity suggests potentiality, the *ability* to perform and not actual performance.[103] Political development must involve then both the will and the capacity to initiate, absorb, and sustain continuous transformation.

The Dialectics of Development

The literature of political development remains heavily laden with the stability orientations of democratic pluralism and its emphasis on modifying change. Modernization, inherently destabilizing, is too often seen as a threat rather than as an opportunity. Unequipped conceptually to deal with radical change and fundamental system transformation, American social science has been imbued with a normative commitment to order.

The commitment to modernization in the new nations has given primacy to politics. "Seek ye first the political kingdom," Kwame Nkrumah of Ghana declared, "and all things shall be added unto you."[104] Development, however, involves not merely the will but the capacity to control and direct change, and the institutional capacity to absorb change may be disproportionately small in comparison to the aspiration for change. The low level of institutionalization may be seen "in the weakness of the administration, in the lack of stability and continuity of basic political symbols and administrative and political frameworks, and also in the relative weakness and underdevelopment of various autonomous interest groups."[105] The forces of modernization are frequently initiated by a government to enhance its capacities, but once unleashed, the forces may proceed with autonomy and far outstretch

---

[102]Manfred Halpern, "The Rate and Costs of Political Development," *Annals* 358 (March 1965): 22. Also see Halpern, "The Revolution of Modernization in National and International Society," in Carl J. Friedrich, ed., *Revolution* (Nomos VIII, New York: Atherton, 1966), pp. 178–214.

[103]Verba, "Sequences and Development," p. 293.

[104]Kwame Nkrumah, *Ghana: The Autobiography of Kwame Nkrumah* (Camden, N.J.: Thomas Nelson and Sons, 1957), p. 163.

[105]Eisenstadt, "Initial Institutional Patterns of Political Modernization," in Welch, *Political Modernization,* p. 261.

the capacity of the government to control or regulate, much less respond, to them in any positive way. Many aspects of modernization may be irreversible, but development is always problematic. The alternative to development does not lie in the absence of change—for that option simply does not exist. No society is so hermetically sealed as to be insulated from the impact of external change, or so stagnant as to be unaffected by the pressures of internal demands.

Political modernization may involve increased differentiation and widespread participation. It may be characterized by the emergence of an effective military organization, modern bureaucratic forms, and an elaborate infrastructure of interest groups and parties. It cannot be assumed, however, that because "modernization is taking place, political development also must be taking place."[106]

Modernization represents both an opportunity and a challenge, for those forces which may enhance the capacity of the political system may at the same time heighten the demands on the system. The same forces which serve to create an identity with the nation-state may also sustain and strengthen primordial identities of religion, language, caste, and tribe. The same forces—education, communications, and economic growth—which may foster participant citizenship may act to increase the demands made on government beyond any capacity to meet them.

The processes of social change represented by modernization have unleashed a concomitant process of social mobilization. Karl Deutsch defines social mobilization as "the process in which major clusters of old social, economic and psychological commitments are eroded or broken and people become available for new patterns of socialization and behavior."[107] In political terms, social mobilization is translated into the demand for equality, for participation and a better life. "The process of social mobilization generates strong pressures toward increasing the capabilities of government, by increasing the volume and range of demands made upon the government and administration, and by widening the scope of politics and the membership of the politically relevant strata."[108]

The rising level of political demands may so strain the limited capacity of the system that institutionalization becomes increasingly difficult as participation expands. The process of modernization may unleash a "revolution of rising frustrations,"[109] as the gap widens between aspi-

---

[106]Huntington, "Political Development and Political Decay," p. 391.

[107]Karl Deutsch, "Social Mobilization and Political Development," *American Political Science Review* 55 (September 1961): 494.

[108]Ibid., p. 501.

[109]Daniel Lerner, "Toward a Communication Theory of Modernization," in Lucian Pye, ed., *Communications and Political Development* (Princeton: Princeton University Press, 1963), pp. 327–50.

ration and achievement. Reform may serve to foster in the masses aspirations that become the catalyst of revolution. The promise of political equality through universal franchise, mass education, the development of communications, welfare measures, and the pursuit of distributive justice all serve to bring forth new demands. They serve to create an awareness of poverty among the poor, to sustain a sense of relative deprivation, and to deepen group conflict as the social and economic inequities of the society are exposed and deepened. Insofar as the system can respond to newly mobilized groups and to accelerating demands, participation strengthens the system and reinforces its legitimacy. When the system is unable—or unwilling—to absorb new demands, participation may simply overwhelm performance capacity.

The nature and form of participation is of critical concern. Participation may involve, minimally, media exposure—simply being informed. It may expand along continua of both scope and intensity. It may involve "interest" in politics, voting, demonstration, or revolutionary activity. Participation, however, does not in itself reflect demands. Indeed, participation may be structured by the regime for the mobilization of support. Participation may become mandatory, as in China, for socializing citizens into a new political culture. The scope of participation in terms of demand formation may remain highly restricted, limited to the various elements of the political elite, but mass participation as mobilized support may be extensive. The modern society is participant, but not necessarily democratic.

"The primary problem of politics," writes Samuel Huntington, "is the lag in the development of political institutions behind social and economic change."[110]

> Political modernization involves the extension of political consciousness to new social groups and the mobilization of these groups into politics. Political development involves the creation of political institutions sufficiently adaptable, complex, autonomous, and coherent to absorb and order the participation of these new groups and to promote social and economic change in the society."[111]

The development of any political system depends on the relationship between political institutionalization[112] and political participation. As

---

[110]Samuel P. Huntington, *Political Order in Changing Societies* (New Haven: Yale University Press, 1968), p. 5.

[111]Ibid., p. 266.

[112]"Institutions are stable, valued, and recurring patterns of behavior." "Institutionalization is the process by which organizations and procedures acquire value and stability. The level of institutionalization of any political system can be defined by the adaptability, complexity, autonomy, and coherence of its organizations and procedures." Ibid., p. 12.

participation expands, the capacity of the political institutions to absorb change must also increase if stability is to be maintained.

Modernization itself is destabilizing, and Huntington is haunted by the spectre of political decay. "The primary problem is not liberty but the creation of a legitimate public order," Huntington argues, "Men may, of course, have order without liberty, but they cannot have liberty without order."[113] "The public interest," he writes, "is whatever strengthens governmental institutions."[114] If stability becomes the highest value, however, increased institutionalization may serve to create repressive order in which the expansion of participation is limited by the attempt to slow the process of social mobilization. This might be accomplished, by Huntington's prescription, through the reinforcement of horizontal divisions within the society, slowing the entry of new groups into politics; through limitations on communications, reducing exposure to mass media and access to higher education; and through suppression of competition among political elites, minimizing uncontrolled mobilization of the masses, as factions or parties appeal for new bases of support.[115]

In seeking to control and regulate the impact of modernization, Huntington seems to rely almost solely on the beneficence of the ruling elite to expand participation as the capacity to respond is enhanced. "In many, if not most, modernizing countries elections serve only to enhance the power of disruptive and often reactionary social forces and to tear down the structure of public authority."[116] Preferring the gov-

---

[113]Ibid., pp. 7–8.

[114]Ibid., p. 25.

[115]Huntington, "Political Development and Political Decay," pp. 419–21. In regard to Huntington's emphasis on order, perhaps the most important facet of institutionalization is the capacity of highly institutionalized political systems to maintain their autonomy by socializing newly politicized social groups so that they identify with and acquiesce to accepted (institutionalized) patterns of political activity. See *Political Order in Changing Societies,* pp. 20–22, 82–83.

The management of demands in the context of the modifying change orientation is imaginatively examined as strategies of political survival by W. Howard Wriggins, *The Ruler's Imperative* (New York: Columbia University Press, 1969). From the cases of Sukarno, Nasser, Bourguiba, Nkrumah, Bandaranaike, Nehru, and Ayub, Wriggins explores the premise that "the ruler's first imperative, and his most urgent desire, is to retain his position at the apex of government, for only from there can be affect the future of the polity he seeks to rule." p. vii. On the problem of demand response, also see Weiner, "Political Participation," in SSRC Committee, *Crises and Sequences,* pp. 159–204.

[116]Huntington, *Political Order in Changing Societies,* p. 7. Robert E. Welch, Jr., has distilled Huntington's argument down to nine asymmetric propositions. In the construction of a causal model, the explanation of political decay depends primarily on a chain of multiplicative (ratio) linkages: (1) An increase in the stress of social mobilization relative to the want-satisfaction capacity of economic development will produce an increase in social frustration. (2) An increase in the stress of social frustration relative to the

ernment of the day to an unknown alternative, he seems prepared to risk the danger of repressive order rather than to expose the system to instability and possible revolution. Here Huntington confronts the classic political problem: In preferring the philosopher king, he has no guarantee that wisdom will not be supplanted by tyranny.

A political elite committed to economic growth may stimulate the formation of demands in the process of inducing social change. Development programs may seek to create "felt needs" within the traditional society in order to facilitate innovation, but in an environment of scarcity, resources are limited, and the system will be most responsive to those commanding political capital—wealth, status, votes. Traditional elites may be reinforced to ensure stability and to suppress widening popular involvement. Repressive rule supplants democratic response in the name of order. Stability bought through repression, however, rather than through higher levels of institutional capacity in response to expanding participation, is the harbinger of chaos—for in the long run, no political system can insulate itself from the challenge of modernization.

If any government is to confront effectively the challenge of modernization, and meet the demands of expanding participation, it must have both the will and the capacity to initiate, absorb, and sustain continuous transformation. The critical factor in the developmental process is the ratio between capacity and demands. As demands increase, capacity must be enhanced to meet those demands (see figure 3). This capacity may be in the form of a positive response—or of negative response, that is, repression. Development, defined in terms of the ratio between capacity and demands, may require a dynamic gap between the two variables. Albert Hirschman sees economic development in terms of a sequence of disequilibria. The process of development involves "backward" linkage to the supply side of the economy and "forward" linkage to the demand side.[117] In terms of the political system, with participation somewhat beyond the capacity of the institutions to respond, the attempt to close the gap serves as the stimulus to higher levels of institutionalization. The interaction between capacity and demands, between institutionalization and participation, thus involves a staggered process of development, as each reacts to the other.

"economizing" capacity of vertical mobility opportunities will produce an increase in politicization. (3) An increase in the stress of politicization relative to the socializing capacity of political institutions will produce a decrease in value integration and consequently a decrease in political order. "A Causal Model of Political Modernization," unpublished paper, Department of Government, University of Texas, 1971, pp. 11–12.

[117] Albert Hirschman, *The Strategy of Economic Development* (New Haven: Yale University Press, 1968), and *Journeys Toward Progress* (New York: Doubleday Anchor, 1965). Also see Almond, "Political Development: Analytical and Normative Perspectives," pp. 456–57.

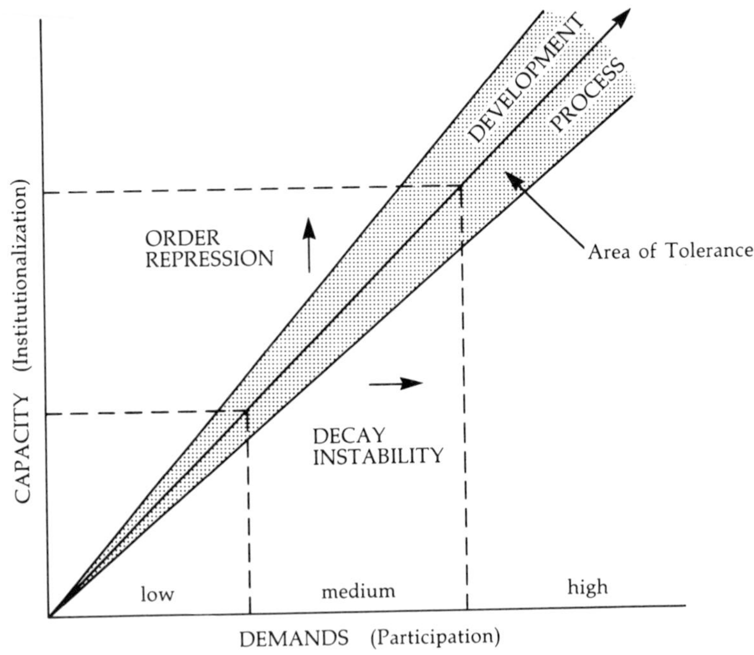

FIGURE 3 THE DEVELOPMENT PROCESS

The development process is dialectical, and the imbalance in demand serves as the incentive for enhanced capacity. The process involves a dynamic equilibrium, in which imbalance is the motive force of change. Beyond a critical range, however, an imbalance may be increasingly difficult to correct. Over-institutionalization is conducive to the establishment of repressive order; participation far beyond institutional capacity may foster unacceptable instability and political decay.[118]

The success of a political system in coping with the challenge of development is dependent upon its capacity to affect horizontal and vertical integration. The task of horizontal integration, of nation building, is the creation of a new sense of community and common identity among those who previously may have shared only the oppression of

[118]In a similar formulation, Fred Riggs states that, in general, the wider the gap between capacity and demands, "the more violent, irreconcilable and ideological the conflict between the competing values of equality and capacity; the narrower this gap, the more is this conflict rational, pragmatic, and susceptible to compromise." "The Dialectics of Development Conflict," *Comparative Political Studies* 1 (July 1968): 205. Also see Riggs, "The Comparison of Whole Political Systems," in Robert T. Holt and John E. Turner, eds., *The Methodology of Comparative Research* (New York: Free Press, 1970), pp. 73–121.

a common colonial master. The people of the polyglot states of Africa and Asia must extend their identity beyond the primordial bonds of tribe, caste, language, and religion to embrace a more inclusive national community. Horizontal integration does not require that traditional sources of identity be abandoned, but they must be transcended. Ideology, perhaps combining elements of tradition and modernity, is the instrument for the creation of a new political culture of shared values, common goals, and a minimum consensus on the institutions of conflict resolution.

Horizontal integration may take place only to the degree that vertical integration is extensive in scope and penetrating in depth. The capacity of the system to generate and absorb change, to respond to demands of expanding participation, requires effective channels of linkage between mass and elite. The institutions of government must command confidence and be regarded as legitimate. They must have the capacity to initiate change and to control its direction and intensity. Channels of access and communication must be available if the system is to respond successfully to continuous change. The political system cannot be simply the dependent variable in a changing world. It must possess the will and the capacity to intervene actively in its environment. Through the formal institutions of government, as well as through interest groups and parties, the political system must provide an infrastructure capable of accommodating the rapidly increasing numbers seeking entry. The success of the developmental effort, within the range of available resources, will depend on the ability of these structures to acquire legitimacy and stability and to provide meaningful access and effective response. What for the West took centuries the new nations seek now to accomplish in decades. The fundamental crises of integration and institutionalization, met sequentially in the West, confront the new nations simultaneously and imperatively.[119]

The dialectical model of political development posits a dynamic equilibrium of change. The interaction of capacity and demand involves a continuously readjusted ratio, as increased demands require enhanced response capacity. Within a critical range of stability (to be determined empirically), change is incremental and reformist in character. Beyond that range, it becomes increasingly revolutionary, requiring fundamental and systemic change in the relationships of power. Conceptually, these forms of change may be distinguished as *modification* or modifying change and as *transformation* or transforming change.

---

[119]For the use of this framework in the analysis of a single system, see Robert L. Hardgrave, *India: Government and Politics in a Developing Nation* (New York: Harcourt Brace Jovanovich, 1970).

The developmental literature reveals a one-sided emphasis on modifying change. Stability, order, balance, equilibrium, and harmony have been both the fundamental reality and fundamental goal for most development scholars. The popular and prevalent "systems" and "structural-functional" approaches to the study of politics have decidedly emphasized such variables as homeostasis, equilibrium, and self-maintenance. Although the group approach has considered conflict within its theoretical purview, the bias has always been towards a balancing and countervailing competition that has enabled systems to resist transformation. The main strains of political culture and socialization literature have stressed benevolence and cooperation that have in turn promoted system-preservation. Even the elite approach, despite concern for revolutionary elites and counter elites, has cultivated an attachment for the study of modification. By focusing analysis most frequently on the politics and policies of elite actors within "the system," this approach accounts well for the conscious development of moderate programs designed to preserve the ongoing sociopolitical system.

The preoccupation with and glorification of modification in American social science has resulted in a serious state of underdevelopment in the overall study of political change. Patterns of conflict, tension, competition, and violence have been considered as aberrations and abnormalities in the political process. These abnormalities are intellectually tolerated only when they contribute to system stability, preservation, and maintenance. This stability orientation arises, in part, from the self-image of social science itself, as inquiry directed to the analysis of "the usual," (recurrent behavior about which general theories may be constructed). Revolutionary change is usually regarded, both by the revolutionaries themselves as well as by those who may suffer, as a breach of normalcy—and thus, almost by definition, outside the purview of social science.

The sterility of this exercise has become increasingly evident. The definition of development and modernization in terms of order in the midst of a world of change and in terms of stability in the midst of a world of instability was first criticized and questioned by those who studied either non-Western societies or subcultures within Western societies. Malevolent orientations and conflictual activities were frequently integral and dominant characteristics of sociopolitical relations in such settings.

In the recent drive to understand the more radical features of change, a number of social scientists have returned to the study of conflict and violence as fundamental processes in social and political relations. Imbalance, inequality, and discontinuity are increasingly considered at least as important as symmetry, congruence, and continuity. This current trend can be seen in the proliferation of studies concentrating on class analysis and dialectical analysis in general.[120]

Modernization and political development are among the fundamental problems that confront man today. In assessing theoretical inquiry, our conceptual and methodological tools must be shaped with these problems in mind. The quest for theory must also be a quest for a profound understanding of societies caught in the midst of change.

---

[120]A slightly differing version of the above three paragraphs can be found in James A. Bill, "Political Violence and Political Change: A Conceptual Commentary," in Herbert Hirsch and David Perry, eds., *Political Microviolence* (New York: Harper and Row, forthcoming).

CHAPTER III

Political Culture and Socialization

The concept of political culture provides a new name for one of the oldest subjects of concern in political science—the cultural milieu in which political behavior takes place and to which it is systemically related. The term *political culture,* adapted from anthropology,[1] embraces much that has long been associated with such concepts as political ideology, public opinion, modal personality, and national character. More than simply offering a new label for long-standing concepts, the political culture approach seeks an explicit and systematic understanding of political orientations and behavior.[2]

Political Culture

Political culture, as a concept, was introduced by Gabriel Almond in his 1956 article, "Comparative Political Systems."[3] Sensitive to the am-

---

[1]See, for example, Alfred L. Kroeber and Clyde Kluckhohn, *Culture: A Critical Review of Concepts and Definition* (New York: Vintage Books, 1963); Alfred L. Kroeber and Talcott Parsons, "The Concepts of Culture and of Social System," *American Sociological Review* 23 (1958): 532–83; and Milton Singer, "The Concept of Culture," *International Encyclopedia of the Social Sciences,* vol. 3, pp. 527-43.

[2]Lucian Pye, "Political Culture," *International Encyclopedia of the Social Sciences,* vol. 12, p. 218.

[3]Gabriel Almond, "Comparative Political Systems," *Journal of Politics* 18 (1956): 391–409.

biguities in the anthropological use of the term *culture,* Almond specifically limited his concept to one of its many meanings, the "psychological orientation toward social objects." The term is used by Almond to refer to "specifically political orientations—attitudes toward the political system and its various parts, and attitudes toward the role of the self in the system."[4]

Sidney Verba describes political culture as consisting of "the system of empirical beliefs, expressive symbols, and values which define the situation in which political action takes place. It provides the subjective orientation to politics."[5] For Lucian Pye, "political culture is the set of attitudes, beliefs, and sentiments which give order and meaning to a political process and which provide the underlying assumptions and rules that govern behavior in the political system. It encompasses both the political ideals and the operating norms of a polity. Political culture is thus the manifestation in aggregate form of the psychological and subjective dimensions of politics. A political culture is the product of both the collective history of a political system and the life histories of the members of that system, and thus it is rooted equally in public events and private experiences."[6]

Every political system, Almond tells us, is "embedded" in a set of meanings and purposes. In seeking to define these psychological "orientations to political action," both explicit and implicit, Almond turned to one of the most influential works of contemporary social science, Parsons and Shils' *Toward a General Theory of Action.* Parsons and Shils contend that any orientation of the actor to his situation may be broken down into a set of analytical elements. These elements are not separate, but are rather different aspects or ingredients of orientation. Any orientation involves three components or modes: the cognitive, the cathectic (or affective), and the evaluative. The cognitive component is that of perception; the cathectic is that of feeling, by which the object is endowed with affective significance; and the evaluative is that of choice,

---

[4]Gabriel Almond and Sidney Verba, *The Civic Culture* (Princeton: Princeton University Press, 1963), pp. 13–14. In this chapter, the critical concepts of "attitude" and "orientation" are used synonymously. In any operationalization of the approach, however, it may be essential to introduce a clear conceptual distinction between these terms.

[5]Sidney Verba, "Comparative Political Culture," in Lucian Pye and Sidney Verba, eds., *Political Culture and Political Development* (Princeton: Princeton University Press, 1965), p. 513.

[6]Lucian Pye, "Political Culture," p. 218. Pye offers a schema for the comparative analysis of political culture, suggesting that there are "certain universal problems or themes with which all political cultures must deal in one manner or another." These problems are (1) the scope and function of politics; (2) concepts of power and authority; (3) political integration; (4) status of politics and politicians; (5) evaluating performance; (6) the affective dimension of politics; and (7) the balance between cooperation and competition. Ibid., pp. 221–23.

combining cognitive and cathectic orientations in judgment about the object.[7] Almond and Verba translate this frame of reference into three types of political orientation:

> (1) "cognitive orientation," that is, knowledge of and about the political system, its roles and the incumbents of these roles, its inputs, and its outputs;
> (2) "affective orientation," or feelings about the political system, its roles, personnel, and performance, and
> (3) "evaluational orientation," the judgments and opinions about political objects that typically involve the combination of value standards and criteria with information and feeling.[8]

The political culture of a society is defined operationally as the particular distribution of patterns of cognitive, affective, and evaluational orientations among the population toward political objects. These objects are divided into three broad classes: "(1) specific *roles* or *structures,* such as legislative bodies, executives, or bureaucracies; (2) *incumbents* of roles, such as particular monarchs, legislators, and administrators, and (3) particular public *policies, decisions,* or *enforcements* of decisions." These structures, incumbents, and decisions may be further distinguished in terms of their involvement in either the "input" process (the flow of demands from the society into the polity) or "output" processes (the conversion of these demands into authoritative policies).[9] Almond is concerned not only with the orientations to the system as a general object, its inputs and outputs, but also with political orientations to the self as an object, that is, with the individual as he views his own role in the political system.

Almond and Verba formulate a series of specific questions in such a way as to facilitate comparison and measurement: "The political culture becomes the frequency of different kinds of cognitive, affective, and evaluative orientations toward the political system in general, its input and output aspects, and the self as political actor."[10] On this basis, three ideal types of political culture are constructed: the parochial, the subject, and the participant. The *parochial political culture* is characterized by an absence of specialized political roles, as in many African tribal societies, and by the comparative absence of expectations among individuals that the political system will be responsive to their needs. The *subject political*

---

[7]Talcott Parsons and Edward Shils, *Toward a General Theory of Action* (Cambridge: Harvard University Press, 1951), pp. 58–60.

[8]Almond and Verba, *The Civic Culture,* p. 15.

[9]Ibid.

[10]Ibid., p. 17.

culture is characterized by a high frequency of orientations toward the system as a general object and toward the output processes of the system, but orientations toward input processes and toward the self as an active participant are minimal. The subject orientation to the political system, and especially to the output objects, involves cognitive recognition of specialized governmental authority, but affective and evaluative orientations may be either favorable or unfavorable. The *participant political culture* is one in which the members are explicitly oriented to the political system in all its aspects. Though their feelings and evaluations may range from acceptance to rejection, individual members of society always assume an "activist" role.[11]

The three political cultures represent a cumulative extension of orientation: One does not displace the other, but is combined with it. In this additive process, each of the "earlier" orientations are necessarily changed and affected. "The parochial orientations must adapt when new and more specialized orientations enter into the picture, just as both parochial and subject orientations change when participant orientations are acquired."[12]

In empirical reality, every political culture is a "mix," and the classification of parochial, subject, and participant cultures does not suggest homogeneity or uniformity, but the statistical frequency of particular orientations. Thus, even the most participant political culture may include parochials and subjects. Every political culture is characterized by a distribution of parochials, subjects, and participants. Political cultures are mixed in yet another sense: each member is himself a particular mix of parochial, subject, and participant orientations.

When the political culture is congruent with political structure, that is, when the cognitive, affective, and evaluative orientations reinforce the political institutions of a society, the culture is said to be "allegiant."[13] Many political cultures, however, are "systemically mixed," with significant portions of parochial, subject, and participant patterns of orientation. Distinguishing elite and mass political cultures within a society is usually possible, for example. If the gap is wide, this may pose a serious challenge to national identity. Myron Weiner has characterized India as having two political cultures, each operating at a different level. The first is that of "an emerging mass political culture," the second, an elite political culture. The mass culture is in the districts, permeating "local politics, both urban and rural, local party organization, and local administration. It is an expanding political culture which

---

[11]Ibid., pp. 17–19.

[12]Ibid., p. 20.

[13]Ibid., p. 21.

reaches out into the state legislative assemblies, state governments, and state administrations." The elite culture is shared by most of the English-speaking intelligentsia. It predominates in New Delhi and "is personified by India's planners, many of the national political leaders, and the senior administrative cadre." "Critical of the emerging, more popular, mass culture, which in large measure is its own creation," the elites have a defensive culture being superseded gradually by that of the mass.[14]

The process of nation building, of welding a cohesive political culture, involves the creation of a political community (a sense of identity among fellow citizens). Integration must be both vertical and horizontal, linking both mass and elite and the various groups of the society one with another in fellow feeling.[15] The mass political culture, particularly in the new nations, is rarely homogeneous and is, more often than not, highly fragmented. Racial, religious, linguistic, tribal, caste, ethnic, class, or geographic cleavages among the population may serve to sustain separate political subcultures. In a pluralistic society, these cleavages cut across each other, and the salience of any one in determining political identity is reduced accordingly. On the other hand, if the various cleavages of a society reinforce each other in a pattern of congruence, the emergence of a distinct and separate political subculture may provide the catalyst for the disintegration and dismemberment of the political system.[16]

The persistence of a systemic mix involves, Almond and Verba suggest, "inevitable strains between culture and structure, and a characteristic tendency toward structural instability."[17] Curiously, however, they make no attempt to determine subcultural variation. The most serious weakness in their data is that the national samples are undifferentiated. The distribution of participants, subjects, and parochials would almost seem to be random, although Almond and Verba are clearly sensitive to the fact that parochial responses are not random. Such responses are systemically related to socio-economic variables.

---

[14]Myron Weiner, "India: Two Political Cultures," in Pye and Verba, eds., *Political Culture and Political Development* p. 199.

[15]See Myron Weiner, "Political Integration and Political Development," in *Annals* 358 (March 1965): 52–64; Clifford Geertz, "The Integrative Revolution," in Clifford Geertz, ed., *Old Societies and New States* (New York: Free Press, 1963), pp. 105–57; Leonard Binder, "National Integration and Political Development," *American Political Science Review* 58 (September 1964): 622–31.

[16]See Seymour M. Lipset and Stein Rokkan, eds., *Party Systems and Voter Alignments: Cross-National Perspectives* (New York: Free Press, 1967), pp. 1–64, and Robert Dahl, ed., *Political Oppositions in Western Democracies* (New Haven: Yale University Press, 1966), pp. 332–401.

[17]Almond and Verba, *The Civic Culture*, p. 23.

Nevertheless, they make no attempt to determine just *who* are the people within each nation who diverge in orientation, nor do they relate the responses to socio-economic variables. Education and sex are the only elements introduced as factors of differentiation within each nation. Rural-urban differences, income, media exposure, ethnicity, and race, as variables, remain to be exhumed in secondary analysis.[18]

The Civic Culture

In their comparative study of political culture, Almond and Verba examine five democracies representing a wide range of political and historical experience: the United States, Great Britain, Germany, Italy, and Mexico. Out of their analysis of British political development, they construct a model of an ideal democratic culture—"the civic culture." It is neither traditional nor modern, but partakes of both; it is a culture of pluralism, of consensus and diversity.[19] It is an allegiant culture, but "more important, in the civic culture participant political orientations combine with and do not replace subject and parochial political orientations. . . . The nonparticipant, more traditional political orientations tend to limit the individual's commitment to politics and to make that commitment milder." In a sense, Almond and Verba argue, "the subject and parochial orientations 'manage' to keep in place the participant political orientations. . . . The maintenance of these more traditional attitudes *and their fusion* with the participant orientations lead to a balanced political culture in which political activity, involvement, and rationality exist but are balanced by passivity, traditionality, and commitment to parochial values."[20]

The civic culture is a particular mix, representing an ideal pattern of parochial, subject, and participant orientations at a particular moment in time. One would assume that the dialectical forces of change which produced the "mix" would continue to act and that parochial and subject orientations would steadily decline in favor of more purely participant orientations. Indeed, Almond and Verba contend that "a successful shift from a subject to a participant culture involves the diffusion of positive orientations toward a democratic infrastructure, the acquisition of norms of civic obligation, and the development of a sense of civic

---

[18]Using the Almond-Verba survey data, Giuseppe Di Palma has examined the pattern of political participation in four nations—Great Britain, Germany, Italy and the United States. See *Apathy and Participation: Mass Politics in Western Societies* (New York: Free Press, 1970).

[19]Almond and Verba, *The Civic Culture,* pp. 6–9.

[20]Ibid., p. 31–32.

competence among a substantial portion of the population."[21] Yet their ideal civic culture, best approximated by "the two relatively stable and successful democracies, Great Britain and the United States,"[22] rests on the maintenance of a distribution of parochial, subject, and participant orientations, not just within the individual, but among individuals within the population.[23] "The civic culture is a mixed political culture. In it many individuals are active in politics, but there are also many who take the more passive role of subjects. More important, even among those performing the active political role of the citizen, the roles of subject and parochial have not been displaced."[24]

The civic culture, with all its contradictions in political attitudes, seems for Almond and Verba "particularly appropriate for democratic political systems"[25] because it sustains a balance between governmental power and responsiveness, between consensus and cleavage, between citizen influence and citizen passivity. It is a political culture of "moderation," maintained by "the democratic myth of citizen competence."

> The decision maker must believe in the democratic myth—that ordinary citizens ought to participate in politics and that they are in fact influential. If the decision maker accepts this view of the role of the ordinary citizen, his own decisions serve to maintain the balance between governmental power and responsiveness. On the one hand, he is free to act as he thinks best because the ordinary citizen is not pounding on his door with demands for action. He is insulated by the inactivity of the ordinary man. But if he shares the belief in the influence potential of the ordinary man, his freedom to act is limited by the fact that he believes there *will* be pounding on his door if he does not act in ways that are responsive.[26]

This concept of the civic culture thus serves as an ideological justification for apathy and non-participation in democratic systems. The parochials are assumed to be uninvolved not because of the cumulative deprivations—poverty, lack of education, low media exposure—which may deny them effective political capital nor because they may be systematically prevented from gaining political access, but because they are regarded as fundamentally satisfied with the system: if they were not satisfied, they would be "pounding at the door."

---

[21]Ibid., p. 27.

[22]Ibid., p. 473.

[23]See ibid., chapter 6, "Functionalism and Systems Analysis," pp. 208–9.

[24]Almond and Verba, *The Civic Culture,* p. 474.

[25]Ibid., p. 476.

[26]Ibid., p. 486.

Orientation and Behavior

Almond has described the political system as "embedded" in the political culture, suggesting culture as the independent variable, but the relationship between system and culture remains ambiguous. Political culture is offered as "the connecting link between micro- and macro-politics." Almond and Verba contend that "the relationship between the attitudes and motivations of the discrete individuals who make up political systems and the character and performance of political systems may be discovered systematically through the concepts of political culture . . ." Political psychology is related to system performance by locating attitudinal and behavioral propensities in the political system as a whole, in its various parts, among subcultures, and at key points of initiative or decision in the political structure.[27] The frequent lack of congruence between political culture and political structure raises serious questions concerning the direction of causality, and Almond and Verba provide little guidance in terms of explanation.

Samuel Beer identifies political culture as one of four main interdependent variables, along with power, interests, and policy. The political culture shapes and conditions the interests and goals pursued, accounts for the origins of changes in the patterns of the political system, and may, in turn, be influenced by those patterns as unplanned and unintended behavior remakes values and beliefs.[28] Each clearly influences the other: the political culture may in considerable degree determine political structure, at the same time the political structure shapes the political culture. Pye warns, however, that the "danger of tautology is particularly great in precisely the area which is now the most important for the future development of theory—the relationship between political culture and political structures and institutions."[29]

If a political system is defined as all those interactions predominantly oriented to the authoritative allocation of values, the system would seem to be one of *behavior,* and not of attitudes. The "raw want" does not enter the political system until it has been articulated as a demand. The unarticulated orientations—what Robert Lane has called the "latent ideology"—would then seem to lie outside the political system. Easton's discussion of political culture in *A Systems Analysis of Political Life* seems

---

[27] Almond and Verba, *The Civic Culture,* p. 33.

[28] Samuel H. Beer, "The Analysis of Political System," in Samuel H. Beer and Adam B. Ulam, eds., *Patterns of Government,* 2nd ed. (New York: Random House, 1962), pp. 30, 41, 67. For an examination of Beer's breakdown of the principal components of political culture as values, beliefs, and attitudes, see Young C. Kim, "The Concept of Political Culture," *Journal of Politics* 26 (May 1964): 324–31.

[29] Pye, "Political Culture," p. 224.

limited to his concern with cultural limitations on demand-formation. What Almond understands to be political culture would constitute, in part, an important ingredient in Easton's notion of "support" insofar as such latent ideology or orientations affect behavior toward the political system.

Some sort of relationship between these orientations and actual behavior is assumed by both Easton and Almond. Almond's position is that people act in ways that can be variously categorized *because* they have internalized certain orientations of action. The problem is then to determine the nature of this relationship, i.e., what are these orientations and how are they related to behavior?

In an attempt to refine the notion of political culture for a more precise exploration of the relationship between orientations and behavior, Lane's study of the ideology of the common man is suggestive. "There should be no doubt," he writes, that "the common man has a set of emotionally charged political beliefs, a critique of alternative proposals, and some modest programs of reform. These beliefs embrace central values and institutions; they are rationalizations of interest (sometimes not his own); and they serve as moral justifications for daily acts and beliefs."[30] Lane admits, however, that for the common man, ideology is "latent," suggesting, perhaps more properly, a diffuse, often vague, orientation on the part of the common man toward those objects to which ideologies speak with self-conscious and systematic articulation. The beliefs of the common man, insofar as they are present, often remain unconscious, to be brought to the fore only by symbolic stimulation. His attitudes may remain dormant, his opinions nonexistent. Diffuse, amorphous, unconscious, these orientations to the political world nevertheless give to each individual a political identity.

The concept of political culture emphasizes that each individual has some sort of orientation to the political world. He does not, however, necessarily have *opinions* about it. Philip Converse, in "The Nature of Belief Systems in Mass Publics," explores orientations toward a number of designated issues. On the basis of his analysis, he presents a sharply dichotomous model of the population. For some, a "hard core of opinion on a given issue crystallizes and remains stable over time. For the remainder of the population, response sequences over time are statistically random." The mass public contains significant proportions of people who, for lack of information about a particular dimension of

---

[30]Robert E. Lane, *Political Ideology* (New York: Free Press, 1962), p. 16. Also see James C. Scott, *Political Ideology in Malaysia: Reality and the Beliefs of an Elite* (New Haven: Yale University Press, 1968), pp. 31–56; and Milton Rokeach, *Beliefs, Attitudes and Values* (San Francisco: Jossey-Bass, 1969).

controversy, offer opinions that vary randomly in direction during repeated inquiries over time.[31]

This indicates not so much *random* opinion as no opinion at all. In survey research, the question, in demanding a verbal response, may itself stimulate the formation of an opinion, creating one where none existed before. Thus, as the reservoir of political orientations, or latent ideology, is tapped by the question stimulus, the opinion is formed. There is always the danger, however, that the stimulus itself, no matter how sophisticated, will affect the response: the opinion elicited may be a distorted image of the orientations from which it is drawn. Some of these problems are revealed in *The Civic Culture,* especially in the data on Mexico, but they are endemic in survey research generally.

What is critical, and all too frequently ignored in the evaluation of survey data, is that all responses are given equal weight. In the responses of a single individual, considered and deeply-felt opinions may be indistinguishable from those reflecting little thought or concern. By the same token, in the aggregate, the stable opinion of an individual on a given issue is given equal weight to what may be simply the random or distorted response of another.

Problems in Cross-Cultural Methodology

The gap between orientation and behavior, discussed in the previous section, possesses methodological as well as theoretical difficulties of the first magnitude. The basic concept of the political culture approach is *orientation.* Therefore, one must be able to gain empirical, first hand knowledge of this critical phenomenon. Basically two developed methods enable the researcher to gather data concerning attitudes and orientations. One relies on verbal response; the other attributes specific attitudes on the basis of observed behavioral patterns. In both methods, the researcher remains one stage removed from his data, and no matter how sophisticated the technique, the gap remains unbridged. Even in the attempt to reach the latent orientations of the individual through physiological techniques (e.g., eye dilation measurement or galvanic skin response), the problem remains in linking orientation to action. Closely entwined with this general problem are a number of more specific methodological difficulties.

The problem of constructing a design that ensures equivalency confronts every scholar engaged in cross-cultural research. Equivalency is especially important when translating the survey instrument from one

---

[31]Philip Converse, "The Nature of Belief Systems in Mass Publics," in David Apter, ed., *Ideology and Discontent* (New York: Free Press, 1964), p. 242.

language into another for comparative purposes. Even more difficult than asking exactly the same question in different languages is the problem of subjective meaning. Party identification, for example, so long an object of survey research in the United States and Western Europe, may have a very different meaning in Mexico, Tunisia, or India. Differences may be traced to the structures of various party systems, but they may also be rooted in the individual's experience with that system and the associations he attaches to it. Even within the same system, the problem of equivalency may arise in the comparative analysis of subcultures. A standardized survey instrument may elicit similar response patterns from, for example, ghetto blacks and middle class white intellectuals, but whether these responses accurately reflect the orientation from which they are drawn is another matter altogether.

Attitudes cannot be compared in a vacuum. Alasdair MacIntyre, following Wittgenstein, underscores the fact that we can identify and define attitudes only in terms of the objects toward which they are directed: "The ability to construct comparative generalizations about attitudes depends on our already having solved the problem of how to construct comparative generalizations about institutions and practices."[32] To suggest, for example, that "trust" is an attitudinal characteristic of the politically modern man is meaningless unless we know something about the trustworthiness of the object in question. The belief of an individual that the authorities in a particular society are scoundrels may well be an accurate perception of reality. Participation, rather than necessarily fostering positive orientations to the political system, may involve increasing cynicism in a series of reality-testing experiences.

Cross-cultural research, between societies or within a single society, necessarily deepens the uncertainty which occurs even in monocultural research and infinitely expands the danger of error in design, implementation, and interpretation. In the actual conduct of research, the problem of the impact of the interview situation on the respondent and of the danger of response set (a disposition to answer in a certain way) remains. In some cultures, it might be considered impolite to respond to any question negatively. Thus each question, to the increasing frustration of the interviewer, may be greeted with enthusiastic affirmation. In other situations, the respondent, assuming that there must surely be a *right* answer to each question, will answer accordingly. Others, in an effort to please the interviewer, may simply offer what he thinks the interviewer would most like to hear.

---

[32]Alasdair C. MacIntyre, *Against the Self-Images of the Age* (New York: Schocken, 1971), pp. 261–62.

Errors in interpretation may be related to the analyst's lack of familiarity with the culture. They may be simply erroneous conclusions drawn from the data, as in Almond and Verba's implication that Italians have low system affect because they have little national pride.[33] These methodological problems are likely to be present in the development of any analytical tools for the study of political culture, but sensitivity to their presence can help to minimize them.[34]

The Concept of Sentiment

While sharing some of the methodological problems of "opinion" and "attitude," the concept of sentiment, as developed by the social psychiatrist Alexander Leighton, offers a tool for the analysis of latent ideology—for the analysis of the political identity of the individual and the political culture of the society. The concept "rests on the assumption that personalities operate as wholes, that both conscious and unconscious factors may be significant, that sentiments can have both constructive and destructive effects in personalities, and that they tend to be organized into systems."[35]

The political identity of an individual may be viewed as a syndrome of sentiments, each sentiment being a union of thought and feeling, of cognition and affect. Drawing upon the concept of sentiment, *cognition* is the process of thought, involving comprehension, memory, and reasoning, and *affect* includes emotion and feeling.[36] In the union of cognition and affect, sentiment is *evaluative.* Through these three elements,

---

[33]"Italians in the overwhelming majority take no pride in their political system, nor even in their economy or society." This conclusion is unwarranted. Their question asked, "Speaking generally, what are things about this country that you are most proud of?" While 27 percent said either that they were proud of nothing or didn't know and only 3 percent said they were *most proud* of their government and political institutions, 25 percent said they were most proud of the physical attributes of the country and 16 percent mentioned Italy's contributions to the arts. Almond and Verba, *The Civic Culture,* pp. 102–3.

[34]The literature in the social sciences on the problems of cross-cultural research is extensive. In political science, see, for example, Robert T. Holt and John E. Turner, eds., *The Methodology of Comparative Research* (New York: Free Press, 1970); Robert Ward, ed., *Studying Politics Abroad: Field Research in the Developing Areas,* (Boston: Little, Brown, 1964); Richard L. Merritt and Stein Rokkan, eds., *Comparing Nations: The Use of Quantitative Data in Cross-National Research* (New Haven: Yale University Press, 1966). For a discussion of some problems specifically relating to the study of political culture, see Robert L. Hardgrave, Jr., "Political Culture and Projective Techniques," *Comparative Political Studies* 2 (July 1969): 249–55.

[35]Alexander Leighton, *My Name is Legion: Foundations for a Theory of Man in Relation to Culture* (New York: Basic Books, 1959), p. 396.

[36]Ibid., p. 19.

cognition, affect, and evaluation—identified by Leighton as perception, expression, and assessment—Almond and Verba speak of the political culture of a society.

The collection of sentiments constituting the political identity of an individual forms a syndrome, each sentiment in systemic relationship to the other. A change in one area, through unconscious factors or conscious affective components, initiates stress, leading potentially to change in other areas. Sentiments are also mutually related in their cognitive aspects. This relationship may range from mere compatibility (a lack of contradiction) to a tight logical interdependence (as in a philosophical system).[37] The range of the continuum encompasses both manifest and latent ideology. Leighton notes, however, that "it may be expected that the totality of sentiments in any given personality will never constitute a rationally congruent system."[38] The rational and the non-rational, the cognitive and affective, while analytically separable, are never wholly distinct in reality. The concept avoids the danger of monocausal, exclusive extremes: "Man is both a thinking and a feeling animal, and he does both simultaneously in one integrated act as he recollects, experiences, and anticipates."[39]

Sentiment is "fundamentally private." But while each individual is unique in his own particular constellation of sentiments, the elements of this pattern are not unique. "Most complexes of sentiment . . . are not idiosyncratic, but are shared, to varying degrees, with other people, family, village, class, or nation."[40] The extensions of shared sentiment are circumscribed by an identity horizon. Within the scope of this horizon lies the body of shared sentiments which Almond has called the political culture.

In speaking of the political culture, distinguishing the system under analysis is necessary. Any society will embrace a variety of political cultures in a "nesting system." In analyzing the Indian political system, for example, it is possible to speak, at a fairly low level of generality, of the Indian *national* political culture as constituting a body of shared sentiments. One may, however, also speak of the political culture in terms of a region, district, village, class, or caste. Insofar as any group of individuals shares a body of sentiments, one may speak of the political culture of that group. An individual may be at once a member of a number of different political cultures. His identity horizon denotes the

[37]Ibid., pp. 240–41.

[38]Ibid., p. 241.

[39]Ibid., p. 246.

[40]Ibid., pp. 252–53.

boundaries of the political world in which he meaningfully shares a body of sentiments.

As the political identity of an individual is a syndrome of interrelated and mutually dependent sentiments, so the political culture of a community is systemic in character. It is affected by changes in the political sentiments of individuals within the system. The political identity of an individual and the political culture of the community are interactive systems, the former being a subsystem of the latter. Each, considered separately, interacts with its environment and is responsive to it. Thus, changes in the environment, insofar as the parameters affect the system, demand an adaptive response on the part of the system. As the social, economic, and political structures of a community change, political sentiment must also change if the political identity of the individual or the culture of the political system is to remain congruent with its environment. Congruence may be taken here as an "ideal" condition, for in the process of change some degree of incongruence is inevitable. Indeed, rapid change may be characterized by a high degree of incongruence. The structure of political sentiment, however, is related systemically to the structure of society.

Political Socialization

The link between orientation and culture is provided by the concept of socialization. Political socialization is the process which inducts the individual into the political culture of shared orientations. In this process, the body of orientations common to the community is internalized and patterned. This patterning is unique in terms of the individual's life experiences, but patterning is necessarily limited to those "raw" orientations of the political culture to which the individual is exposed. Thus, the individual is always socialized to a *particular* political culture. His political world is circumscribed by an identity horizon.

"Political socialization shapes and transmits a nation's political culture," write Dawson and Prewitt. It may maintain a nation's political culture insofar as it transmits that culture from one generation to the next, but it may also transform the political culture as it leads the population, or parts of it, to view and experience political life in new ways. Under special circumstances, as in the emergence of a new political community, socialization processes may create a political culture where before none had existed.[41]

Concern for the training and education of citizens goes back at least to Plato's *Republic,* but only recently, as Herbert Hirsch notes, "has

---

[41]Richard E. Dawson and Kenneth Prewitt, *Political Socialization* (Boston: Little, Brown, 1969), p. 27.

empirical research begun to transform early philosophical speculation and the assumptions of political practice into more concrete knowledge of the factors involved in political learning."[42] Herbert Hyman, with the publication of *Political Socialization* in 1959, stimulated the initial development of political socialization as a special field of inquiry in political science.

Hyman describes political socialization as a continuous learning process involving both emotional learning and manifest political indoctrination, and as being mediated by all of the participations and experiences of the individual.[43] "Socialization is a learning process (and) political socialization is the gradual learning of the norms, attitudes, and behavior accepted and practiced by the ongoing political system."[44]

"All political systems," as Almond argues in *The Politics of the Developing Areas,* "tend to perpetuate their cultures and structures through time, and they do this mainly by means of the socializing influences of the primary and secondary structures through which the young of the society pass in the process of maturation." The product of political socialization is a set of orientations—cognitive, affective, and evaluative—toward the political system. The sources of political attitudes are many. They include early socialization experiences, as well as adult socialization. They may include both political and non-political experiences. They may be specific or diffuse, latent or manifest, with the rate of manifest political socialization accelerating as the child matures.[45] Fred Greenstein sees political socialization as encompassing "*all* political learning, formal and informal, deliberate and unplanned, at every stage of the life cycle, including not only explicitly political learning but also nominally nonpolitical learning that affects political behavior, such as the learning of politically relevant social attitudes and the acquisition of politically relevant personality characteristics."[46]

"Although there is no generally accepted approach to the study of political socialization," Greenstein writes, "much of what is known and

---

[42]Herbert Hirsch, *Poverty and Politicization: Political Socialization in an American Sub-Culture* (New York: Free Press, 1971), p. 1. Also see Fred Greenstein, *Children and Politics* (New Haven: Yale University Press, 1965), pp. 2–5. During the 1920s and 1930s, largely out of the inspiration of Charles E. Merriam, there was considerable stress on civic education. See, for example, Charles E. Merriam, *The Making of Citizens* (Chicago: University of Chicago Press, 1931). This literature is briefly reviewed in Greenstein, pp. 5–9.

[43]Herbert Hyman, *Political Socialization: A Study in the Psychology of Political Behavior* (New York: Free Press, 1959), pp. 17–20.

[44]Roberta S. Sigel, "Assumptions About the Learning of Political Values," *Annals* 361 (September 1965): 2. Hirsch, as does Sigel, emphasizes social learning theory in political socialization. *Poverty and Politicization,* pp. 20–24.

[45]Almond and Coleman, *The Politics of the Developing Areas* (Princeton: Princeton University Press, 1960), pp. 27–29; 326.

[46]Fred Greenstein, "Political Socialization," *International Encyclopedia of the Social Sciences,* vol. 14, p. 551.

much of what ought to be known can be summed up in the following paraphrase of Lasswell's formulation of the general process of communication: (a) who (b) learns what (c) from whom (d) under what circumstances (e) with what effect?"[47]

The agents of political socialization include family, school, church, peer groups, social class, ethnic group, the work-life situation, and the mass media.[48] Of these, the family and the school have received the closest attention as the most salient agents of socialization.

The Family's Role in Socialization

The process of political socialization begins first in the family, and these early experiences are deeply influential on later political orientations because they are rooted in primary family loyalties. The family, according to Hess and Torney, acts as an agent in three ways: it transmits attitudes to the child; the parent serves as a model to the child; and role definitions and expectations within the family structure are generalized to political objects.[49]

The role of the family in political socialization is reflected in the strong relationship in voting preferences between American adults and their parents.[50] Converse and Depeux, in a comparative study of France and the United States, argue that there is a lower level of political communication between parent and child in France. Only 30 percent of French adults were able to remember their parents' party preferences, in contrast to 80 percent of the Americans sampled.[51] The difference,

---

[47]Ibid., p. 552. This formulation serves to structure Greenstein's review of the literature, pp. 552–55; *Children and Politics,* pp. 12–15. With the same formulation, Hirsch casts a critical eye on the body of socialization research in political science, *Poverty and Politicization,* pp. 2–12. For extensive bibliographies on political socialization, see Hirsch, *Poverty and Politicization,* and Kenneth P. Langton, *Political Socialization* (New York: Oxford University Press, 1969).

[48]Robert D. Hess and Judith V. Torney examine these agents in three socializing contexts in *The Development of Political Attitudes in Children* (Chicago: Aldine, 1967), pp. 93–94.

[49]Robert D. Hess and Judith V. Torney, *The Development of Basic Attitudes and Values Toward Government and Citizenship During the Elementary School Years,* pt. I (Chicago: University of Chicago Press, 1965), p. 184, cited in Hirsch, *Poverty and Politicization* pp. 6–7. Also see James C. Davies, "The Family's Role in Political Socialization," *Annals* 361 (September 1965): 10–19; Langton, *Political Socialization,* pp. 21–83.

[50]See the extensive literature on voting behavior, the classics of which are Paul Lazarsfeld et al., *The People's Choice,* 2nd ed. (New York: Columbia University Press, 1948), p. 142; Bernard Berelson et al., *Voting* (Chicago: University of Chicago Press, 1954), p. 89; Angus Campbell et al., *The American Voter* (New York: John Wiley and Sons, 1965), pp. 120–67. Also see Hyman, *Political Socialization,* pp. 71–95.

[51]Philip E. Converse and George Depeux, "Politicization of the Electorate in France and the United States," *Public Opinion Quarterly* 26 (Spring 1962): 1–23.

however, may suggest not so much a lower saliency for the family as an agent of political socialization in France as the considerably less significant role of party identification in that society.

Surely the most controversial aspect of the study of political socialization has been the attention given to the relationship of child rearing practices and the development of political personality. During the 1940s, it was something of an anthropological fad to isolate toilet training and breast feeding as keys to personality formation, and, in a giant leap from child rearing to the structure of society, to "national character."[52] The recent interest in child rearing among political scientists has arisen primarily out of the richly imaginative work of Erik Erikson[53] and from the influence he has had upon Everett Hagen and Lucian Pye.

Interest in early child rearing in the process of political socialization has focused on the developing areas. Hagen, an economist, is concerned with the relationship between early indulgence of the child and the development of entrepreneurial orientations.[54] In its political mode, the argument links an adult's sense of political efficacy with his infantile experience of the world. The passive child, indulged with lack of toilet training, constant handling, and late weaning, gains little sense of mastery over his environment. This is allegedly translated in adulthood into a low level of political efficacy, a feeling that the individual has little power or influence. (This may, indeed, be an accurate perception of a political system offering little meaningful access.) The explanation of efficacy solely in terms of childhood experience is inadequate, and courts the danger of simplistic reductionism.

Lucian Pye, examining political culture in Burma in an effort to locate attitudes and practices which inhibit and impede the process of modernization and nation building, focused on some of these problems in his discussion of socialization in *Politics, Personality, and Nation-Building: Burma's Search for Identity.* Pye writes that "from the time of his earliest experiences the child exists in a world in which there is no rational relationship, no recognizable cause-and-effect connection between his

---

[52]For a review of the literature, see, for example, Alex Inkeles and Daniel J. Levinson, "National Character: The Study of Modal Personality and Sociocultural Systems," in Gardner Lindzey, ed., *Handbook of Social Psychology* (Cambridge: Addison-Wesley, 1954), vol. 2, pp. 977–1020; Alex Inkeles, "National Character and Modern Political Systems," in Francis L. K. Hsu, ed., *Psychological Anthropology* (Homewood, Ill.: Dorsey Press, 1961), pp. 172–208; H. C. J. Duijker and N. H. Frijda, *National Character and National Stereotypes* (Amsterdam: North Holland Publishing, 1960); George A. DeVos, "National Character," *International Encyclopedia of the Social Sciences* vol. 9, pp. 14–9.

[53]See Erik H. Erikson, *Childhood and Society* (New York: Norton, 1950); *Young Man Luther* (New York: Norton, 1958); *Gandhi's Truth* (New York: Norton, 1969).

[54]Everett Hagen, *On the Theory of Social Change* (Homewood, Ill.: Dorsey Press, 1962). See especially pp. 123–60.

powers of action and choice and the things he most desperately wants. . . . At every state in life the Burmese child is taught to be completely submissive before any form of authority and to expect that a passive and yielding attitude is most likely to please those in power."[55] The Burmese child seeks insulation from a hostile world over which he has no control. He acquires "absolute faith and loyalty in his family and unrestrained suspicion of strangers."[56] Shifting continents, the political world of Edward Banfield's southern Italy underscores the pervasive lack of trust in the "amoral familism" of a "backward society."[57]

Going beyond the first experiences of the infant with the environment around him, Easton and Hess suggest the process of political socialization begins most clearly at about the age of three. From this age, political learning in the family, as later in school, may be the product of deliberate conscious teaching or may be acquired incidentally and almost unknown to the learner himself. The parents, for example, may specifically inform their children about politics and government. More likely, and perhaps more meaningfully, the child may simply overhear his parents talking about political life.

Lawrence Wylie, in *Village in the Vaucluse,* describes the impact of an overheard adult conversation. The French attitude toward government, he says, is summed up in the use of the word *ils* (they). The "they" outside the village are "dangerous because they are anonymous, intangible, and over-powering." The people of Wylie's village agree that "a man with power over you is essentially evil." Most of the villagers view politicians as "a pile of bandits." The children "constantly hear adults referring to Government as a source of evil and to the men who run it as instruments of evil. There is nothing personal in this belief. It does not concern one particular Government composed of one particular group of men. It concerns Government everywhere and at all times. . . . Some are less bad than others, but all are essentially bad." The result of all this, Wylie says, is an extreme form of individualism, with forty million Frenchmen each demanding to be left alone to cultivate their own gardens.[58]

---

[55]Pye, *Politics, Personality, and Nation-Building,* pp. 182–84. The book aroused considerable controversy, focusing on Pye's heavy reliance on psychoanalytical intuition and on the small sample from which his judgments on Burma are drawn. The study of attitudes is based on 79 interviews with people from the Burmese political elite in Rangoon: 34 administrators, 27 politicians, and 18 journalists, businessmen, and educators. The deductive power of Pye's thesis is analyzed in Robert T. Holt and John E. Turner, *The Political Basis of Economic Development* (Princeton: Van Nostrand, 1966), pp. 24–34.

[56]Pye, *Politics, Personality, and Nation-Building,* p. 205.

[57]Edward Banfield, *The Moral Basis of a Backward Society* (New York: Free Press, 1958).

[58]Lawrence Wylie, *Village in the Vaucluse* (Cambridge: Harvard University Press, 1961), pp. 206–8.

The child's relationship with the parents—particularly with the father—may have a latent impact on later political orientations. From infancy onward, the child becomes aware of authority as he is the object of parental discipline. During the 1940s and 1950s, in the inquiries into the rise of Nazi Germany and the causes of World War II, there was much contradictory speculation on the relationship between the authoritarian personality and the father-centered Prussian family. On the one hand, it was argued that the Third Reich was the logically congruent political manifestation of the German family structure: Hitler was to the *volk* as the father was to his children. With evidence that the stereotyped German family was considerably less authoritarian than the model suggested, the rise of Hitler was then "explained" in terms of compensation for the declining role of the traditional father.[59] A contemporary version of such reductionism may be seen in the attempts to "explain" the New Left movement on American college campuses. Conventional wisdom attributed the radicalism of youth to generational conflict, to a reaction formation against the more politically and socially conservative father. The campus revolutionary was simply "testing his wings" as an autonomous individual and would soon "grow out of it." With data that the parents of the young members of the New Left were in fact sympathetic to their cause and were themselves predominantly liberal, explanation was revised. The roots of radicalism were now to be found in the permissiveness of child rearing and specifically in the advice of Dr. Benjamin Spock.[60]

Psychoanalytical explanations of political behavior can easily run amuck and must be approached with caution. Such is surely the case with Freud and Bullitt's study of Woodrow Wilson. Presidential political behavior is explained in terms of an unresolved relationship with an "incomparable father."[61] In explaining everything, nothing is explained.

The experience of the child within the family environment does have a critically formative influence on the later development of attitudes and on behavior. In *The Civic Culture,* Almond and Verba found statistical evidence suggesting that if an individual participates in making decisions within his family, and later in school and at work, he is more likely

---

[59]See Sidney Verba, "Germany: The Remaking of Political Culture," in Pye and Verba, *Political Culture and Political Development,* pp. 154–60.

[60]See Lewis S. Feuer, *The Conflict of Generations: The Character and Significance of Student Movements* (New York: Basic Books, 1969); and Seymour M. Lipset and Sheldon S. Wolin, eds., *Berkeley Student Revolt: Facts and Interpretations* (New York: Doubleday Anchor, 1965).

[61]Sigmund Freud and William C. Bullitt, *Thomas Woodrow Wilson: A Psychological Study* (Boston: Houghton Mifflin, 1966).

to feel capable of influencing government. He will have a greater sense of political efficacy. "Thus, *the how as well as the what* of the familial socialization process contributes to political socialization in that it may or may not teach the child the skills which will facilitate adult political effectiveness."[62] The participation of the child in family decision making is essentially a middle class phenomena and may suggest there is something to be allocated—that is, the middle class child is more likely than the lower class child to have his "demands" satisfied.

In the family, as in later life, the individual is socialized to a wide range of attitudes which are not specifically political, but which may have a deep impact on his political orientations. The child's orientations regarding his relationship to other people, his attitudes toward money and fiscal responsibility, and so on, may all spill over into politically salient adult orientations.

The School in Political Socialization

Together with the family, the early school experiences of the child constitute particularly important elements in the formation of political orientations. A study of political socialization among American children by Easton and Hess indicates that by the time the child has completed elementary school, many basic political attitudes and values—particularly with regard to the regime and the community—have become firmly established. "The truly formative years of the maturing member of a political system would seem to be the years between the ages of three and thirteen. It is this period when rapid growth and development in political orientations take place. . . ."[63]

Fred Greenstein, in his study of *Children and Politics,* confirms these findings. Greenstein also found that the first conceptions of political authority have more affective than cognitive content. This is particularly apparent in partisan orientations: the American child knows which political party he likes before he can make distinctions between them.[64] In the words of Easton and Dennis, "He learns to like the government before he really knows what it is."[65] The first objects of the political system to which the child attaches affect seem to be personalized—the policeman, the mayor, and most of all the president. In a process of

---

[62]Sigel, "Assumptions About the Learning of Political Values," p. 6.

[63]David Easton and Robert D. Hess, "A Child's Political World," *Midwest Journal of Political Science* 6 (August 1962): 236.

[64]Fred Greenstein, *Children and Politics,* pp. 55–84.

[65]David Easton and Jack Dennis, "The Child's Image of Government," *Annals* 361 (September 1965): 56.

transference from an ideal parental model, the child endows the president with a benevolent image, according to Easton and Hess. This contributes "to the ease with which maturing members of the American political system develop a strong attachment to the structure of the regime." They contend that "the first point of contact children are likely to have with the overall structure of authority is through their awareness of the President." He is seen as all-virtuous: "benign, wise, helpful, concerned for the welfare of others, protective, powerful, good, and honest." Although this highly favorable orientation declines as the child matures, the absolute levels of positive response remain quite high.[66] Greenstein confirms the child's positive response in the image of the "benevolent leader."[67]

Both the Easton-Hess and Greenstein studies were conducted during the Eisenhower presidency, with a chief executive who had a distinctly *benevolent* image in comparison to those who followed. However, a replication of the Easton and Hess survey in a cross-cultural survey (Chile, Puerto Rico, Australia, and Japan) revealed the same pattern of favorable orientations to their own leader.[68] Greenstein notes that "there are interesting variations from nation to nation in the absolute levels of idealization, but the tendency for younger children to display more idealized conceptions of leaders than do older children is consistent from nation to nation."[69] The evidence, however, suggests cultural variation, and the work of Wylie in France or Banfield in Italy certainly presents a less positive orientation to authority than the Easton-Hess and Greenstein studies. Moreover, the data from these studies is derived almost entirely from white, middle class, and suburban school children, who might well be expected to have more favorable images of the political world than the children of rural, racial, or ethnic subcultures. In a study of political socialization in the relatively poor and isolated Appalachian region of Kentucky, Jaros, Hirsch, and Fleron found that the children "are dramatically less favorably inclined toward political

---

[66]Easton and Hess, "A Child's Political World," pp. 240–44. Also see Robert D. Hess and David Easton, "The Child's Changing Image of the President," *Public Opinion Quarterly* 24 (Winter 1960): 632–44; Robert D. Hess and Judith V. Torney, *The Development of Political Attitudes in Children,* pp. 32–59; David Easton and Jack Dennis, *Children in the Political System: Origins of Political Legitimacy* (New York: McGraw-Hill, 1969), pp. 165–208; Roberta S. Sigel, "Image of a President: Some Political Views of School Children," *American Political Science Review* 62 (March 1968): 216–26.

[67]See Greenstein, *Children and Politics,* pp. 27–54. Also see Greenstein's earlier articles, "The Benevolent Leader: Children's Image of Political Authority," *American Political Science Review* 54 (December 1960): 934–43; "More on Children's Images of the President," *Public Opinion Quarterly* 25 (1961): 648–54.

[68]Robert D. Hess, "The Socialization of Attitudes Toward Political Authority: Some Crossnational Comparisons," *International Social Science Journal* 15 (1963): 542–59.

[69]Greenstein, *Children and Politics,* p. 42 fn.

objects than are their counterparts in other portions of the nation." The president specifically emerges in a far less benevolent image.[70]

Political socialization is normally homogeneous, and although there surely might be conflict among socializing agents, the school experiences most frequently reinforce the early socialization experiences within the family. As participation in family decision making may lead to a greater sense of political efficacy, so also do involvement and participation in the schools. A greater amount of child participation in family decision making occurs in middle and upper middle class homes; a lesser amount among the working classes. This pattern may be reinforced in the schools, where there may be less scope for the child to participate in urban, lower class or ghetto neighborhood schools than in suburban schools. The differences in schools are reflected in instruction—in the deliberate socialization of the child into the political culture. Edgar Litt found in a study of the texts used in the schools of an upper class, a lower middle class, and a working class community that the "students in the three communities were being trained to play different political roles, and to respond to political phenomena in different ways."

> In the working-class community, where political involvement is low, the arena of civic education offers training in the basic democratic procedures without stressing political participation or the citizen's view of conflict and disagreement as indigenous to the political system. Politics is conducted by formal governmental institutions working in harmony for the benefit of citizens.
>
> In the lower middle-class school system . . . training in the elements of democratic government is supplemented by an emphasis on the responsibilities of citizenship, not on the dynamics of public decision-making.
>
> Only in the affluent and political vibrant community . . . are insights into political processes and functions of politics passed on to those who, judging from their socio-economic and political environment, will likely man those positions that involve them in influencing or making political decisions.[71]

These differences correspond closely to Almond and Verba's parochial, subject, and participant orientations. Richard Rose, writing about the norms of inequality in English political culture, emphasizes the differing

---

[70]Dean Jaros, Herbert Hirsch, and Frederic J. Fleron, Jr., "The Malevolent Leader: Political Socialization in an American Subculture," *American Political Science Review* 62 (June 1968): 574–75. Also see Hirsch, *Poverty and Politicization.*

[71]Edgar Litt, "Civic Education, Community Norms, and Political Indoctrination," *American Sociological Review* 28 (February 1963): 69–75. Also see Langton, *Political Socialization,* pp. 84–139, and the chapter on "Social Class Differences in Political Learning" in Greenstein, *Children and Politics,* pp. 85–106. Significant differentiation by sex is also described by Greenstein, pp. 107–27.

socialization experiences in modern secondary schools and the elite grammar and public schools, as they prepare children to assume distinct but complementary roles in life as followers and as leaders.[72]

Adult Socialization

Socialization does not cease as the child matures, although its most formative stages may have passed. The work situation and adult experiences generally continue to act upon the individual in a continuous process. Adult orientations have their roots in early learning, and while the effects of that learning may be attenuated by later experience, "the concepts, information and feelings that are first acquired serve as 'filters' through which later perceptions must pass."[73]

One aspect of adult socialization involves a more specialized function: role socialization or recruitment. This is the process by which individuals are inducted into the specialized roles of the political system, training them in the appropriate skills, providing them with a pattern of values, expectations, and affects. For most people, their specialized political role may be no more than that of voter. Other individuals who are more participant may be socialized into various roles of leadership. Donald Matthews has analyzed the political culture of the United States Senate, for example, and the process by which the freshman Senator acquires orientations which enable him to operate affectively in that august body. "There are unwritten rules of behavior," which Matthews calls the folkways of the Senate. "These rules are normative, that is, they define how a senator ought to behave. Nonconformity is met with moral condemnation, while senators who conform to the folkways are rewarded with high esteem by their colleagues. Partly because of this fact, they tend to be the most influential and effective members of the Senate."[74]

---

[72]Richard Rose, *Politics in England: An Interpretation* (Boston: Little, Brown, 1964), pp. 65–72. For an examination of the role of education in political socialization in the developing areas, see James S. Coleman, ed., *Education and Political Development* (Princeton: Princeton University Press, 1965).

[73]Greenstein, "Political Socialization," p. 554. Also see the discussion of the funnel of causality in Campbell et al., *The American Voter,* pp. 18–37.

[74]Donald R. Matthews, *U.S. Senators and Their World* (New York: Vintage Books, 1960), p. 116. Also see Herbert Hirsch, "The Politicization of State Legislators: A Reexamination," in Herbert Hirsch and M. Donald Hancock, eds., *Comparative Legislative Systems: A Reader in Theory and Research* (New York: Free Press, 1971), pp. 98–106; and Heinz Eulau et al., "The Political Socialization of American State Legislators," in John C. Wahlke and Heinz Eulau eds., *Legislative Behavior: A Reader in Theory and Research* (Glencoe, Ill.: Free Press, 1959), pp. 305–13; James David Barber, *The Lawmakers* (New Haven: Yale University Press, 1964); Allan Kornberg and Norman Thomas, "The Political Socialization of National Legislative Elites in the United States and Canada," *Journal of Politics* 27 (1965): 761–75.

The Problem of Change

"Political socialization," Roberta Sigel writes, "is essentially a conservative process facilitating the maintenance of the *status quo* by making people love the system under which they are born."[75] It provides stability from generation to generation. Nevertheless, the political world of one generation differs—often significantly—from that of the next, and there are significant differences within each generation. Individual personality accounts for variation, but the pattern of variation must be sought in the structure of society and of the political system. In situations of rapid social change, the homogeneity of the traditional socializing processes may be disrupted. Conflict may arise as the various agents socialize the same person toward different, mutually exclusive norms. Perhaps the most fundamental source of conflict, and one yet to be systematically examined, lies in the contradiction between political reality and the political norms to which an individual may be socialized. "The child who experiences police brutality, sees school doors closed to him because of race, or observes his father pay protection money to the police (and grow prosperous) cannot easily internalize the norms taught by society at large but rather will experience culture conflict or will develop attitudes learned from his personal experience."[76]

As the individual begins to encounter the political world in reality-testing experiences, what he finds may be in sharp contrast to the values and beliefs he acquired during early socialization. The contradiction is not easily resolved, but in strain toward consistency, the individual will attempt to minimize dissonance.[77] His response to contradiction may be one of selective retention, wherein he simply blocks out any political reality which may conflict with his expectations. He may recede into cynicism or a cultivated apathy. He may readjust his belief system, so as to bring his values into more sympathetic alignment with his experience. Alternatively, his encounter with contradiction may be radicalizing, a catalyst for revolutionary change: he may seek to restructure reality in the image of his own values.

The Mass Media

Of all the sources of conflict among socializing agents, the independent role of the mass media is potentially the greatest. Hirsch, in his study of political socialization in the poverty subculture of Appalachia, concludes that "the media are generally more salient agents of information

---

[75]Sigel, "Assumptions About the Learning of Political Values," pp. 7–8.

[76]Ibid., pp. 8–9.

[77]Leon Festinger, *A Theory of Cognitive Dissonance* (Evanston, Ill.: Row, Peterson, 1957).

transmission than the parents, peers, or school,"[78] and this influence is not affected by the variable of age. Underscoring the cultural differences of Appalachia, where the mother occupies a higher rank as an agent of information transmission than the father, females have a higher exposure to the media and, in contrast to middle class culture, are more likely to be oriented to political stimuli than the male.[79]

Dawson and Prewitt, while recognizing the mass media as "becoming increasingly important as shapers of political orientations,"[80] qualify the media's role by reference to broad conclusions of communications theory:

> First, more often than not the media act as transmitters of political cues which are originated by other agencies. Second, the information carried by mass media goes through a two-step flow. Third, the media tend to reinforce existing political orientations rather than create new ones. Fourth, the messages of the mass media are received and interpreted in a social setting, and in the context of socially conditioned predispositions.[81]

Considerable evidence supports these observations in terms of the transmission of specific content.[82] However, in McLuhan's terms the media *experience* may be more significant than the manifest content involved (the medium is the message).[83] Perhaps the most significant finding in Hirsch's Appalachia study is that "the media seem to operate as latent rather than manifest agents. The media content to which the child is exposed had no relationship to the media's performance as an agent, while the hours of exposure did. Thus, the rate of exposure was a more salient variable than content."[84]

Media participation is an opening wedge in the emergence of a modern, participant society. It is the vehicle of an expanding identity horizon, or of what Daniel Lerner has called the "mobile personality." Independent of content, mass media participation may serve the development of an empathetic capacity, opening a wider world of experience to the individual. Mass communication, in speeding and expanding the spread of knowledge, becomes "the great multiplier" in modernization.

---

[78]Hirsch, *Poverty and Politicization,* p. 120.

[79]Ibid., pp. 118–35.

[80]Dawson and Prewitt, *Political Socialization,* p. 194.

[81]Ibid., p. 197.

[82]See Joseph T. Klapper, *The Effects of Mass Communications* (New York: Free Press, 1960).

[83]Marshall McLuhan, *Understanding Media* (New York: McGraw-Hill, 1964).

[84]Hirsch, *Poverty and Politicization,* p. 135.

Emphasizing the potential of cinema, for example, in the process of change in the Middle East, Lerner writes that "where the impact of movies has been massive and sustained, as in modern Lebanon, the results are highly visible." The movies "teach new desires and new satisfactions. . . . They portray roles in which . . . richer lives are lived, and provide clues as to how these roles can be enacted by others.[85]

Although "the nations most in need of such modernizing communication are those least likely to have such resources,"[86] Herbert Hyman has argued that in transitional societies, the media as instruments of socialization are

> efficient and their sweep is vast enough to cover the huge populations requiring modernization. Their standardization . . . [is] suited to producing widespread national uniformities in patterns of behavior; and their spirit is modern, no matter what else is wrong with it. By contrast, while the conventional agencies of socialization in society—parents, teachers, peers, neighbors, and the like—can be more flexible in suiting the lesson to the capacities and needs of the particular learner and more potent an influence, the outcomes cannot be as uniform, and their efforts are often directed against modernization.[87]

Socialization in the New Nations

The lack of congruence among agents of socialization is likely to be particularly acute in the new nations. "The more rapidly a country is trying to change, the more likely will the various socialization agents be out of phase with one another."[88] Robert LeVine, in an analysis of the literature on Asia and Africa, hypothesizes that in these new nations, the majority of parents socialize their children for participation in the local authority systems of the rural areas rather than for roles in the national citizenry.[89] The political world of most people in these devel-

---

[85]Daniel Lerner, *The Passing of Traditional Society: Modernizing the Middle East* (New York Free Press, 1958), pp. 399–400. Also see Robert L. Hardgrave, Jr., "Film and Society in Tamil Nadu," *Monthly Public Opinion Surveys of the Indian Institute of Public Opinion* 15 (March, April 1970): 1–62, and "The Celluloid God: M. G. R. and the Tamil Film," *South Asian Review* 4 (July 1971): 307–14.

[86]Dawson and Prewitt, *Political Socialization,* p. 195.

[87]"Mass Communications and Political Socialization: The Role of Patterns of Communication," in Pye, *Communications and Political Development,* p. 142.

[88]Kenneth Prewitt, "Political Socialization and Political Education in the New Nations," in Roberta S. Sigel, ed., *Learning About Politics* (New York: Random House, 1970), pp. 615–16.

[89]Robert LeVine, "Political Socialization and Culture Change," in Geertz, *Old Societies and New States,* p. 282.

oping areas is narrowly circumscribed by the limited extensions of primordial sentiment—attachment to family, village, caste, or tribe.[90] The individual is socialized to a world of ascriptive, particularistic, and diffuse political values.

One of the fundamental problems of political development is to break this pattern, release the individual from this narrowly defined perspective, and extend his political horizons in a process of social mobilization. The Cuban elite, for example, has sought to direct socialization processes toward the creation of "new values and behavior in the context of new political settings. Political socialization under the Revolutionary Government," Richard Fagen writes, "has not been used primarily for settling citizens into the ongoing system. It has been a directed learning process through which the elite seeks to create a new political culture. . . . In Cuba there has been a planned attack on the cultural fabric itself."[91]

The acquisition of new patterns of behavior, of a new image of personal identity, is dependent on new patterns of socialization, socialization to an unknown future. The old patterns, however, are not easily broken. Primordial sentiments are among the first orientations acquired by the individual, and even when the broader cultural environment and political system no longer reinforce certain traditional orientations, the behavioral dispositions acquired in the milieu of the family or ethnic enclave (caste or tribe) may persist.[92] Bruner, on the basis of his studies of American Indians, concluded that culture patterns learned early in life are most resistant to change in contact situations.[93] Easton and Hess and Greenstein, in their studies of political socialization, found that affective orientations toward political authority precede the cognitive orientations, and that these affective orientations are never wholly lost.

Primordial sentiments, those early orientations acquired in the family, seem likely to persist in the new nations of Africa and Asia for a long time to come—even in the face of rapid social, economic, and political change. Perhaps a major cause is the disparity between the sexes in response to modernization. Although most of the new nations seek to stress female emancipation, and countries like India have provided a role of national political importance for women, the women of

---

[90]See Geertz, "The Integrative Revolution," in Geertz, *Old Societies and New States,* pp. 105–57.

[91]Richard Fagen, *The Transformation of Political Culture in Cuba* (Stanford: Stanford University Press, 1969), p. 6.

[92]LeVine, "Political Socialization and Culture Change," p. 285.

[93]Edward M. Bruner, "Cultural Transmission and Cultural Change," *Southwestern Journal of Anthropology* 12 (1956): 191–99.

these areas are generally far more traditional in orientation than men. Their contacts are far more limited and so their perspectives are more narrowly defined. Education is a rarely stressed and often negative value for a wife, eliminating another opportunity for modernizing influence. In the new nations, even among the "modernized" elite, traditional patterns of marriage alliance (arranged marriages) continue to persist. When modernized males marry traditionally-oriented females, the children are likely to acquire traditional orientations from their mother since they usually spend more time with her. The earliest orientations of the individual, even among the most modernized segment of the society, are thus likely to be strongly parochial and primordial in character. The modern work-life situation, in the factory or office, also removes the father from the home for the greater portion of the day, leaving the children more exclusively with the mother than would have been the case in the traditional setting.

Many of the patterns associated with modernization do not necessarily lead to dissolution of traditional cultures and the development of new patterns of socialization. Urbanization, for example, need not immediately overturn traditional values. The city itself may be traditional. Ghetto communities in the city may preserve traditional values and behavior. Indeed, urbanization may lead to intensification of certain types of primordial sentiments, as they are threatened in an environment of change.

The impact of change in the new nations must inevitably affect these early socialization patterns, but it may take several generations. In the United States, even after two or three generations, immigrant communities have not lost their distinguishable characteristics: they have not melted in the pot.[94] Parochial patterns are not likely to change quickly in the new nations of Africa and Asia, either. The process of nation building, however, depends in part on breaking these primordial patterns of attitude and behavior, and creating a new sense of political identity. In the new nations, as LeVine points out, "political leaders striving for change will attempt to create national institutions for the countersocialization of individuals whose orientations have already been formed to some extent along traditional lines. The kinds of institutions that have been used in this way are youth movements, schools and universities, the military forces, and special training villages. Any of these can become an assimilating institution, attempting to reorient young adults, adolescents, or even children, and resocialize them to a new national ideology and a new way of life. In their more coercive

---

[94]See Nathan Glazer and Daniel P. Moynihan, *Beyond the Melting Pot* (Cambridge, Mass.: M.I.T. Press, 1963).

forms, associated with totalitarian governments, such institutions may explicitly attempt to destroy family and other traditional groups as well as inculcating new values."[95]

The institutions for adult socialization are likely to be most effective in resocialization if they are able to isolate the trainees, "to maintain consistent goals with the institutions, to manipulate rewards and punishments in the service of official training goals, and to use both formal instruction and opportunities for imitation and practice of new roles. . . . A complete social environment in which the individual becomes temporarily involved may be necessary to affect drastic alterations in his motives, habits, and values after childhood."[96] The army is perhaps the most effective such institution and has been consciously used in the new nations, especially in Africa, as a primary agent of adult socialization to national political culture. The college may also provide such a socialization agent. Students can be isolated in an atmosphere of homogeneous political values, with conformity pressures and rewards for acquisition of the new values, and a great deal of exposure to and practice with the new political orientations. Socialization to a new political culture is critical in the process of nation building, and it cannot always be attained by fiat or even by the most enlightened program of political education. As with the child in his encounter with the political world, the unplanned and unintended may have the greatest impact.

Evaluation of the Approach

The political culture approach has assisted in recovering historical perspective in comparative analysis. As with the traditional historical and configurational emphasis on the uniqueness of each political system, however, political culture stresses the unique character of each society. "Studies of different political cultures therefore tend to emphasize different themes,"[97] as in the varying analyses among the contributions to Pye and Verba's *Political Culture and Political Development.* All too often studies of political culture and socialization are insensitive to cultural variation, both among and within nations. The findings of limited samples within the United States have been projected into universal laws of socialization, limited in applicability not only to the nations of Africa and Asia, but to American subcultures as well. The major findings of political socialization research remain "culture bound"

[95]LeVine, "Political Socialization and Culture Change," p. 301.

[96]Ibid., pp. 301–2.

[97]Pye, "Political Culture," p. 221.

and can be broadened only with far greater sub- and cross-cultural data than we now have.[98] "The ultimate test of the utility of a theory of political culture will depend upon its value for comparative and generalized analysis."[99]

For all the ethnocentricism of *The Civic Culture,* Almond and Verba's operationalization of "political culture" marks a major advance in developing the concept as a useful tool in comparative politics. It does not, however, resolve the fundamental problem of the relationship between the political culture and the political system, between orientation and behavior. Political culture does not constitute a theory of explanatory power. It remains tautological, generally failing to distinguish analytically its use as either a dependent or independent variable vis-á-vis the political system. It does not provide the analytical capacity to explain why political systems evolve as they do or why they differ, nor does it account for subcultural variation. Insofar as it has explanatory value, it is largely residual: "Political culture is that which accounts for the inter-systemic differences in responses of political systems to identical stimuli when all other variables have been accounted for."[100] Such "explanation" may well be meaningless, as in psychological reductionism, where the hypotheses can neither be verified nor proved false.

One of the most serious problems in the study of political socialization, particularly as it relates to change, is the fact that research has seldom been longitudinal. In a single time continuum, children of different ages are examined regarding the content of their political orientations. The differences observed between the various ages are inferred to constitute a developmental sequence. The socialization process within an individual is assumed to involve change over time which can be measured at a single moment in time by the differences among children of progressively older age. Such an assumption, however, is unwarranted, for it ignores the fact that individuals of all ages, children and adults, experience events, such as depression, war, or presidential assassination, at a single moment in time. The mass media—in exposing everyone to the same stimuli at the same time—expand this influence.

Without longitudinal perspective, we may only speculate about the process of political socialization, and the argument that the early years of childhood are "the 'truly formative years' in the development of

[98]Hirsch, *Poverty and Politicization,* p. 9. Also see Prewitt, "Political Socialization and Political Education," pp. 614–15.

[99]Pye, "Political Culture," p. 221.

[100]Delos D. Hughes and Edward L. Pinney, "Political Culture and the Idioms of Political Development," in Edward L. Pinney, ed., *Comparative Politics and Political Theory* (Chapel Hill: University of North Carolina Press, 1966), pp. 72–73.

political attitudes has not been, and cannot be, answered from the data gathered by any of the studies thus far concluded." Hirsch contends that "while early socialization experiences may be important, concentration of attention on children of a particular age group, as has characterized political science research, threatens to trap the investigator in a static conception of socialization. By so restricting their attention, scholars have been unable . . . to answer what is perhaps the key theoretical question: 'How does early socialization relate to later political behavior?' "[101]

Because of the focus on the socialization of children, far too little attention has been devoted to adult socialization and to the agents of change which may deflect the normally homogeneous course of experiential learning. How, for example, do deviant orientations from the cultural norm themselves act as agents of political change?[102] With the broader functional concern for system maintenance and persistence, socialization research has been endowed with an orientation to the cultural status quo.

The assumption of homogeneity among agents and the emphasis on socialization as a process of perpetuating a given culture from one generation to the next has given research on political culture and socialization a static bias. The circularity of influence between the political culture and the political system may explain incremental change and modification, but it is less able to account for revolutionary change. The psychological variables of the political culture approach are "useful in investigating and explaining how and why certain political institutions function or fail to function in specific national settings. It is much less useful," Fagen contends, "when the focus of inquiry is on the directed transformation of institutions themselves."[103] In the process of social mobilization and directed change, "political culture cannot be isolated from the study of citizenship participation and institutional change."[104]

As an approach, political culture is necessarily limited. Its focus is almost wholly on the "input" side of the political system—on the determinants of political behavior rather than on political behavior as such. The approach stresses political culture as an independent variable, affecting, conditioning, or determining political behavior.[105] The other

---

[101]Hirsch, *Poverty and Politicization,* pp. 3–4. Also see Langton, *Political Socialization,* pp. 16–20.

[102]Rexene Hanes, "Political Culture: An Approach to Comparative Politics," unpublished paper, Department of Government, University of Texas, 1970.

[103]Fagen, *The Transformation of Political Culture in Cuba,* p. 5.

[104]Ibid., p. 10.

[105]See Kim, "The Concept of Political Culture," pp. 334–36.

side of the analytical perspective—the ways in which political structure and behavior shape the pattern of political culture—is frequently ignored. Politics remains a dependent variable of culture and personality, with no autonomy or independence. The "pre-political" focus on states of mind is essential to an understanding of political behavior, but unless the two are effectively linked in the development of explanatory theory, much of the intellectual energy devoted to research in political culture and socialization may be dissipated in a psychological inquiry that bears little relation to political life.

CHAPTER IV

Group Politics

The group approach to the study of politics was first explicitly and systematically developed by Arthur F. Bentley in his ground breaking work, *The Process of Government,* published in 1908.[1] Prior to this, important aspects of group analysis had been applied by political scholars through the centuries and throughout the world. James Madison and John C. Calhoun analyzed early American political processes through the lens of group cooperation and conflict. The great Arab political philosopher, Ibn Khaldun, developed a powerful explanation of the rise and fall of Islamic civilizations on the basis of the dynamics of group cohesion.

Explicit studies of group analysis as it has developed as a theoretical approach have been relatively rare. Although there are innumerable studies of particular interest groups and systems of groups, few scholars have concerned themselves with detailed conceptual and theoretical evaluation of the approach. Indeed, nearly half a century passed before Bentley's lead was seriously pursued by David B. Truman in his important study, *The Governmental Process.*[2] Since then, important theoretical contributions concerning group analysis have been made by Earl Latham (1952), Charles B. Hagan (1958), Samuel J. Eldersveld (1958),

---

[1]Arthur F. Bentley, *The Process of Government* (Cambridge, Mass.: Belknap Press of Harvard University Press, 1967). This is the latest reprinting of the 1908 study. All quotations are taken from this most recent issue.

[2]David B. Truman, *The Governmental Process* (New York: Knopf, 1951).

Robert T. Golembiewski (1960), Gabriel Almond (1958, 1966), Mancur Olson, Jr. (1965), and Jean Blondel (1969). Harry Eckstein (1963) and Oran R. Young (1968) have written concisely stimulating commentaries on the group approach, while Joseph LaPalombara (1960, 1964), Myron Weiner (1962), and Fred W. Riggs (1963) are three of an embarrassingly small number who have sharpened this theoretical approach from a non-Western perspective.[3]

The group perspective as an explicitly developed theoretical approach appeared in direct reaction to the traditional institutional and legalistic approach to the study of politics. It also represented one part of a more general drive to move political analysis away from normative emphases and towards a concentrated concern with the empirical elements. The work of Bentley is crystal clear in this regard. He defined the political science of his day, therefore, as "a formal study of the most external characteristics of governing institutions."[4] Bentley warned that the raw material of government could not be found in lawbooks, constitutional conventions, essays, appeals, and diatribes.[5] In general, "he desired to direct scholars from the fluff of utopian work toward the 'hard stuff' of empirical reality."[6] Considering the history of political study in America, it is not surprising that Bentley's work went ignored for so long.

[3]The relevant references are the following: Earl Latham, *The Group Basis of Politics* (Ithaca, New York: Cornell University Press, 1952); Charles B. Hagan, "The Group in a Political Science," in Roland Young, ed., *Approaches to the Study of Politics* (Evanston, Ill.: Northwestern University Press, 1958), pp. 38–51; Samuel J. Eldersveld, "American Interest Groups: A Survey of Research and Some Implications for Theory and Method," in Henry W. Ehrmann, ed., *Interest Groups on Four Continents* (Pittsburgh: University of Pittsburgh Press, 1958), pp. 173–96; Robert T. Golembiewski, " 'The Group Basis of Politics': Notes on Analysis and Development," *American Political Science Review* 54 (December 1960): 962–71; Gabriel A. Almond, "A Comparative Study of Interest Groups and the Political Process," *American Political Science Review* 52 (March 1958): 270–82; Gabriel A. Almond and G. Bingham Powell, *Comparative Politics: A Developmental Approach* (Boston: Little, Brown, 1966), pp. 73–97; Mancur Olson, *The Logic of Collective Action: Public Goods and the Theory of Groups* (New York: Schocken, 1968); Jean Blondel, *An Introduction to Comparative Government* (New York: Praeger, 1969), pp. 59–97; Harry Eckstein, "Group Theory and the Comparative Study of Pressure Groups," in Harry Eckstein and David Apter, eds., *Comparative Politics: A Reader* (New York: Free Press), pp. 389–97; Oran Young, *Systems of Political Science* (Englewood Cliffs, N.J.: Prentice Hall, 1968) pp. 79–92; Joseph LaPalombara, "The Utility and Limitations of Interest Group Theory in Non-American Field Situations," *The Journal of Politics* 22 (February 1960): 29–49; LaPalombara, *Interest Groups in Italian Politics* (Princeton: Princeton University Press, 1964); Myron Weiner, *The Politics of Scarcity: Public Pressures and Political Response in India* (Chicago: University of Chicago Press, 1962); and Fred W. Riggs, "The Theory of Developing Polities," *World Politics* 16 (October 1963): 147–71. Theoretical literature concerning groups is abundant in psychology, social psychology, and sociology. For an idea of what has been done in these disciplines, see A. Paul Hare, Edgar F. Borgatta, and Robert F. Bales, eds., *Small Groups: Studies in Social Interaction*, rev. ed. (New York: Knopf, 1965).

[4]Bentley, *Process of Government*, p. 162.

[5]Ibid., p. 179.

[6]Robert T. Golembiewski, " 'The Group Basis of Politics,' " p. 964.

Following the referral to and general endorsement of Bentley's work by David Truman, Bentleyan group analysis moved from a position of being greatly ignored to a position of being roundly attacked. Consecutive articles published in the *American Political Science Review* in 1960 accused Bentley of cynicism, and one scholar decried the "evil effect of Bentleyism."[7] R. T. Golembiewski took a rather exceptional stance when he wrote: "The time is ripe, in short, to leap to Bentley's shoulders with newly available knowledge; it is not a time to nip at his heels because he did not do what he did not intend to."[8] Scholars are only now beginning to heed Golembiewski's call.

Themes and Definitions

Group studies focus upon collectivities of individuals who interact in pursuance of common political goals. Basic attention is centered upon the collectivity and not upon the individual since the former is assumed to have more influence than the latter in shaping political processes. Although a fluctuating emphasis is placed upon the individual or the group depending upon the particular practitioner of the approach, the fundamental unit of analysis must necessarily be the group. Arthur Bentley, for example, went so far as to refer even to the individual actor in group terms. He wrote that " 'President Roosevelt' does not mean to us, when we hear it, so much bone and blood, but a certain number of millions of Americans tending in certain directions."[9] David Truman occupies a middle position in this respect as he recognizes the autonomy of the individual but at the same time chooses to concentrate attention upon the group. Mancur Olson, Jr. represents the other extreme as he

---

[7]See R. E. Dowling, "Pressure Group Theory: Its Methodological Range," *American Political Science Review* 54 (December 1960): 944–54; Myron Q. Hale, "The Cosmology of Arthur F. Bentley," *American Political Science Review* 54 (December 1960): 955–61. See p. 954 of the Dowling article for the statement of the "evil effects of Bentleyism."

[8]Golembiewski, " 'The Group Basis of Politics,' " p. 971. Bentley's analysis of group and politics must be evaluated in terms of his entire social and philosophical framework and not only in terms of passages selectively drawn from *The Process of Government.* The serious Bentleyan scholar ought to examine the following two books written by Bentley: *Relativity in Man and Society* (New York and London: G. P. Putnam's Sons, 1926); and *Behavior Knowledge Fact* (Bloomington, Ind.: Principia Press, 1935). See also Richard W. Taylor, ed., *Life, Language, Law: Essays in Honor of Arthur F. Bentley* (Yellow Springs, Ohio: Antioch Press, 1957). This edited collection contains a statement made by Bentley late in his life which underlines the point we raise in this note: "One of the questions that has most frequently been asked me is why, after having made something of a start in the study of government, I did not continue it. My answer has regularly been that I did continue, and that I recognize no break between my earlier and later inquiries." (p. 210).

[9]Bentley, *Process of Government,* p. 322.

analyzes group behavior by spending considerable time examining individual relations in an intragroup context.[10]

Group scholars view the political system as a gigantic network of groups in a constant state of interaction with one another. This interaction takes the form of pressures and counterpressures, the outcome of which defines the state of the political system at any given time. Group theoreticians develop elaborate taxonomic schemata to assist them in their drive to understand group configurations. Groups are classified, therefore, according to degree of organization, field of interest, style of articulation, and location of activity. The basic questions of power, authority, continuity, and change are directly confronted by the group approach. According to the group theorists, the result of group competition determines who governs, and changes in the political system follow upon changes in group formations.

The literature on group analysis abounds with various and sundry definitions of the basic concept itself. Most of the definitions, however, are variations of the definitions of group proposed by Bentley and Truman. According to Bentley, a group is " . . . a certain portion of the men of a society, taken, however, not as a physical mass cut off from other masses of men, but as a mass activity, which does not preclude the men who participate in it from participating likewise in many other activities."[11] Bentley's writing indicates that for him a group is a mass of activity that tends to move for "some definite course of conduct."[12] For Bentley, the essence of group is activity and interest. David Truman first provided a definition of a categoric group as "any collection of individuals who have some characteristic in common."[13] He then defined interest group as "any group that, on the basis of one or more shared attitudes, makes certain claims upon other groups in the society for the establishment, maintenance, or enhancement of forms of behavior that are implied by the shared attitudes."[14] Truman briefly defines interest groups as "patterns of interaction" and points out that "it is the interaction that is crucial, however, not the shared characteristic."[15]

Although the Bentley and Truman definitions of group are often contrasted, the core of their views are similar. An interest group is, first of all, a collectivity of individuals. Bentley speaks about "a certain portion of the men of a society" while Truman uses the phrase "collec-

---

[10]See Olson, *The Logic of Collective Action.*

[11]Bentley, *Process of Government,* p. 211.

[12]Ibid., p. 214.

[13]Truman, *Governmental Process,* p. 23.

[14]Ibid., p. 33.

[15]Ibid., p. 24.

tion of individuals." Second, the key characteristic of this aggregate of individuals is their interaction. Bentley's "mass of activity" is very similar to Truman's "patterns of interaction." Finally, both theoreticians agree in their own particular terminology that this collectivity seeks to act towards a common good. This goal may be as specific as pursuing a particular interest or as general as moving in some common direction.

A group may be defined as an *aggregate of individuals who interact in varying degrees in pursuance of a common interest.*[16] For purposes of comparative *political* analysis, this particular collectivity should have some impact upon the political system. This definiton of group carries the basic ingredients that most analysts include in their conceptualization of group. It is consistent with the important definitions of Bentley and Truman, and makes no arbitrary judgments about levels of interaction or kinds of organization. It is, therefore, conceptually possible to develop a definition of group that scholars might agree upon as they attempt to build empirical theory from this perspective.

The Group Approach and Comparative Analysis

As an approach explicitly designed to generate empirical political theory, group analysis has developed out of an extremely parochial intellectual background. With one or two partial exceptions, the pioneering theoreticians have founded their studies on considerable expertise in American or Western European political systems. As a result, culture bound imprints have been left upon all stages of the theory-building process in which group analysts have worked. The major partial exception to this is the work of Gabriel Almond who in collaboration with scholars such as James S. Coleman and G. Bingham Powell has developed a typology of groups that carries broad comparative meaning. According to Almond, there are four types of "interest articulation structures" or "interest groups."[17]

Associational interest groups are highly organized and specialized aggregates that explicitly represent the interests of a particular collectivity. Such groups are well-staffed and relatively tightly-knit. They have been recognized and strongly stressed by scholars in the group tradition. It

---

[16]One might follow David Truman in defining interest as the *shared attitude* of the aggregate whether it concerns material advantage, political power, ideas, or sympathies.

[17] Interest group is defined as "a group of individuals who are linked by particular bonds of concern of advantage, and who have some awareness of these bonds." See Gabriel A. Almond and G. Bingham Powell, *Comparative Politics,* p. 75.

is argued that "their organizational base gives them an advantage over non-associational groups."[18] Examples of associational interest groups include trade unions, business, ethnic, and religious organizations, and civic groups.

Institutional interest groups pursue several goals besides the articulation of their own particular interest. Whereas associational groups exist primarily to further a special interest, institution groups exist because they are assigned to perform certain sociopolitical functions. Their most obvious role as an interest group is to lobby in support of their own existence, as when a department of defense warns of the dire necessity for slashing welfare spending in order to increase the military budget to meet the enemy threat. Institutional interest groups are also formally and officially organized. Like associational groups, they "may occupy particularly powerful positions in the society because of the strength provided by their organizational base."[19] Almond includes legislatures, bureaucracies, political parties, armies, and churches as examples of institutional groups. He also includes subgroups such as legislative blocs, officer cliques, skill groups, and ideological cliques within this category.[20]

Nonassociational interest groups pursue their interests informally and possess highly fluid, relatively concealed, and highly personal interaction patterns. In Almond's terms, nonassociational groups reflect such distinguishing features as "the intermittent pattern of articulation, the absence of an organized procedure for establishing the nature and means of articulation, and the lack of continuity in internal structure."[21] Examples of this group-type include kinship, lineage, ethnic, regional, and status collectivities.

Nonassociational interest groups involve essentially two forms: (1) the informal group or clique; and (2) categoric aggregations to which interests are attributed. Racial, ethnic, class, and religious groups are among the many examples that might be cited. Although left unclear by Almond, the essential character of these nonassociational categories lies in the fact that objective interests are *attributed* to them by, for example, policy makers who then act as if these groups consciously pursued these interests in their own behalf. The Almondian scheme

---

[18]Ibid., p. 78.

[19]Ibid., p. 77.

[20]Institutional interest subgroups would seem to be much less formal or official than institutional groups and as such would more closely approximate the nonassociational interest groups.

[21]Almond and Powell, *Comparative Politics,* pp. 76–77.

focuses almost exclusively on nonassociational groups as categories, largely ignoring the informal collectivity as an action group.

Anomic interest groups: Spontaneous and eruptive aggregations such as riots, demonstrations, and other manifestations of mob activity are examples of anomic groups. These may not be in self-conscious pursuit of an interest even though a particular interest may be attributed to the group activity. A riot, for example, may not involve the presentation of specific demands but it may, in an ultimate catharsis of frustration, be a signal of diffuse demands to which political decision makers need respond. Anomic groups are usually disturbing and disordering to the ongoing social and political system. The patterns of group formation are the most dramatically intermittent in the case of this kind of interest group.

The above typology of groups has broad comparative value since it provides an exhaustive categorization developed on the basis of organizational forms of interest articulation. The typology includes the two polar extremes of amorphous and intermittent anomic activity on the one hand, and highly specialized and formally organized associational structures on the other hand. Despite this, however, the Almond typology carries a number of implicit assumptions and explicit judgments that fail to enable it to escape the bonds of parochialism continuing to impede the theoretical advance of group analysis.

In this important typology, certain group types are considered somehow better than and preferable to others. Indeed, the process of political development is viewed as involving a movement from the dominance of one group-type to the dominance of another. This takes the form of a strong built-in value preference for the associational interest group followed in descending order of preference for the institutional, nonassociational, and anomic interest groups. The pro-associational group bias becomes especially evident with the emphasis upon "good and bad boundary maintenance." Associational groups boast the best boundary maintenance and prevail in Western democratic political systems.[22] This distinction later formed the basis for Almond's concern for subsystem autonomy in the process of political development.

In their influential study, *Comparative Politics: A Developmental Approach,* Almond and Powell argue that nonassociational groups have but limited influence in modern societies for two reasons. "First, interest-group studies have shown that organization is highly advantageous for

---

[22]Almond has admitted that this question of boundaries and boundary maintenance "is not that easy." See Gabriel Almond, "A Developmental Approach to Political Systems," *World Politics* 17 (January 1965): 188.

successful interest articulations. In modern societies competition from numerous organized groups is too great to permit a high degree of successful articulation by nonassociational groups. Second, important nonassociational groups with continuing interests soon develop organized structures, and hence fall into one of the two following classes of interest groups [associational, institutional]."[23]

This argumentation contains a number of highly questionable assumptions. While categoric groups may have no organization, clearly informal groups such as factions or cliques do have organizational structure. By assuming that they do not or that it is somehow less than that found in associational groups, the authors exhibit a culture-bound perspective. The difference between associational and nonassociational interest groups resides in the *kind* of organization. The organizational characteristics of nonassociational groups, for example, include such variables as personalism, informality,[24] and covertness. Also difficult to accept is the stark assertion that in modern societies a high degree of successful articulation by nonassociational groups is not permitted. Cliques, caucuses, and personal coteries of advisors play key roles in societies as "modern" as the United States.[25] Finally, little evidence can be found to support the statement that nonassociational groups somehow inexorably evolve into associational groups. One could make quite the opposite point by citing the numerous instances in which associational and institutional groups splinter into factions, cliques, and informal coalitions.

The general preoccupation with associational and institutional groups has carried over to the study of non-Western political systems where the role of nonassociational groups is critical. In an attempt to apply the Almond group scheme to a particular developing nation (India), for

---

[23]Almond and Powell, *Comparative Politics,* p. 77.

[24]From the point of view of many non-Western cultures, these patterns have, of course, been very *formal.* In describing such groups in terms of *in*formality, we risk culture-bound distortion. We, nonetheless, use the term *informal* since it connotes a certain unofficiality and fluidity of organization.

[25]In 1960, the Vice Chairman of the Dallas County Democratic Executive Committee offered his colleagues the following political advice: "The first and usually last political mistake a group of like minded persons can make is to band together into an organization . . . elect a Board of Directors, officers, establish by-laws . . . There are many of us here who know each other. Business leaders know us and we know them. When something needs to be done we caucus. There is no leader. We group loosely around our County Chairman. We don't need or use much money, but when we need it, it is easy to find." *Report on the Conference of Business and Professional Leaders,* Dallas, Texas, 1960, pp. 46–48 as quoted in James R. Soukup, Clifton McCleskey and Harry Holloway, *Party and Factional Division in Texas* (Austin, Texas: University of Texas Press, 1964), p. 4. Also, as one senior American lobbyist declared in 1972 in referring to the memo attributed to ITT lobbyist Dita Beard: "You never, never write it down. That's the first rule of the business." See *Time,* 27 March 1972, p. 33.

example, Myron Weiner has centered all attention upon the group Almond himself had stressed—the associational interest group.[26] In a plea for the development of an infrastructure of associational groups, he excludes not only the nonassociational groups but the institutional groups as well from his consideration. Fred W. Riggs writes that by excluding institutional groups, Weiner deliberately omits the key centers of decision making in India.[27]

Riggs calls for a "two-tiered" model or "one which distinguishes between 'formal' or 'effective' structures, i.e., between what is described ideally and what actually happens."[28] He points out that Leonard Binder takes one more step in the right direction when he includes the influence of institutional groups in his study of Iran.[29] Yet, scholars continue to fail to move on to the business of in-depth analysis of nonassociational group networks. In non-Western societies it is the least formal and least visible structures of interest articulation that are the major focal points of political decision making. This is the case for a number of reasons.

Several preconditions must be met if the formal and visible type of organization reflected in associational and institutional groups is to develop. Certain *technical conditions* such as a charter, organizational expertise, and officials are essential. Crucial *social conditions* including uninterrupted communication and a certain level of trust and cooperation must also be present. The *political conditions* of organization are especially significant as certain political elites suppress, limit, or deter the emergence of associational groups. Finally, financial resources and equipment are essential to the successful operation of associational and institutional groups. These *economic conditions* are especially important to these types of collectivities since formal organization requires more elaborate facilities.[30]

In many societies, these four kinds of conditions are often exactly those conditions that cannot be met. In most Latin American, Middle Eastern, African, and Asian societies it is extremely difficult to find even

---

[26]Weiner, *The Politics of Scarcity.* In another volume, Weiner explicitly and sensitively relates factions to a political party structure. See his *Party Building in a New Nation: The Indian National Congress* (Chicago: University of Chicago Press, 1967), esp. pp. 133–60.

[27]Riggs, "The Theory of Developing Polities."

[28]Ibid., p. 154.

[29]See Leonard Binder, *Iran: Political Development in a Changing Society* (Berkeley and Los Angeles: University of California Press, 1962). Besides an emphasis upon institutional groups, Binder discusses such personal interaction as bargaining, legitimizing, consulting, and lobbying.

[30]Ralf Dahrendorf provides the basic analysis of the conditions of organizations but his list excludes the economic category. See Dahrendorf, *Class and Class Conflict in Industrial Society* (Stanford, California: Stanford University Press, 1959), pp. 185–88.

two or three of these sets of conditions present. Business, therefore, gets done in fluctuating networks of cliques or factions. Political demands flow through informal interest-articulating structures.

Informal group politics occur, of course, in all societies. Such processes, however, take on varying forms and hold quite different significance from society to society. Preliminary research by these writers indicates that the patterns of factional politics are most prevalent in Latin American societies such as Brazil and Middle Eastern societies such as Iran. They are of only slightly less import in Asian societies such as Japan and the Philippines. They would appear to be relatively less significant in Western societies such as Great Britain and the United States, while in countries like Italy they assume a much more prominent role.[31] In certain contexts, the informal group structure is so prevalent

---

[31]For two important theoretical studies concerning the comparative analysis of informal groups, see Ralph W. Nicholas, "Factions: A Comparative Analysis," in *Political Systems and the Distribution of Power* (A.S.A. Monographs 2; London: Tavistock; New York: Praeger, 1965), pp. 21–61; and Adrian C. Mayer, "The Significance of Quasi-Groups in the Study of Complex Societies," in M. Banton, ed., *The Social Anthropology of Complex Societies* (A.S.A. Monographs 4, London: Tavistock, 1966), pp. 97–122. The following are stimulating discussions of informal politics although they do not explicitly reflect a group approach: Rene Lemarchand, "Political Clientelism and Ethnicity in Tropical Africa: Competing Solidarities in Nation-Building," *American Political Science Review* 66 (March 1972): 68–90; James C. Scott, "Patron-Client Politics and Political Change in Southeast Asia," *American Political Science Review* 66 (March 1972): 91–113; and James C. Scott, *Comparative Political Corruption* (Englewood Cliffs, N.J.: Prentice-Hall, 1972). For a discussion relating informal groups and small groups, see Sidney Verba, *Small Groups and Political Behavior* (Princeton: Princeton University Press, 1961), pp. 11–22.

For studies of informal group politics that are anchored in the contexts of particular societies throughout the world, see the following analyses: Anthony Leeds, "Brazilian Careers and Social Structure: A Case History and Model," in Dwight B. Heath and Richard N. Adams, eds., *Contemporary Cultures and Societies of Latin America* (New York: Random House, 1965), pp. 379–404; J. S. Yadava, "Factionalism in a Haryana Village," *American Anthropologist* 70 (October 1968): 898–910; Myron Weiner, *Party Building*, pp. 133–60; Oscar Lewis, *Village Life in Northern India* (Urbana: University of Illinois Press, 1958), pp. 113–54; F. G. Bailey, "Parapolitical Systems," in Marc J. Swartz, ed., *Local-Level Politics: Social and Cultural Perspectives* (Chicago: Aldine, 1968), pp. 281–94; B. D. Graham, "The Succession of Factional Systems in the Uttar Pradesh Congress Party, 1937–68," in Swartz, ed., *Local-Level Politics*, pp. 323–60; Paul R. Brass, *Factional Politics in an Indian State* (Berkeley and Los Angeles: University of California Press, 1965); George O. Totten and Tamio Kawakami, "The Functions of Factionalism in Japanese Politics," *Pacific Affairs* 38 (Summer 1965): 109–22; Arthur Jay Lerman, "Political, Traditional, and Modern Economic Groups, and the Taiwan Provincial Assembly," (Ph.D. diss., Princeton University, 1972); Bernard Gallin, "Political Factionalism and Its Impact on Chinese Village Social Organization in Taiwan," in Swartz, ed., *Local-Level Politics*, pp. 377–400; Melford E. Spiro, "Factionalism and Politics in Village Burma," in Swartz, ed., *Local-Level Politics*, pp. 401–21; James A. Bill, "The Plasticity of Informal Politics: The Case of Iran," *Middle East Journal* 27 (1973); Alan J. Stern, Sidney Tarrow, and Mary Frase Williams, "Factions and Opinion Groups in European Mass Parties," *Comparative Politics* 3 (July 1971): 529–59; and V. O. Key, Jr., *Southern Politics* (New York: Vintage Books, 1949), esp. pp. 298–311.

that it carries a specific appellation. The list below contains examples of informal groups as they are referred to in the languages of some of the societies in which they operate.

INFORMAL GROUPS

A COMPARATIVE VOCABULARY

Society	*Transliterated Term*	*Translation*
Afghanistan	*gerdab*	"whirlpool"
Bolivia	*rosca*	"little kernel"
Brazil	*panelinha*	"little saucepan"
China	*p'ai*	"faction"
Colombia	*la rosca*	[a twisted pastry]
India (Haryana state)	*dharha*	"party"
India (Orissa state)	*dolo*	"flock" or "herd"
Iran	*dowreh*	"cycle"
Japan	*habatsu*	"clique"
Kenya	*nkiguenas*	"discussions"
Liberia and Sierra Leone	*poro*	[secret society]
Mexico	*equipo*	"team"
Panama	*combo*	"clique"
Taiwan	*p'aihsi*	"faction"
United States (Mexican—American)	*palomilla*	"butterfly"

The importance of factions in sociopolitical systems throughout the world is attested to by the following statements by anthropologists and political scientists who have immersed themselves in the cultures and societies of their interest.[32] "Factionalism is endemic on all structural levels of Burmese society . . ."[33] In Mexican villages, "the faction is the

[32]We use the terms informal group and faction synonymously. In this sense, a faction is an informal collectivity of individuals who relate to one another in highly personalistic terms in the pursuance of a shared interest. These are noncorporate and, in Almond's terms, nonassociational groups.

[33]Spiro, "Factionalism and Politics," p. 404.

political group *par excellence* . . . [34] In discussing factions in Brazil, one authority concludes that "without knowing this informal organization, one cannot understand how Brazil functions, economically or politically."[35] In Japan, political parties are defined as "factional federations."[36] In the Guntur district of India, factions are the basic units of political action, while in Rampur in Northern India factions compose "the very heart of village life."[37] In Iran, a kaleidoscopic network of informal groups underlies the entire social and political system.[38] Even the mass parties of Europe are the sites where factions "flourish" and continually increase in number.[39] And in the American south, "factions of the Democratic party play the role assigned elsewhere to political parties."[40]

By focusing upon the informal group or faction as the major conceptual tool for theory building, one might investigate the following issues in attempting to understand comparative political systems. What is the relationship between informal groups and formal groups, and how does this relationship affect the operation of the political system? Are factions organized along the lines of personalistic ties, geographic proximity, ideological commitment, or a combination of these considerations? What is the capacity of informal groups to persist and how does this durability influence the stability of the political system? How do factions relate to kinship and class structures within particular societies? And does the existence of important networks of informal groups promote or impede the processes of political development and modernization?

With few exceptions, leading group scholars recognize the existence of the nonassociational group and reserve a place in their typologies for it. Various manifestations of this significant group-type are referred to in the literature by the following kinds of terms: *quasi-group, near group,*

---

[34]Paul Friedrich, "The Legitimacy of a Cacique," in Swartz, ed., *Local-Level Politics,* p. 254.

[35]Leeds, "Brazilian Careers and Social Structure," p. 387.

[36]Allan B. Cole, George O. Totten, Cecil H. Uyehara, *Socialist Parties in Postwar Japan* (New Haven and London: Yale University Press, 1966), p. 273.

[37]See Weiner, *Party Building,* pp. 133–60 and Lewis, *Village Life in Northern India,* p. 113.

[38]J. A. Bill, "The Plasticity of Informal Politics," and William Green Miller, "Political Organization in Iran: From Dowreh to Political Party," *Middle East Journal* 23 (Spring and Summer 1969): 159–67, 343–50.

[39]Stern, Tarrow, and Williams, "Factions and Opinion Groups," pp. 529–30.

[40]Key, *Southern Politics,* p. 298. The cross-cultural comparative potential of informal group analysis is rather colorfully seen in the case where V. O. Key compares faction leaders in the American south to Mexican generals and where one observer terms Louisiana "the western-most of the Arab states." See Key, ibid., p. 305; and T. Harry Williams, *Huey Long* (New York: Bantam Books, 1970), p. 194.

demi-group, clect, informal group, communal group, incipient group, and *unofficial group.*[41] Terms more commonly used to refer to nonassociational group types include clique, faction, and coterie. But despite this general recognition of the existence of nonassociational collectivities, scholars too often ignore the phenomenon in their attempts to analyze politics and to build theory.

The major explanation for our ignorance of the formation and function of informal groups concerns the inherent research difficulties involved. Such structures are difficult to locate and even more difficult to observe. This is, of course, precisely the reason why such groups retain their effectiveness. Low profile and limited access promote secrecy and protect the membership. Outsiders are distrusted, and scholars are no exception to this. Only anthropologists have had a modicum of success in penetrating these groups, since they have been the social scientists who have expended the most time and energy in order to gain entry into social communities other than their own. In their emphasis upon quantitative techniques and measurement, political scientists have frequently been among those least willing to move into field situations where access is difficult and precise measurement is practically impossible.

Yet if the practitioners of the group approach seek to build empirical theory, then they must conquer ethnocentricity and begin serious analysis of the informal or nonassociational group. Developing comprehensive and consistent taxonomies and typologies is an important stage in the theory-building process. By focusing attention almost solely within one or two categories of the taxonomic scheme and thereby ignoring the other categories, one risks generating narrow hypotheses and weak theory. Much of the strength of taxonomies resides in the tendency that develops for the research to compare and contrast types. One must take alternating perspectives and spend considerable time analyzing each of the categories he has developed. Group analysts have adequate taxonomies. It remains for them to examine all categories contained therein. This is especially urgent in comparative political analysis where the major structures of political decision making in many communities throughout the world remain to be seriously explored.

The Theory of Collective Goods

The group approach has been recently jarred by an embryonic literature that has developed out of economics and the study of public goods.

[41]These terms have been used by Morris Ginsberg, Lewis Yablonsky, Harold Lasswell, Abraham Kaplan, Fred W. Riggs, Joseph Kahl, Jean Blondel, and Earl Latham respectively. The last two terms listed belong to Latham.

Because this new analysis carries universal applicability, i.e., it is portrayed as relevant to all societies at all times, it carries special significance for the field of comparative politics. Thus, although the mainstream of comparative political study has yet to be perceptibly touched by the developing logic of collective action, it is impossible to ignore the latter much longer.

The core of the theoretical literature concerning collective goods (as this literature relates specifically to the group approach and the study of politics) is *The Logic of Collective Action,* by Mancur Olson, Jr.[42] In this study, Olson mounts a formidable attack on certain dimensions of traditional group study. Because it is based on principles of self-interest and rationality, the Olson formulation is indeed a direct extension of the trend in which group analysts have reacted against the "fluff of formalism." The crucial differences between the views of Olson and scholars such as Bentley and Truman lie in their conclusions about the manner in which members of collectivities seek after and achieve their goals. There are many examples of a collective good. One example is the goal shared by all members of a group. According to Olson, "the very fact that a goal or purpose is *common* to a group means that no one in the group is excluded from the benefit or satisfaction brought about by its achievement."[43] Group analysis has traditionally assumed that individuals band together in order to enhance their chances of obtaining a common goal or good. The fundamental conclusion concerning this drive to aggregate is that individuals have indeed been able to achieve their ends through group membership and group activity. This is, after all, the major reason why individuals continue to join groups.[44] Earl Latham writes, for example, that "groups organize for the self-expression and security of the members that comprise them."[45] He even argues that group goals (or collective goods) such as security mean "the maintenance of the existence of the group."[46] Implicit in the reasoning pro-

---

[42]Olson, *The Logic of Collective Action.* For other important studies that support the Olson thesis, see James Buchanan, *The Demand and Supply of Public Goods* (Chicago: Rand McNally, 1968); Robert H. Salisbury, "An Exchange Theory of Interest Group," *Midwest Journal of Political Science* 13 (February 1969): 1–32; and Albert Breton and Raymond Breton, "An Economic Theory of Social Movement," *The American Economic Review* 59 (May 1969): 198–205.

[43]Olson, *The Logic of Collective Action,* p. 15.

[44]The other reason usually given for the formation of collectivities is the posited existence of some innate human proclivity or instinct. As Olson correctly points out, however, this interpretation "merely adds a word, not an explanation . . . " See Ibid., p. 19.

[45]Latham, *The Group Basis of Politics,* p. 28.

[46]Ibid.

cess of the traditional practitioners of the group approach is the assumption that groups pursue their self-interest in the same manner that individuals seek their self-interest. The political system is viewed, therefore, as a network of competing groups of individuals who work through their group in order to insure that they obtain certain common benefits.

Basing his argument on the premise that individuals act rationally and in their own self-interest, Olson concludes that individuals within large groups will not act to achieve the common or group interest. This is true despite the fact that each individual in the group stands to benefit if the collective good is obtained. Since individuals often do not act towards collective good acquisition, groups often do not achieve the goals for which they strive. In the end, Olson states that it is not rational for individual members of large groups to attempt to further group interest. Olson summarizes his thesis as follows:

> If the members of a large group rationally seek to maximize their personal welfare, they will *not* act to advance their common or group objectives unless there is coercion to force them to do so, or unless some separate incentive, distinct from the achievement of the common or group interest, is offered to the members of the group individually on the condition that they help bear the costs or burdens involved in the achievement of the group objectives. Nor will such large groups form organizations to further their common goals in the absence of the coercion or the separate incentives just mentioned. These points hold true even when there is unanimous agreement in a group about the common good and the methods of achieving it.[47]

Why should a person who is one small figure in a large group expend his energy in seeking to further the common goal when as a member of the group he will share in the fruits of the achieved good in any case? Why should an individual pay the cost of a good when he need not do so? In very large groups, the contribution of a single individual will make no *perceptible* difference in whether or not the good will be supplied. Why should a person work for the common good when, as measured against the action of a huge aggregation, his efforts can have no noticeable effect? If the contribution of an individual is bound to be miniscule and if one is to receive a share of the common reward in any case, then the rational path for the self-interested individual is to refrain from contributing to the common effort. Such everyday expressions as "What can I do? I am only one person" and "Let the other guy do it" are reflective of this process of reasoning.

---

[47]Olson, *The Logic of Collective Action,* p. 2.

Olson builds three major exceptions into his conclusions concerning group activity, i.e., he explains that the collective good *will* be supplied under certain conditions. As Olson points out, in many obvious instances groups achieve in varying degrees the common good sought. We are told in the first instance that the formulation does not apply to "small groups" but only to "very large" or "latent" groups. Small groups will attain their common interest more effectively than large groups for the following three reasons: (1) the smaller the group, the larger the proportional share for each individual member; (2) in small groups, an individual will more readily recognize that he will in fact gain the share; and (3) individuals in small groups can know one another and can be aware of each other's contributions to the common good. This alone often acts as an incentive for small group members to contribute. The two cases in which *large* groups will successfully achieve the collective good occur when there is coercion to force the members to contribute or when separate incentives are offered to the members individually in order to gain their cooperation. In the absence of these two conditions, "the rational individual in the large group in a socio-political context will not be willing to make any sacrifices to achieve the objectives he shares with others."[48]

In *The Logic of Collective Action,* Olson directly measures his conclusions against traditional group analysis. In arguing that rational and self-interested members of large groups do not work for the common good and that as a result groups often do not successfully obtain their goals, this formulation stands as a devastating critique. Comparative political analysts have already begun to use it as a reason to avoid adopting the group approach to the study of politics.[49]

Although the Olson thesis will remain a major contribution to our understanding of the manner in which individuals and groups interact in society, it does not effectively destroy the group approach to the study of politics for three major reasons. First, the study is not applicable to an entire universe of group-types, i.e., the small groups.[50] The

---

[48]Ibid., p. 39.

[49]See, for example, Carle H. Landé, "Networks and Groups in Southeast Asia: Some Observations on the Group Theory of Politics," paper presented for discussion at a meeting of the Political Development Seminar, Southeast Asia Development Advisory Group, The Asia Society, New York, March 20–21, 1970, p. 4. Landé has been a stimulating pioneer in the development of the study of informal politics.

[50]For instances in which Olson emphasizes the fact that small groups are excepted from his theory, see *The Logic of Collective Action,* pp. 3, 21, 52, 65, 76, 167. Besides this, it remains a highly debatable issue whether or not size is an important and meaningful distinction in contrasting group activity. Olson himself is not convincing about this. He introduces, for example, a distinction between intermediate groups and small groups and defines the small group as one "in which one or more members gets a large fraction of

analysis is not, therefore, a theory of groups, but a theory of a tiny segment of groups, i.e., the "very large" or "latent" groups.[51] Yet one of the great strengths of the group approach is the concentration upon the politics of small group interaction. Viewed in comparative perspective, the small informal (nonassociational) group discussed in the section above is a critically important decision making structure in most of the world. The group approach is not undermined because it is not synonymous with "large" group analysis.

The second reason why Olson's analysis of collective goods does not successfully challenge the group approach as an approach concerns the very nature of the Olsonian formulation. Despite the fact that it challenges important aspects of traditional group study, it is still essentially a variant of group analysis. The theory of collective goods is based upon the construction of both a group typology and individual interaction vis-á-vis the group itself. As such, the Olson study represents both a re-examination of ongoing group approaches and a reformulation founded primarily upon the group as the basic unit of analysis. Despite the depth of its critique, therefore, it in the end remains itself a group approach.

Finally, a successful argument challenging the Olson formulation strictly on logical and theoretical grounds has been developed by Frohlich, Oppenheimer, and Young.[52] They conclude that it is in fact logical for rational, self-interested group members to contribute to group goals in certain important instances. It is maintained that an individual will shape his calculations concerning whether or not to contribute to the common good on the basis of his assessment of what other group members will contribute. "The individual member will contribute whenever he expects others to make contributions toward the provision of the good, which when combined with his own contribution, will leave him better off than if he had decided not to contribute."[53] In other words, a group member will occasionally feel that his effort towards the

---

the total benefit that they find it worthwhile to see that the collective good is provided." An intermediate group is one "where two or more members must act simultaneously before a collective good can be obtained." See Olson, *The Logic of Collective Action,* p. 46. This kind of distinction makes it logically possible for a small group to be larger than an intermediate group. One can find the first characteristic in the intermediate group and the second characteristic in the small group.

[51]In this regard, it is significant that some of Olson's most important hypotheses are the two or three he generates offhandedly concerning small groups. Perhaps his best analysis of the political process is his discussion of small exclusive groups and his passing references to strategic interaction "in a reasonably small organization." Ibid., pp. 42–43.

[52]Norman Frohlich, Joe A. Oppenheimer and Oran R. Young, *Political Leadership and Collective Goods* (Princeton, N.J.: Princeton University Press, 1971).

[53]Ibid., p. 23

common good will have a perceptible impact. He may, for example, calculate that the situation is such that slightly more effort will achieve the good and that if he does not make the contribution, no one else will. In these kinds of situations, it may be quite rational for the individual member to contribute to the common good.

The final link in the Frohlich-Oppenheimer-Young thesis concerns the fact that the information that any group member has about the expectations of the other members is bound to be imperfect. In order for the individual to act for the collective good, therefore, a mechanism must exist which assists the members in coordinating their expectations concerning one another. This mechanism can take various forms including, for example, cultural patterns and traditions. In a situation, however, where the costs of permanent coordination are high or where there is a continual need for costly collective goods, then the mechanism could come to exist in the form of a political leader.[54] Such a leader can shape the relative expectations of group members in order that they contribute to the acquisition of the collective good.

Despite the fact that the theory of collective goods as formulated by Olson can be challenged both on empirical and logical grounds, it remains a major contribution to the continuing development of the group approach to politics. It raises fundamentally significant questions concerning patterns of collective behavior and also provides new stimulating insights into the politics of group interaction. As such, the theory of collective goods and the theoretical reactions that continue to develop in its wake carry special relevance to the study of comparative politics.

The Group Approach Analyzed

One of the greatest strengths of the group approach is the position it holds in the general development of explicit theoretical approaches to the study of politics. This approach was the first to begin undermining the traditional emphasis upon formal institutions and legal structures. Initially through the work of Bentley and later through the formulations of an impressive number and variety of other scholars, group analysis has provided an appealing alternative to the traditional modes of studying politics. In an attempt to uncover the "real" or "basic" forces of political life, group scholars ruthlessly cut through the formal and institutional trappings of government and focused their attention upon structures of competition. Group analysis helped to draw such concepts

[54]See Norman Frohlich and Joe A. Oppenheimer, "I Get By With a Little Help From My Friends," *World Politics* 23 (October 1970): 104–20.

as "power," "interest," and "conflict" into the mainstream of the systematic study of politics. Although more recently developed approaches have also helped reorient political study, the group approach significantly and systematically shook political analysis loose from the traditional mold.

With the sudden and dramatic developments in the field of comparative political analysis in the 1950s and 1960s, the group approach was one of the few ongoing approaches that experienced a renaissance.[55] In non-Western societies where formal-legal institutions were only of slight import and impact in the political system, group analysis looked very appealing indeed. Group study continues, in fact, to be very popular in the cross-cultural study of political systems. Besides the fact that it is more obviously relevant in non-Western contexts than approaches of the formal-legal variety, it also carries the advantage of being readily applicable in *all* contexts. Groups are evident wherever human beings congregate, thereby investing this approach with the broadest possible relevance. Although particular practitioners of group analysis may adopt parochial perspectives through narrow definitions and typologies, this is a valid criticism only of the practitioner and not of the approach. As an approach to the study of comparative politics, group study has the important strength of wide-range applicability.

In the early stages of theory building, where questions are raised and issues are selected, the group approach is extremely valuable. Among the important questions raised within this approach are the following: How and why do individuals form groups? What are the different types of groups and how do they relate to the political system? What is the relationship between the group structure and the formal structure in any political system? What are the different patterns of conflict and cooperation that prevail within groups and between groups? How does group size and organization relate to the attainment of group goals? How does group activity enable one to understand the processes of social change and political development? Questions such as these reflect an emphasis upon the basic issues of cooperation, conflict, continuity, and change. The group approach raises from the beginning questions about the dynamics of decision making and the distribution of rewards and priorities in society. As such, it attempts to confront the core of the political process.

As an approach systematically designed to provide social and political explanation, group analysis represents an explicit attempt to be rigorous

---

[55]See Gabriel A. Almond, "A Comparative Study of Interest Groups and the Political Process," Joseph LaPalombara, "The Utility and Limitations of Interest Group Theory in Non-American Field Situations," and Roy C. Macridis, "Interest Groups in Comparative Analysis," *The Journal of Politics* 23 (February 1961): 25–45.

and scientific. The group approach is founded on a concern for empiricism and a drive to imitate the style of sciences such as physics. Although the approach has fallen considerably short of achieving the status of anything that might be called theory, it has made substantial progress in the earliest phases of the theory-building process. At the level of taxonomies and typologies, a great deal of stimulating work has been done.[56] The collection and ordering of data concerning group politics is now reaching the stage where sets of interesting hypotheses may be increasingly generated. As group scholars continually gather more data in non-Western contexts, these crucial early stages of theory building will be refined and strengthened even more.

The group approach to comparative political analysis, therefore, has focused a great deal of attention upon the related processes of problemation, conceptualization, and classification. For this reason, Charles B. Hagan refers to the group approach as a "descriptive system," while Oran Young praises its "descriptive power."[57] The greatest strengths of group analysis, in short, reside in what Peter Caws refers to as "the scientific activity of description."[58]

The most serious shortcoming of the group approach is the very fact that it consistently fails to construct theoretical formulations. Its practitioners appear unable to move beyond conceptual frameworks and elaborate typologies. Systematically related sets of testable generalizations are conspicuously absent in the writings of group analysts. Harry Eckstein, therefore, writes that the group approach "does not relate any variables to one another, nor specify any possible relation between variables. For that reason also it does not 'explain' anything in reality. It links no causes and effects; it specifies no formal relations (equations, for example) to which actual phenomena tend to correspond. Nothing in it can be correlated, nothing depicted on a two-dimensional or multidimensional graph."[59] Although this particular critique tends to overstate the case against group analysis, it is nonetheless a generally accurate characterization.

Although a number of other approaches to political study are severely lacking in the production of testable generalizations, the group approach is most prone to criticism on this basis for one peculiar reason.

---

[56]See, for example, Jean Blondel, *An Introduction to Comparative Government* pp. 59–97.

[57]Charles B. Hagan, "The Group in a Political Science," p. 40; and Young, *Systems of Political Science,* p. 88.

[58]Peter Caws, *The Philosophy of Science: A Systematic Account* (Princeton: D. Van Nostrand, 1965), p. 91.

[59]Eckstein, "Group Theory and the Comparative Study of Pressure Groups," in Eckstein and Apter, eds., *Comparative Politics,* p. 392.

Group analysts make highly extravagant claims for their approach (the approach itself is usually referred to in the literature as group "theory"). Critics of the approach are fond of quoting Bentley's statement that "when the groups are adequately stated, everything is stated. When I say everything I mean everything."[60] Group theorists have tended to see society and political systems as nothing more than gigantic networks of interacting groups. They have also exhibited great resourcefulness in translating most of the vocabulary of politics into group terms. In short, they end up claiming the ability to explain political activity of any type, anytime, anyplace. When promise is measured against performance, however, group analysis reflects the largest gap of any theoretical approach.

Built into the group approach are a number of difficulties that help explain the scarcity of sets of testable generalizations. The seeming inability to move beyond conceptual schemes and typological exercises is traceable to certain inherent weaknesses in the approach itself. A major set of problems rests in the area of researchability. This point is attested to by the huge gap that separates two types of group study along the road to theory. The exercises that most closely approximate theory, such as the collective good analysis of scholars like Mancur Olson, remain distant from the empirical world. The most logically and formally developed group analysis is remote from the environment where comparative political processes develop and operate. Such formulations remain to be applied and tested in the "real world." The other kind of study remains mired in empirical description. Most of this literature focuses upon particular interest groups or sets of interest groups within particular societies. Such studies seldom generate empirical generalizations concerning group relations and the political system.

Group structures and relations are difficult to research and even more difficult to measure with any kind of precision. This is especially true in the broad arena of comparative political analysis. The key group constellations in many societies resist discovery, observation, and measurement. Even in those cultures where key political groups are officially and manifestly evident, however, there has been very little systematic study that has resulted in precise discussion of intragroup and intergroup patterns. The shrouded, fluctuating, and complex nature of group relations even in the most formal collectivities resists techniques both of observation and quantification.

Besides the problem of particular research techniques, there is the closely related issue of the narrow research context. Young writes that

---

[60]Bentley, *The Process of Government,* pp. 208–9. Critics of Bentley have, however, overdone their emphasis on this quotation.

"the fact that the approach was developed largely by persons interested in the American political system has left a considerable imprint on its conceptualizations."[61] Yet, even group analyses applied outside the American experience tend to proceed on a society by society basis.[62] Because most group studies remain monocontextual rather than multicontextual, hypotheses that cut across cultures remain relatively rare. This hinders the development of generalizaton and hampers the spirit of stimulation.

The shortcomings of research technique and the limitations of research context combine to invest the group approach with problems that seriously impede the theory-building process. These two major difficulties are mutually supporting. The problem of researchability is especially pronounced in precisely those societies in which group study remains to be seriously applied. The approach, therefore, continues to be practiced mainly in the circumscribed context of America and Western Europe. The advances made here suggest that the theoretical work will continue to be applied primarily in these contexts. As a result, the suggestive and stimulative insights that might be gained by the simultaneous examination of group politics in other societies have been minimal. The jump from description to explanation and from typology to theory has yet to be made within the framework of the group approach to political analysis.

The Challenge of Modernization

Despite the prevalent criticism that group theorists have ignored the issue of change, many of the leading group scholars have been explicitly sensitive to this important subject. Certainly, nothing intrinsic to the approach precludes the analysis of change per se. The group approach, in fact, carries a number of advantages for the analysis of change. First, group analysis permits one to focus upon the *actual* processes of power and authority, or as Eckstein points out, it calls attention to the "real forces."[63] Surface change that marks the level of formal-legal structures is not the target of group scholarship. As a result, legalistic and formalistic modes of modifying change need not deflect the attention of those who adopt a group perspective.

Second, the group approach when properly employed fosters concentration upon relationships and interaction. Groups are studied in refer-

[61] Young, *Systems of Political Science,* p. 88.

[62] For one of the best studies of this kind, see Philippe C. Schmitter, *Interest Conflict and Political Change in Brazil* (Stanford, Calif.: Stanford University Press, 1971).

[63] Eckstein, "Group Theory," p. 393.

ence to other groups. These relations may be conflictual as well as cooperative in nature, and either tension or harmony may be the outcome that prevails. Since the study of the patterns and processes of cooperation and conflict is crucial to the understanding of modernization and development, the group approach is relevant in this area. A third contribution is the fact that group analysis lends itself to broad comparison if its practitioners are willing to make a serious effort to apply it in this manner. The approach, therefore, can be utilized in societies in which the challenge of modernization is most dramatically evident. As the context of analysis is broadened and as this expansion includes more societies in which the developmental process is highlighted in different ways, the opportunities for explaining this process are greatly increased.

Finally, the group approach allows one to include the important *political* dimensions of modernization within the field of analysis. Questions that focus upon the aggregation and articulation of interests, the role of groups in national decision-making processes, and the patterns of division and coalition of collectivities as they impinge on power and authority relations are basic political issues. The demand for priorities and the ultimate distribution of values can be effectively understood within group terms regardless of whether the units involved are political cliques or political parties.

The group theoreticians account for political development and modernization in terms of the changes that occur in the group structure. Each scholar defines modernization according to a particular direction in which the group configuration moves. Some examples of the kinds of changing group patterns that signal political modernization are the following: (1) specialization, differentiation, and development of associational group-types (Gabriel Almond); (2) intricacy and complexity of group relations (David Truman); (3) increasing number of highly differentiated groups (Harry Eckstein); (4) greater solidification and representation of group interests (Arthur Bentley); (5) appearance of new groups performing specific functions (Leonard Binder); (6) movement from communal to associational group types (Jean Blondel); and (7) increasing integration of the group system (Lucian Pye). In sum, modernization is explained by leading group scholars as the process in which groups become more formal, complex, differentiated, specialized, and integrated structures. The presence of these characteristics is usually interpreted as signifying that the process of modernization is underway. They are among the same characteristics often presented as the prerequisites for system stability and system maintenance. At this point group analysis reveals certain important inadequacies for dealing with the issue of modernization.

The group approach places a heavy emphasis upon such concepts as *equilibrium* and *balance.* When the equilibrium is threatened, the process is described as *disturbance* or *disruption.*[64] Within the group perspective, the important patterns and functions are *integrative* in nature. The literature reflects a preoccupation with the following kinds of concepts: consensus, cohesion, coalition, coalescence, combination, alliance, agreement, bargaining, reciprocation, negotiation, uniformity, and conformity. These kinds of concerns dominate group analysis whereas such processes as disintegration, division, and disagreement are often treated as aberrant patterns. This equilibrating and integrating focus is intrinsically intertwined with the failure of the approach to account for the transforming dimensions of change. Thus, although group analysis has been oriented to the study of modifying change, it has not addressed itself to the deeper and more radical forms of change.

The fundamental problem of the group approach in this regard lies in the assumption that political life consists of a bargaining process in which the various groups interact in negotiation and compromise. Groups are assumed willing to compromise because their members are divided in their loyalties. A pluralistic situation occurs in which each individual is divided in his interests among various crosscutting groups, and because each has relatively low salience, he is willing to bargain for something less than his full demand. The pluralist model of American democracy does not account for and cannot deal with the demands of high salience which are regarded, by their nature, as threatening to the system.

Group scholars view the sociopolitical system as a huge fluctuating but stabilizing web of groups. Although conflict and competition are oftentimes central to the approach, they always serve the end of system preservation. The system is taken as a given, and its maintenance is explained in terms of checks and balances between and among groups. Countervailing pressures and equilibrating tensions may in the short run account for modifications in power relations, but in the long run

[64]For an example of what we consider an inordinate emphasis upon the concept "equilibrium," see Truman, *The Governmental Process,* esp. pp. 26–33. Embedded in this section of Truman's work, however, is a reference to a deeper form of change. Truman points out on p. 28 that "although institutionalized groups are characterized by stability, that is, by the tendency to revert to an equilibrium among the interactions of the participants following a disturbance from outside the group, not all disturbances are followed by a return to such a balance." Despite this insight which is unusual in group scholarship, Truman smothers the observation with two dozen surrounding references to such concepts as "stability," "balance," uniformity," and "equilibrium." The more radical change is explained away with a terminology that includes words such as "disturbance" and "disruption" and phrases such as ". . . inappropriate or aberrant or compensatory substitute activities . . ." (See p. 30).

they always contribute to system stability. This is the reason why one writer criticizes the group approach for stressing "cynical conservatism," while another concludes that the approach relates primarily to " 'middle range' changes rather than to more fundamental or systemic change."[65] In the group framework, pushing and pulling and checking and balancing explain both modifying *change* and system *continuity.*

Group scholarship treats the political system as a mosaic of groups held together by a checking competition and cooperation. There has been little analysis of the process whereby the mosaic crumbles and is rebuilt. Part of the difficulty here stems from the fact that the group approach tends to take groups as the given and basic elements of analysis. The roots of group origination and group formation are often left unexplored. As a result, a number of key questions that lead directly to the study of radical or transforming change remain outside the purview of the group approach. How are groups grounded? What is the relationship of groups to the social structure? How are group patterns related to the basic lines of stratification that cut across social and political systems? What is the relationship between attitudinal change and group dynamics? One distinguished commentator on group analysis writes, therefore, that very little attention ". . . has been devoted to demonstrating the roots of the interest group system in the social structure, and to exploring the implications of social change on interest group organization, ideology, membership, role structure, and internal process."[66]

Although a number of scholars have incorporated segments of the group approach in outlining typologies and models of development, few analysts have attempted to explain the phenomenon of revolution through a group emphasis. While alterations of group structures are sometimes related to modifications of political systems, they have not been used to explain the processes of system transformation. An approach that assumes system maintenance and analyzes in terms of equilibrium and balance cannot confront the transforming dimensions of developmental change.

---

[65]The writers referred to are Myron Q. Hale and Oran Young respectively. See Hale, "The Cosmology of Arthur F. Bentley," p. 958; and Young, *Systems of Political Science,* p. 89.

[66]Samuel J. Eldersveld, "*American Interest Groups,*" pp. 184–5.

CHAPTER V

The Political Elite Approach

Elite analysis has become an increasingly popular approach to the study of politics and society. In the field of comparative politics, the cross-cultural study of elites has become an especially dynamic mode of inquiry. A recent bibliography of writings on political elites from 1945–67, for example, includes 4200 different references.[1] The elite approach has coexisted with the formal-legal approach for centuries. Only since the mid-nineteenth century, however, has elite analysis acquired a more explicit and rigorous theoretical standing. Systematic attempts by scholars to place the elite approach squarely within the comparative theory-building process have accelerated greatly during the last two decades.

Elite analysis has always presented a serious threat to the formal-legal approach since it has sought to focus attention upon the behavior of a relatively small number of political decision makers, rather than stressing the formal and institutional apparatus of government. Elite scholars also challenged group theorists by emphasizing conflict and stratification and by assuming the particular significance of one special group. Finally, the elite approach has presented a serious alternative to class

[1]Carl Beck and J. Thomas McKechnie, *Political Elites: A Select Computerized Bibliography* (Cambridge: M.I.T. Press, 1968).For a more manageable and discriminating bibliography on political elites, see William B. Quandt, *The Comparative Study of Political Elites,* Sage Professional Paper, Comparative Politics Series (Beverly HIlls, Calif.: Sage Publications, 1970). The Quandt study includes a useful bibliographic essay.

analysis by concentrating study at a level of stratification considered to be of preeminent importance since it is the locus of political leadership. Perhaps more than any other approach to the study of politics, elite analysis has served to challenge and question other theoretical approaches.

The fundamental perspective of the elite approach is summarized by the assertion that all political systems are divided into two strata—those who rule and those who are ruled. The rulers are labeled the political elite, and this elite is the most significant aspect of any political system. The political elite is that group which possesses most political power and which makes most important political decisions in a society. It is composed of that minority of individuals who are most active in political affairs. By focusing analysis upon this particular group within the political system, one can best understand the patterns and processes of political life.

Since all political systems can be by definition stratified into rulers and ruled, elite analysts argue that their approach is well-suited for comparative study. The existence of a political elite is held to be common to all political systems regardless of location, time, or culture. While the existence of an elite permits a common basis for cross-national comparison, the actual structure of each elite can be used to account for differences in political systems. The formations and activities which distinguish elites one from another are said to be what determine the differing character of political systems. Thus, the elite approach provides both a common basis for comparative analysis and a method for explaining the differing characteristics of political systems.

The Pioneers of Elite Analysis

The key to the development of the political elite approach to the study of comparative politics is held by three early modern political sociologists—Gaetano Mosca, Vilfredo Pareto, and Robert Michels.[2] The theoretical explorations of these classical elite scholars exist as the major orienting landmarks of elite analysis. Their work represents a culmination and supercession of the elite investigations that preceded it and at the same time stands today as the fountainhead of behavioral elite

---

[2]Gaetano Mosca, *The Ruling Class (Elementi di Scienza Politica),* trans. Hannah D. Kahn, (New York: McGraw-Hill, 1939); Vilfredo Pareto, *The Mind and Society (Trattato di Sociologia Generale),* trans. Andrew Bongiorno and Arthur Livingston, 4 vols. (New York: Harcourt, Brace, 1935); Robert Michels, *Political Parties: A Sociological Study of the Oligarchical Tendencies of Modern Democracy,* trans. Eden and Cedar Paul (Glencoe, Ill.: Free Press, 1949).

study. In order to assess the strengths and shortcomings of the elite approach, the theoretical formulations of these three European political sociologists must be explored and evaluated.

Early Foundations

In the late nineteenth century, Mosca and Pareto presented their first systematic and comprehensive analysis of the political elite. Although the roots of elite study extend back to the writings of Aristotle, a number of other writers helped shape the approach. Among those whose work had a direct impact upon the studies of Mosca, Pareto, and Michels were Henri Comte de Saint-Simon, Hippolyte Taine, Ludwig Gumplowicz, and Karl Marx.

Mosca credits Henri Comte de Saint-Simon (1760–1825) with first having systematically traced the fundamental outlines of the political elite approach.[3] Saint-Simon viewed society as a pyramid at the apex of which existed a political elite.[4] Recognizing the fact that such an elite was a permanent and ever-present phenomenon, Saint-Simon proposed to reform the system by changing the elite. He maintained that the pyramid should and indeed would always remain, but that the materials out of which it was constructed should be altered. According to Saint-Simon, the scientists, artists, and industrial leaders should become the political rulers and decision makers. He demanded that the political elite be characterized more by talent than by birth. Thus, Saint-Simon sketched a picture of a stratified society ruled by an elite. He then introduced a strong normative element and foresaw a new society which was to be directed by a quite different political elite.[5]

---

[3]See Mosca, *The Ruling Class,* p. 329. For explicit examples of the Saint-Simonian influence upon Mosca, see pp. 329–30, 334–35, 416, 453. For Michels' evaluation of and debt to Saint-Simon, see Michels, *Political Parties,* pp. 239, 379–81. Although he does not comment directly upon Saint-Simon's views on the political elite, Vilfredo Pareto does refer to Saint-Simon. See Pareto, *Mind and Society,* paragraphs 304, 655, 732, 960 n. 10.

[4]Saint-Simon does not speak of a political elite as such, but rather of a general elite. It is obvious, however, that Saint-Simon considers the primary functions of this elite to be political in nature.

[5]For the key writings of Saint-Simon that directly concern the political elite, see Henri Comte de Saint-Simon, "Letters From An Inhabitant of Geneva to His Contemporaries," in F. M. H. Markham, ed., *Henri Comte de Saint-Simon, 1760–1825: Selected Writings* (New York: Macmillan, 1952), esp. pp. 2, 8, 11; Saint-Simon, "The Reorganization of the European Community," in ibid., esp. pp. 29, 46–48; and Saint-Simon, "On Social Organization," in ibid., pp. 76–80. For pertinent commentaries on Saint-Simon's ideas about the political elite, see Georg G. Iggers, *The Cult of Authority—The Political Philosophy of the Saint-Simonians—A Chapter in the Intellectual History of Totalitarianism* (The Hague: Martinus Nijhoff, 1958), pp. 3, 17, 74–77, 98–101, 139; Emile Durkheim, *Socialism and Saint-Simon,* trans. Charlotte Sattler (Yellow Springs, Ohio: The Antioch Press, 1958), pp. 193–94, 200, 240; and Robert Soltau, *French Political Thought in the Nineteenth Century* (New Haven: Yale University Press, 1931), pp. 140–45.

Hippolyte Taine (1823–93) also exerted considerable influence upon Mosca. In *The Ancient Regime,* Taine minutely describes and analyzes one particular elite and explains a crucial period in the life of the French political system in terms of this elite. This elite, which is referred to by Taine as "the ruling class" and as "the privileged class," was composed of the clergy, the nobles, and the king. Taine points to many causes for the French Revolution, but he sees them all interlaced and subordinate to the actions of the elite, making that group primarily responsible for this fundamental upheaval of the sociopolitical system. Taine poses and then answers the basic questions concerning this elite, and in so doing he provides a perceptive insight into its character and role in the society.[6]

Another important influence upon the thinking of Gaetano Mosca and to a lesser degree upon Michels and Pareto was Ludwig Gumplowicz (1838–1909). Although carefully rejecting much of what Gumplowicz asserted, including the parallelism he draws between social and biological evolution, Mosca showers a great deal of credit upon Gumplowicz for his part in recognizing the existence of the ruling class. Gumplowicz refers directly to a political elite which is mentally superior to the rest in society. He goes so far as to define the state as simply the organized control of the minority over the majority. Gumplowicz also examines the composition of the elite, its functions, and the methods it utilizes to maintain its position.[7]

Despite the fact that he was primarily a class, rather than an elite, analyst, Karl Marx (1818–83) had a great influence upon the writings of Mosca, Pareto, and Michels. Emphasizing the overriding importance of the class struggle, Marx focused attention not only upon those who rule, but also upon those who are ruled. Indeed, Marx affixed the preponderance of emphasis upon those who are ruled. The political element in the Marxian theory cannot be overemphasized since Marx often stressed the fact that all class struggles are political struggles. There is also an aspect to Marxism that envisions the eventual disappearance of stratification from society. In this important sense, the Marxian utopia is quite

---

[6]See H. A. Taine, *The Ancient Regime—Volume I of Les Origines de la France Contemporaire* (London: Daldy, Isbister and Co., 1876). For the internal divisions and heterogeneity of the French elite, see pp. 1–12. For the general characteristics of this same elite, see pp. 13–27, 86–169. For the functions it performed, see pp. 28–85. For Taine's analysis of the decline and destruction of this elite, see pp. 165–69, 297–304, 312–14, 398–400.

[7]For Gumplowicz's own views on the elite, see L. Gumplowicz, *The Outlines of Sociology,* trans. Frederick W. Moore (Philadelphia: American Academy, 1899), esp. pp. 116–54. For a reaction to Gumplowicz and his analysis of elites, see I. Kochanowski, "Ludwig Gumplowicz," *American Journal of Sociology* 15 (November 1909): 405–9. The first thing that Kochanowski recalls about Gumplowicz was his attempt at "a liberation of the political sciences from the misty regions of the juristic state (*Rechtsstaat*) . . ." See ibid., p. 408.

different from the Saint-Simonian utopia. As he developed his theory, Marx came to believe that force and violence must be involved in any solution to the problem of stratification. Although he did not formulate a political elite approach, Marx did see the crucial role played by stratification, and as a result he undoubtedly enjoys a prominent position in the development of political elite analysis.[8]

The above writers have all approached the study of political elites quite differently. Saint-Simon, Gumplowicz, and Marx develop formulations applicable to all societies, while Taine is primarily concerned with one particular society. Taine, Saint-Simon, and Gumplowicz consider the existence of a political elite as inevitable and everpresent, while Marx foresees its eventual disappearance. Marx, Taine, and Saint-Simon see the elite characterized by wealth, education, property, or noble birth, while Gumplowicz views it as a biologically superior group. Gumplowicz, Marx, and Taine provide no indication of the exact size of the elite, while Saint-Simon gives an actual numerical estimate. None of the four men carefully define the key concepts they use, and therefore such terms as "rulers," "bourgeoisie," "ruling class," "privileged class," "superior class," "proletariat," "subject class," and "middle class" as used by these writers are very difficult to compare and understand. It is most difficult to assess just how closely such concepts coincide with the meaning applied to "political elite" in the general perspective outlined above. Finally, these theorists all raise profound questions to which they seek answers through the careful examination of history. Among the key questions they commonly raise are: Who rules society? What are the common characteristics of these rulers? How does this group of rulers maintain its position?

This rather brief exposition of some of the major thoughts of the precursors of Mosca, Pareto, and Michels is intended to serve the following purposes: (1) it will enable one to grasp the state of the development of the political elite approach to comparative politics prior to the writings of Mosca; (2) it will indicate the successes and failures of later elite scholars to improve upon these early studies; and (3) by illuminating the major problems faced by all early scholars of the political elite, it should assist in the vital evaluation and criticism of contemporary elite analysis.

Gaetano Mosca's analysis of the political elite was best expressed in his *Elementi di Scienza Politica* which was first published in 1896. This study is contained in the volume entitled *The Ruling Class* which

---

[8]For Marx's most explicit and direct reference to a political elite, see Karl Marx and Friedrich Engels, *The German Ideology,* ed. R. Pascal (London: Lawrence and Wishart, 1938), pp. 39–41, 48–49, 60, 69.

became available in English in 1939. *The Mind and Society (Trattato di Sociologia Generale),* which was Vilfredo Pareto's prodigious masterpiece and which contains important sections devoted to elite analysis, first appeared in English in 1935. Michels' *Political Parties* was published in 1915 and puts ideas of the political elite to the test by examining certain crucial organizations in light of Mosca's framework. The objects of Michels' study were organizations that were supposedly anti-elite in character—the social democratic political parties in Western Europe.

Mosca: The Political Class

Gaetano Mosca argues that in all political systems there are two strata: the political class and the non-political class. An elite is present in all systems and societies, and the type and level of civilization vary as this elite varies.[9] Perhaps Mosca himself best stated the perspective of his study when he wrote:

> In all societies—from societies that are very meagerly developed and have barely attained the dawning of civilization, down to the most advanced and powerful societies—two classes of people appear—a class that rules and a class that is ruled. The first class, always the less numerous, performs all political functions, monopolizes power and enjoys the advantages that power brings, whereas the second, the more numerous class, is directed and controlled by the first.[10]

The key concepts that Mosca relied upon include "social force," "political formula," "social type," "juridical defense," and "political class." These terms, which are Mosca's own, appear constantly throughout his work.[11] The concept social force corresponds very closely to what is now commonly referred to as power (defined in its broadest dimensions). Included within this are such forces as military strength, land, money, and education. The political formula is a type of myth or uni-

---

[9]In emphasizing the universal presence of the political class, Mosca goes to great lengths to point to its presence in modern representative democracies as well as in "collectivist" systems under which he includes social democratic and communist systems. See Mosca, *The Ruling Class,* esp. pp. 254–70, 283–87.

[10]Ibid., p. 50.

[11]For the most explicit definitions by Mosca of his key concepts, see ibid., pp. 50, 62, 70–73, 103–19, 125–26, 141–47.

versal moral principle upon which the actual exercise of power is justified and rationalized. The social type is the basic factor binding a society together and includes the common race, religion, language, and entire culture of the society. Mosca's "juridical defense" means government by law which regulates and disciplines the moral sense of man. As has been indicated above, the political class is defined by Mosca as the less numerous class that performs all political functions. Besides the above concepts, Mosca also, of course, utilizes such general ones as class, power, status, and influence.

Two groups of questions stand out among the many raised by Mosca. The first deals with the nature of the political elite, while the second concerns its maintenance or displacement. In the first category concerning the nature of the elite, Mosca provides his definition of the political class. He then raises the enormously important question: What are the bases of elite status within a society? In answering this question, he sheds a great deal of light upon the very nature of the political elite and upon both its participation in the decision-making processes and its roles within the authority structure of a society.

Mosca points out that elite bases vary from society to society. In the primitive society, military valor is the key to status. In a more advanced society, competence in the manipulation of religious symbols becomes the most prized value. In the next stage of societal advancement, wealth becomes the prime base. In the most advanced society (bureaucracy or technocracy), specialized knowledge is the outstanding base upon which the elite rests its status. Thus, Mosca sees a military elite, a religious elite, an economic elite, and a merit elite depending on the particular society and its stage of development.[12] It would be a misinterpretation of Mosca's theory, however, to view these four types of political elite bases as completely separate and divorced. In each case, Mosca indicates the principal base leading to status. Elements of the other bases are also undoubtedly present. In the bureaucratic society wealth or economic strength may be part of the reason for the status of the elite. In the primitive society the military elite may also partially rely upon religious instruments or symbols.

Indirectly related to this basic question is another important issue which also concerns the nature of the political elite. What is the relationship between the political elite and the state? According to Mosca, a very basic and key connection exists between the political class and the state. The state is an instrument of oligarchies or "organized minori-

[12]For Mosca's development of this important point, see ibid., esp. pp. 53–59, 70–102.

ties." The theorist goes on to write that "in reality the state is just the concrete organization of a large number of the elements that rule in a given society . . ."[13]

In a second category of questions, Mosca examines elite maintenance. The basic premise here is that by understanding the continued maintenance or change in the political elite, one can also understand continuity and change in the society as a whole. The author spends most of his time attempting to answer the question: Why do elites become weakened? He does this by studying how and why elites maintain their position. In *The Ruling Class,* five reasons are given: (1) close identity of life-ways; (2) use of the political formula; (3) mimetism (imitation); (4) circulation of the elite; and (5) support of the army. Through close identity of life-ways, or in Mosca's terms, social type, the entire society rallies to support the political elite against external threats.[14] Through the political formula, the political class articulates a moral and legal basis for its power. The natural tendency of an individual's values to develop in accord with the environment in which he is reared (mimetism) often occasions the development of feelings of self-abnegation which are exploited by the elite.[15] The elite continually assimilates new members from a second stratum which infuses the ruling class with new blood and ideas. At the same time, this serves to satisfy the always threatening middle class.[16] Finally, the political elite secures the support of the army, thus buttressing loyalty with force.[17]

The answers and solutions that Mosca found for his questions and problems were arrived at through a procedure that involved broad historical comparisons of ruling and non-ruling groups. In Chapter One of his study, the author carefully outlines this methodology. After positing the point that human beings are basically alike the world over, Mosca writes that in comparing political systems it is necessary to have "a broad and thorough knowledge of history."[18] He even points out that the studies of Aristotle, Machiavelli, and Montesquieu were severely limited because their knowledge of history was not comprehensive enough. In his own study, Mosca draws upon a broad knowledge of American, Chinese, Japanese, Indian, Persian, and North African his-

---

[13]Ibid., pp. 161–62.

[14]See ibid., esp. pp. 108–9. See also pp. 72–73, 103–19.

[15]See ibid., pp. 184–87.

[16]For Mosca's treatment of the circulation of the elite, see ibid., esp. pp. 404–9, 425, 474. It is interesting that Mosca is seldom credited for his ideas on elite circulation. His writing in this regard, although not as detailed as Pareto's, is nonetheless a stimulating contribution.

[17]See ibid., pp. 222–43.

[18]Ibid., p. 47.

tory, as well as upon an excellent understanding of ancient, medieval, and modern European history.

Pareto: The Governing Elite

Vilfredo Pareto concisely states the perspective of his approach in two places in the *Trattato.* Early in the first volume of his work, he writes that "every people is governed by an elite, by a chosen element in the population . . ."[19] Towards the end of his gigantic study he states, "it is always an oligarchy that governs . . ."[20]

Among the key concepts in Pareto's theory are "elite," "governing elite," "non-governing elite," "derivations," "residues," and "elite circulation." For Pareto, elite is a broadly defined concept. It is simply a group of people who have the highest indices in their particular field of activity. It is important, however, that this elite be divided into a governing and non-governing elite. The governing elite of Pareto corresponds to the political class of Mosca and to the term political elite in general. The concept of elite circulation refers to the continuous (evolutionary or revolutionary) change in the composition of the elite. The fact that this concept was also developed by Mosca is usually overlooked. Pareto, however, explained it in detail and emphasized its importance. The residues and derivations are integral parts of Pareto's entire analytic system. The residues are manifestations of sentiments or certain qualities of men that are reflected only through certain actions. They fall into six classes, only the first two of which are especially relevant to political elite study. The residues of combination (Class I) reflect intelligence, shrewdness, resourcefulness, and manipulation, while the residues of persistent aggregates (Class II) reflect force, loyalty, patriotism, and conservatism. The derivations of Pareto correspond very closely to Mosca's political formula. They are rationalizations (usually myths) that are used to justify the actions of men. Other characteristic concepts often employed by Pareto are aristocracy, class, strata, and influence.[21]

The central problems and questions to which Pareto sought answers in his development of political elite analysis greatly resemble those raised by Mosca. Although he raises a few scattered basic questions concerning the nature of the governing elite, Pareto devoted most of his attention to the changes that the elite undergoes. He places most em-

---

[19]Pareto, *Mind and Society,* para. 246.

[20]Ibid., para. 2183.

[21]For Pareto's definitions of elites, governing elites, non-governing elites, and elite circulation, see ibid., para. 2027–59.

phasis upon such questions as: Under what circumstances do ruling oligarchies change? How does the elite maintain itself? Pareto, like Mosca, gives several reasons for the ability of an elite to maintain its position in the political system. Perhaps the outstanding key is the sufficient circulation of the elite. According to Pareto, a closed and inaccessible political elite is the greatest cause of instability and always foreshadows revolution and upheaval. Regardless of whether the elite absorbs prominent members of the masses or whether members of the masses force themselves into that elite through violence and revolution, circulation itself is persistently evident. The idea of elite circulation in Pareto's work is integrally intertwined with the more general problems of societal continuity and change—the issues that rest at the heart of the concerns of contemporary social science.

Pareto stresses the relationship between residue changes and elite circulation. When the elite is dominated by combination residues, it governs chiefly by ruse and wit. The reason this elite may fall is because of its inability to be strong at critical moments in its existence. Pareto provides many historical examples in which a certain hesitance on the part of the governing elite to use force resulted in its own destruction.[22] Yet when the elite becomes imbued with persistent aggregate residues, it governs largely by force or the threat of force. This also leads to its downfall, since its overbearing and coercive methods occasion the reaction of revolution.[23] Pareto writes that "if it is true that governments which are incompetent or unable to use force fall, it is also true that no government endures by depending entirely upon force."[24] Pareto also discusses an elite that can balance both types of residue and blend "the same mixture of force and consent."[25]

The procedures adopted by Pareto to find answers to his questions are quite complex. Using terms such as manifestations, sentiments, residues, derivations, instincts, and logico-experimental, he develops a procedure that at times seems to approach present political culture and socialization studies. In his development of political elite theory, however, Pareto relies heavily upon the same procedure used so well by

---

[22]Ibid., para. 2183, 2187–93, 2202.

[23]In developing his idea concerning the role played by the two kinds of residues in the political elite, Pareto uses an interesting analogy which compares the governing elite dominant in persistence of aggregates as lions and the elite dominant in combinations as foxes. See ibid., para. 2178.

[24]Ibid., para. 2202. Joseph Lopreato has already begun to explode the myth that Pareto was a partisan of violence and a preacher of coercion. See Lopreato, *Vilfredo Pareto* (New York: Crowell, 1965), pp. 1–35.

[25]Pareto, *Mind and Soceity,* para. 2252.

Gaetano Mosca—the historical comparison. Pareto possessed an extraordinary knowledge of classical Greek and Roman history as well as of medieval and modern European history. Pareto also had a deep understanding of mathematics, economics, engineering, and the natural sciences in general. This enabled him to draw upon a wide variety of disciplines and fields for a more precise study of man and society.

Michels: The Oligarchy

Robert Michels' book demonstrates that all political parties are organized oligarchically. After spending some time discussing "the inevitability of oligarchy in party life,"[26] Michels explains the basic perspective of his study as follows:

> The democratic external form which characterizes the life of political parties may readily veil from superficial observers the tendency towards aristocracy, or rather towards oligarchy, which is inherent in all party organization.[27]

Michels then broadens this perspective when he posits "the existence of immanent oligarchical tendencies in every kind of human organization which strives for the attainment of definite ends."[28] This two-fold conception of the fundamental nature of Michels' subject matter prevails throughout the study.

Among the key concepts used by Michels are "oligarchy," "organization," "aristocracy," "power," "leaders," "masses," "class," and "stratum." In the best criticism of these concepts as used by Michels, C. W. Cassinelli shows, for instance, that five different meanings are attached to oligarchy in *Political Parties.*[29] The most important concepts used by Michels are "oligarchy" and "organization." One can safely say very little about Michels' exact meaning of these two concepts. His "oligarchy" plays roughly the same role in the internal structure of the political party that Mosca's "political class" and Pareto's "governing elite" play in the general political system. For Michels, the concept "organization" was used to assist him in generalizing his idea of the

---

[26]Michels, *Political Parties,* p. ix.

[27]Ibid., p. 11. Michels also clearly outlines the perspective of his study on pp. 404–5.

[28]Ibid. This broader perspective is best explained by Michels in his section on the "iron law of oligarchy." See pp. 377–92.

[29]Cassinelli, "The Law of Oligarchy," *American Political Science Review* 47 (September 1953): 773–84. Cassinelli attempts to sharpen Michels' concepts by providing his own definitions of them.

tendency to oligarchy. The existence of an organization always indicates the presence of an oligarchy.[30]

Besides touching on the definition of his subject matter, Michels poses three other principal questions in *Political Parties:* (1) Why are political parties (and other "organizations") always organized oligarchically? (2) What are the general characteristics of the oligarchy itself? (3) How does the oligarchy maintain itself?

Among the reasons given for the existence of the oligarchy, Michels stresses three in particular. First, he points out that it is inevitable that representatives and specialists come to exist in large organizations.[31] Representatives are necessary for practical reasons, while specialists are needed for technical reasons. The two, in fact, are usually combined. An oligarchy is formed when such representatives are selected or elected. Michels goes on to show how and why the representatives are more active and influential than the represented.[32] Concerning the social democratic political party in particular, Michels emphasizes its role as a fighting party. Its primary goal is to win. Therefore, it must be characterized by discipline, unity, and the ability to act quickly. This requires the existence of a few full-time leaders. The final cause of oligarchy can be termed psychological. The masses have an inherent need to be guided. Michels also stresses the political indifference as well as incompetence of the majority.

In treating the second major problem which concerns the general characteristics of the oligarchy itself, Michels raises several specific questions. What special personal qualities do its members possess? How is it composed internally and what relationships exist between its members? What is its political orientation? Michels deals at length with the personal qualities that usually characterize the membership of an oligarchy. In these sections, he stresses such qualities as intellectual superiority. In examining the internal relationships of an oligarchy, Michels emphasizes conflict and cooperation. Special attention is called to the fissure between the older and newer members of the oligarchy. He also analyzes the intensity and implications of such inner dissension.[33] In considering the political orientations of ruling oligarchies, Michels

[30]Michels is quite explicit on this point. In the early pages of his book, he writes: "Organization implies the tendency to oligarchy." At the end, he writes: "Who says organization, says oligarchy." See Michels, *Political Parties,* pp. 32, 401.

[31]The key word here is "large." The author indicates that organizations that are not "large" ones are often not organized oligarchically. For an idea of what Michels means by "large" organizations, see ibid., p. 26.

[32]For Michels' examination of the technical-practical causes of oligarchy, see ibid., pp. 26–40.

[33]Concerning this internal structure and activity, see ibid., pp. 74–77, 157, 164–84.

argues that they have an inherent tendency to become conservative. Even those that were the most revolutionary in the beginning soon become conservative. As Michels colorfully sums it up, "The revolutionaries of today become the reactionaries of tomorrow."[34] One final important characteristic of oligarchies that is emphasized in *Political Parties* is their tendency to become self-perpetuating. Nepotism becomes very common.

The final major question raised by Michels involves the maintenance of the ruling oligarchy. The important reasons for the continuing character of an oligarchy are: (1) its use of a "general ethical principle;" (2) the fidelity, dedication, and financial independence of the members of the oligarchy; (3) the ability of the oligarchy to avoid deep inner conflicts as well as to stave off the inevitable tendency to become irresponsible; and (4) the capacity of the oligarchy to absorb and digest new individuals and ideas from the masses.

Michels' reference to the oligarchy's use of a "general ethical principle" or to widely cherished symbols and ideas is equivalent to Mosca's "political formula" and Pareto's "derivations." It is used by all oligarchies to muster support for their policies. According to Michels, oligarchies in democratic societies garner support for themselves and their programs by rationalizing their existence with such terms as "general interest."[35] Michels indicates further that oligarchies characterized by a high degree of fidelity, dedication, and financial independence are better able to maintain their positions. He particularly stresses the importance of press support for the ruling oligarchy. The ability of the oligarchy to preserve its position depends also to a great extent upon its skill in avoiding internal strife. It must, at a minimum, always present a united front towards the masses. According to Michels, all oligarchies tend to abuse their power and to become irresponsible. Any oligarchy wishing to preserve its position must be able to control this tendency. Finally, the core of what Michels terms the "iron law of oligarchy" contains an important reason for an elite's general ability to endure.[36] This is a process by which individuals outside of the oligarchy are absorbed into it. Actually, this process as explained by Michels closely resembles Mosca and Pareto's ideas on the circulation of the elite.

The procedures used by Michels in seeking the answers to the questions he poses require some explanation. First of all, Michels is applying

---

[34]Ibid., p. 184.

[35]On the oligarchy's use of universal moral principles, see ibid., pp. 15–18, 45–48, 215–25.

[36]The "iron law of oligarchy" actually indicates the existence of oligarchies in general rather than the persistence of a particular oligarchy. As such, it is an elaborate statement of the perspective of the study.

his ideas on two levels. He not only attempts to indicate the presence of oligarchies in a particular kind of political party, but in all other "organizations" as well. Although the major portion of his book is devoted to demonstrating the former, substantial sections are devoted to the latter. Michels twice becomes especially concerned with studying the existence of a ruling oligarchy in the political system.[37] One can even safely assume that whenever the author speaks generally of the oligarchical tendency, he is referring to the ruling oligarchy in the overall political system.[38]

In *Political Parties,* Michels is able to follow a much more rigorous procedure than either Mosca or Pareto. Limiting himself to the European social democratic movements, he gathers a great deal of data and is able to present some statistical analysis. This element in Michels' work has caused Renzo Sereno to write that "his statistical approach remains the first, and perhaps the foremost, contribution to a positive study of a group in power . . ."[39] At the same time, it must be remembered that Michels applied this method to only one specific form of organization and thus disclosed one particular kind of oligarchy.

Classical Elite Analysis Evaluated

The strengths and shortcomings of the political elite approach as formulated by Mosca, Pareto, and Michels are generally reflective of the elite approach. One of their major contributions was the questions they raised and the problems they sought to address. (See table 2 for a comparison of these three theorists). All three theoreticians posed the following kinds of problems and questions: Who rules in a political system, i.e., who makes the decisions and who is most active politically? What are the general characteristics of the political elite? What is its relation to the state and to the political system? What connections does it maintain with other groups in society? How does the political elite maintain and buttress its position? These kinds of questions had already begun to be raised by men like Saint-Simon, Taine, Gumplowicz, and Marx; yet Mosca, Pareto, and Michels were the first to relate all the key questions and to pose them in a systematic manner.

---

[37]See ibid., pp. 235–316, 377–92.

[38]For Michels' most extended development of a general theory of a political elite, or ruling oligarchy as he terms it, see Robert Michels, *First Lectures in Political Sociology,* trans. Alfred de Grazia (Minneapolis: University of Minnesota Press, 1949), esp. pp. 63–84, 103–16.

[39]Renzo Sereno, *The Rulers* (New York: Praeger, 1962), p. 38.

TABLE 2 THE CLASSICAL ELITE THEORISTS: A SUMMARY COMPARISON

Gaetano Mosca	*Vilfredo Pareto*	*Robert Michels*
	BASIC PERSPECTIVE	
In all societies, two classes of people appear--a class that rules and a class that is ruled.	Every people is governed by an elite.	Immanent oligarchical tendencies exist in every kind of human organization.
	KEY CONCEPTS	
Political Class Political Formula Social Force	Governing Elite Deprivations Residues	Ruling Oligarchy General Ethical Principles Power
	BASIC QUESTIONS	
What is the nature of the elite? What are the bases of elite status in society? How does the elite maintain itself?	What is the nature of the elite? Under what circumstances do elites change? How does the elite maintain itself?	Why are organizations organized hierarchically? What are the characteristics of the oligarchy? How does the oligarchy maintain itself?
	MAJOR PROCEDURES	
Broad historical comparison	Broad historical comparison and social psychology	Data gathering and statistical analysis

The classical elite scholars ruthlessly cut through the trappings and window dressing that obscured the real processes of politics and that absorbed the full attention of the formal-legal scholar. Instead of attempting to understand a political system by concentrating upon formal structures, they endeavored to discover who actually made the decisions and how and why they did so. Mosca, Pareto, and Michels found the answers to their questions and the solutions to their problems in some kind of a political elite. Then, by raising many more incisive questions about the nature and functions of this elite, they developed a general approach for the comparative study of political systems. Many of these questions are raised by contemporary political scientists about today's political systems. At a certain point in the development of any field, it is critically important that someone raise the relevant questions.

Because he was considering a limited entity with which he was personally acquainted and about which he could gather statistical data, Michels was able to adopt a relatively rigorous methodology. Mosca and Pareto, on the other hand, proceeded through the use of broad historical comparison. Drawing upon evidence gained by analyzing political systems that have existed throughout the world, they found answers to the significant questions they had raised. By proceeding in this manner, Mosca and Pareto did not become preoccupied with and bogged down in the early stages of the theory-building process and were able to avoid the twin dangers of taxonomizing and modelmania. Broad historical analysis is an effective and valuable tool in comparative study when it is used consistently and competently. Such comparisons, however, have been seldom utilized and have become especially rare today. One reason for this is that such processes of investigation require a profound knowledge of a varied array of political systems. The larger the number of systems evaluated, the sounder the resultant theory is likely to be.

Whatever the advantages, however, this kind of procedure lacked rigorous experimental techniques. Observational precision and the measurement of key relations were almost completely absent. Mosca and Pareto relied heavily upon encyclopedic knowledge of world political history as well as upon a great deal of personal insight. Although these qualities served them well, they were only a partially successful substitute for more exact, precise, and refined methodology.

One of the more serious difficulties of the political elite approach as formulated by Mosca, Pareto, and Michels concerns the conceptual framework. Explicit and lucid definitions of the key concepts are not provided. "Power," "influence," "class," and "status," for example, are never defined although they are used by all three scholars. The work of Mosca and Michels, in particular, suffers because of a confusing conceptual apparatus. Different terminology is often used to signify the same concept, and identical terminology is many times applied to quite different concepts. For example, Mosca alternately refers to the same phenomenon as "political class," "ruling class," and "aristocracy," while Michels attaches several meanings to "oligarchy."

This difficulty becomes especially serious when one attempts to extract a political elite approach from the writings of these theorists. What does one do, for example, when confronted with a list of terms such as the following: political class, ruling class, aristocracy, oligarchy, ruling oligarchy, political leaders, elite, and governing elite? All of these terms appear in the basic works of the classical elite theorists. The most that can be said comparatively is that Mosca, Pareto, and Michels refer to essentially the same thing when they speak of "political class," "governing elite," and "ruling oligarchy." The same is true of "political formula," "derivations," and "general ethical principles." To a lesser extent, this also holds concerning their conceptualizations of "elite circulation." Beyond this, conceptual vagueness and inconsistency reign. This detracts significantly from the clarity and value of the elite approach as presented by the classical elite scholars.

The crucial contributions of Mosca, Pareto, and Michels to the study of comparative political systems have too long been ignored by political scientists. The centrality of these formulations to elite analysis is such that contemporary elite study still reflects essentially the same kinds of strengths and shortcomings. This will become evident in terms of the more general analysis that follows.

Elite Analysis and Theory Building

In 1935, Harold D. Lasswell wrote the following at the beginning of his important study *World Politics and Personal Insecurity:* "The few who get the most of any value are the elite; the rest are the rank and file." Lasswell argued that the analysis of politics "necessitates the comparison of world elites in terms of social origins, special skills, personal traits, subjective attitudes, and sustaining assets, such as symbols, goods, and violence."[40] Harold Lasswell, more than anyone else, reexamined, reformulated, and reintroduced many of the ideas and analyses of the classical elite theorists to modern political science. Since Laswell's important study of four decades ago, social science studies have contained a progressively heavier percentage of analyses stressing the central role of the elite. Among the most significant theoretical contributions to elite analysis are studies by T. B. Bottomore, Suzanne Keller, William Kornhauser, and Geraint Parry. Leading theoreticians who have also applied the elite approach empirically to the study of American political processes include Floyd Hunter, C. Wright Mills, G. William Domhoff, and Arnold M. Rose. In the area of cross-national comparative study, distinguished elite analyses are relatively few; prominent among them are the studies of Frederick Frey, Seymour M. Lipset, Lewis J. Edinger, Donald D. Searing, and Carl Beck.[41]

The elite approach to the study of politics has progressed unevenly along the route to theory. In certain stages of theory building, such as procedure and researchability, strides have been taken. In other areas,

---

[40]Harold D. Lasswell, *World Politics and Personal Insecurity*, 1st paperback ed. (New York: Free Press, 1965), p. 3.

[41]See selected bibliography for the key studies of the scholars mentioned in this paragraph.

such as conceptualization and definition, ground has been lost and inconsistency and confusion reign supreme. Partly because of conceptual chaos and partly because of the implicit nature of much of the elite approach, students and scholars have had difficulty in distinguishing this approach from other approaches to the study of politics. One area in which certain analytic distinctions must be drawn is the relationship between the elite and group approaches.

Elite and Group Analysis

Both the group and elite approaches to the study of comparative politics center upon aggregations of political actors and emphasize social forces and relations. Both approaches lean heavily upon such relational concepts as power, influence, pressure, and authority. Both approaches represent specific attempts to analyze the processes at work behind the formal trappings and legal institutions of government. Both approaches, therefore, have served to undermine the traditional emphasis placed upon the formal-legal approach to the study of political processes. Despite these similarities, fundamental analytic distinctions separate the two approaches. The most important of these distinctions resides in the basic perspective of each approach.

Elite analysis is preeminently conflict analysis that stresses vertical stratification. All political systems are stratified into political elites and non-elites, and the tension that inheres in this division is the basis for explaining the similarities and differences in political systems. Conflict and competition are everpresent in a basic situation of inequality between elites and non-elites (or masses), haves and have-nots, those who rule and those who are ruled. At least as important in this perspective is the fact that virtually all emphasis is placed upon one side of the conflict line, i.e., upon the political elite. Thus by its very nature the elite approach assumes stratification with a heavy emphasis upon one side of that which is stratified. The practitioners of comparative elite analysis, therefore, more often draw their comparisons on the basis of intra-elite relations than on the basis of elite–non-elite relations. Elite studies generally reflect concentration upon *elite* attitudes, policies, and configurations.

The group approach stresses patterns of cooperation and conflict *in a nonstratified universe.* The political system is viewed as a seamless web composed of a "limitless criss-cross of groups."[42] The emphasis is upon balances rather than upon inequalities, and relationships reflect reci-

---

[42]Arthur F. Bentley, *The Process of Government* (Cambridge, Mass.: Belknap Press of Harvard University Press, 1967), p. 204.

procity more than disparity. This is precisely the reason why group analysts tend to reach conclusions emphasizing cohesion and stability, while elite theoreticians often conclude with visions of division and instability. Beyond this basic distinction between group and elite analysis rests the more obvious difference involving the elite scholar's more limited universe of inquiry. The group theorist is generally concerned with a myriad of interacting groups which may be located at any point in the political system. The elite approach, however, focuses attention upon one very special aggregation: the elite. Because it involves a limited unit and one that is central to political decision making, the elite approach is often concerned with attitudes and orientations. Socialization and decisional patterns of elite actors are sought and analyzed. An intimate relationship exists between the elite approach and the political culture approach.[43] The group approach, on the other hand, is a fundamental method of studying political outcomes. The emphasis here is upon action and reaction, pressures and balances.

Elites and the Road to Theory

The greatest strength of the elite approach rests in the early stages of theory building where questions are raised and problems are sketched. This approach seems naturally designed to locate those who wield most political power or who make the fundamental political decisions in society. It also asks important questions about the goals and orientations of the individuals who compose the political elite. By concentrating upon decision makers and power holders, elite analysis provides an attractive alternative to studies of formal institutions. By locating and observing the activities of those who wield power, one has taken an important stride in the direction of understanding political behavior. Although elite analysis does not easily lend itself to the study of political outcomes, it does raise key questions concerning the inputs of policy making and decisional attitudes. The emphasis is upon human actors—people who create institutions and write constitutions; personalities who plan, plot, dedicate, and decide.

The elite approach to the study of politics carries two further advantages. It involves a universe of manageable proportions for the focus of study; and its comparative applicability is of the broadest dimensions. By limiting the concentration of analysis upon one relatively circumscribed group within the political system, the student is able to bring

[43]In this regard, it is instructive to note that elite analysts from Vilfredo Pareto to Harold Lasswell to Frederick Frey have also done extensive work in the areas of political socialization and political psychology. Many of the leading elite scholars have also been among the best practitioners of the political culture approach.

more intellectual tools to bear upon his study. More in-depth investigation is possible in this situation, and quantitative techniques can be used to analyze the subject matter. Finally, since elites are present in all political systems, the possibilities for broad comparative study are numerous. Political systems need not be confined to nation-states, but can include units that range from small associations to tribes to city governments to international organizations. If elite analysis concerns a research unit of rather limited size and if it has broadly comparative meaning, then one must raise the question of why so few comparative studies have been developed utilizing the elite approach. The search for the answer to this question takes one directly to those stages in the theory making process where elite study reflects serious weaknesses.

The first apparently inherent difficulty of the elite approach continues to be one that plagued the classical elite theorists. The conceptual framework, which is the basic skeleton without which powerful theory cannot be built, is extremely shaky. Despite continuing concerted efforts to define and differentiate the key concepts as explicitly and consistently as possible, the situation has seemed to deteriorate rather than improve. The conceptualizations of the classical elite scholars were if not consistent at least not obviously inconsistent. Contemporary elite research reflects conceptual confusion, and an entire literature has grown up which contains a less than productive debate over concepts. The construction and destruction of conceptual frameworks has to a large extent become an end in itself. The crucial concepts "elite," "power," "influence," and "authority" remain to be defined and differentiated clearly and consistently and in a way that will permit them to be operational to building elite theory. Surely there must be some strong understanding and agreement of what an "elite" is if one is utilizing an "elite" approach.

Harold D. Lasswell, who has been the greatest contemporary contributor to the development of elite analysis, has defined elite as follows:

> The few who get the most of any value are the elite.[44]
> The elite are those with most power in a group.[45]
> Most simply, the elite are the influential.[46]

Thus, one theorist can define elite as those who have the most of *any* value and also as those who have the most of a *particular* value. The nature of this particular value apparently differs from one writing to the

---

[44]Lasswell, *World Politics and Personal Insecurity,* p. 3.

[45]Harold D. Lasswell and Abraham Kaplan, *Power and Society* (New Haven: Yale University Press, 1950), p. 201.

[46]Harold D. Lasswell and Daniel Lerner, eds., *World Revolutionary Elites* (Cambridge: M.I.T. Press, 1965), p. 4.

next. By 1965, Professor Lasswell could write that "by this time most scientific observers realize that any single definition for such a key term as 'elite' is inadequate."[47] "Most scientific observers" also realize that there is little chance for building theory by viewing the heart of one's conceptual apparatus in different ways at different times. If one scholar handles his basic concepts inconsistently, the situation of various scholars employing the same approach cannot be expected to be much better. And in the case of the elite approach it is not.

C. Wright Mills writes about a "power elite," meaning those "political, economic, and military circles which as an intricate set of overlapping cliques share decisions having at least national consequences."[48] For William Kornhauser, an elite "is composed of people who by virtue of their social position have special responsibility for standards in a given social context."[49] Geraint Parry views elites as "small minorities who appear to play an exceptionally influential part in political and social affairs."[50] Suzanne Keller writes that the term elite refers "first of all to a minority of individuals designated to serve a collectivity in a socially valued way."[51] T. B. Bottomore sees elites as "functional, mainly occupational, groups which have high status (for whatever reason) in a society."[52] Robert Dahl talks about a "ruling elite" which "is a controlling group less than a majority in size that is not a pure artifact of democratic rules. It is a minority of individuals whose preferences regularly prevail in cases of differences in preference on key political issues."[53] G. William Domhoff defines power elite as "persons who are in command positions in institutional hierarchies controlled by members of the American upper class."[54]

In attempting to abstract a common meaning out of various definitions such as these, little more can be said than that elite usually refers to a minority of individuals who have the most of what there is to have or who get the most of what there is to get in society. Few agree on *what* the elite has most of, but it is generally termed as power, influence, or status. Very few concur on the definition of these terms. The differences over the meaning of "elite," for example, are mild compared to

---

[47]Ibid.

[48]C. Wright Mills, *The Power Elite* (New York: Oxford University Press, 1959), p. 18.

[49]William Kornhauser, *The Politics of Mass Society* (New York: Free Press, 1959), p. 51.

[50]Geraint Parry, *Political Elites* (New York: Praeger, 1969), p. 13.

[51]Suzanne Keller, *Beyond the Ruling Class: Strategic Elites in Modern Society* (New York: Random House, 1963), p. 4.

[52]T. B. Bottomore, *Elites and Society* (New York: Basic Books, 1964), p. 8.

[53]Robert A. Dahl, "A Critique of the Ruling Elite Model," *American Political Science Review* 52 (June 1958): 464.

[54]G. William Domhoff, *Who Rules America?* (Englewood Cliffs, N.J.: Prentice-Hall, 1967), p. 8.

the disagreements concerning the concept "power." Talking about power elites or political elites or ruling elites, therefore, is at least as confusing as talking about elites. The "power" in "power elites" has referred to everything from institutional position to decision-making abilities. But which institutions contain the prerequisites of elitism, and does this mean that those who do not enjoy a position within a certain institution cannot be members of the power elite? Surely not all decision making processes involve a power elite, but how does one decide what the key decisions are and where they are being made?

Theory building is a cooperative and cumulative enterprise in which scholars observe and consider the research of others and then build and improve upon it. In a situation where everyone uses his own vocabulary and erects his own conceptual framework, building meaningful generalizations is difficult. But in a case where everyone continually changes the content of his conceptual framework and where everyone uses the same terminology to refer to numerous quite different concepts, it is virtually impossible to engage effectively in the business of theory.

Not unrelated to the problem of conceptual clarity is the large question of researchability. How does one locate members of the elite? Many contemporary elite scholars settle for choosing them according to their formal positions, but in doing this they return directly to the formal-legal approach. In many societies, those who really wield power and make the key decisions prefer to remain behind the scenes. Here they are less exposed to the criticism and inevitable misfortune that plague those in formal posts. One of the fashionable criticisms of the elite approach is that the arguments against the existence of a particular elite can always be countered by the reply that it is there but is resting behind the scenes. It is suggested that this argument can be used ad infinitum, and thus one can never falsify the nonexistence of an elite. Actually, few elite theorists defend their analysis this way. Far more commonly, those utilizing the elite approach actually include in their designated elite a number of individuals who do not hold important formal positions. It is extremely difficult business, however, to locate certain important elite members who have a vested interest in remaining behind the scenes. The criticism is not so much that elite analysts justify their approach by pointing to invisible elites as it is that the analyst himself has difficulty in locating the elite. If one cannot even adequately pinpoint the elite, how is it possible to apply effectively the elite approach to the study of politics? There is also the related and serious difficulty of gathering comparable data about the personal and social characteristics of elite members.

A second series of difficulties involves analyzing the elite's political behavior. Even if one surmounts the first series of obstacles and succeeds in locating the elite, the crucial patterns and processes of political activity engaged in by elite members must still be identified. How does one relate elite characteristics, e.g., social background, to elite political performance? It has yet to be satisfactorily demonstrated that social background determines political behavior. In his penetrating review of the state of elite study, Dankwart Rustow makes this point by quoting Frederick Frey who writes that "to leap from some knowledge of the social backgrounds of national politicians to inferences about the power structure of the society is quite dangerous. Even to proceed from such knowledge to judgments about the political behavior of these same politicians can be treacherous . . ."[55] Moving from describing elite configurations to analyzing elite political behavior is a difficult procedural task. For this reason most elite studies terminate with detailed description of particular elites. Partly for this reason also, the elite approach has generated very little systematic theory. Progress has bogged down in the area of finding out who governs. Dankwart Rustow concludes that "theories with little factual support therefore have been replaced by masses of facts with little theoretical structure."[56]

In the area of elite identification, several techniques have been developed and refined through time. They can be divided into the following categories: observational, formal-positional, reputational, decisional, and historical. The observational and historical procedures are the least rigorous and most flexible methods. The success of the observational technique depends greatly upon the skill of the particular researcher and the resources and access that he can command. Although greatly lacking in systematization and precision, it has the strength of lending itself best to the identification of more concealed members of the particular elite. The historical technique used so effectively by Mosca and Pareto also lacks precision. It is only as strong as the historical records it rests upon and requires knowledge of an unusual depth and breadth by the researcher. The utilization of this method is further complicated by the fact that the data was not gathered in terms of an elite framework. If skillfully implemented, however, the historical technique can often lead to novel insights into the political role of elites.

The formal-positional, reputational, and decisional methods of elite identification have been developed relatively recently and represent an attempt to introduce a modicum of precision into elite analysis. Positional study involves a decision concerning what institutional positions

[55]Frederick W. Frey, *The Turkish Political Elite* (Cambridge: M.I.T. Press, 1965), p. 157 as quoted in Dankwart A. Rustow, "The Study of Elites: Who's Who, When, and How," *World Politics* 18 (July 1966): 702.

[56]Rustow, "The Study of Elites," p. 716.

are the crucial ones and then designating the occupants of these positions as members of the elite. This listing of formal officeholders is the easiest method of elite identification, and it also lends itself to quantitative analysis. The great difficulty, of course, is that elite membership is not necessarily congruent with the occupancy of high formal positions. The decisional technique concentrates on case studies of particular issues considered to be fundamental or key. Through meticulous analysis of these decision-making processes, the researcher identifies the elite. This method contains a more subtle version of the same difficulty that confronts the formal-positional technique. Is the formal decision-making process the "real" one, or is it possible that decisions have already been made on an informal basis elsewhere with different participants involved? Even in the formal setting, decisions may be reached on the basis of implicit pressures exerted on those present by absent powerful individuals. Thus, in a classic article, Peter Bachrach and Morton S. Baratz emphasize the existence of a "nondecision-making process."[57] Both the formal-positional and decisional methods are particularly weak in the study of non-Western societies where the most influential tend to rest behind the scenes and where the important decisions are made in informal settings.

Perhaps the most widely utilized procedure in contemporary elite study is the reputational method. In this technique, the researcher relies upon informants who nominate those they consider to be members of the elite. The elite is eventually identified on the basis of what most of the informants and interviewees believe the elite to be. This method has the advantage of being able to enlist the support of informed members of the community or society under examination. This, in turn, may lead to the identification of some less obvious elite members. Reputational analysis also has the strength of being susceptible to statistical precision and sophistication. However, it also contains severe inadequacies. On what basis does one select the informants, and how does one protect

---

[57]Peter Bachrach and Morton S. Baratz, "Two Faces of Power," *American Political Science Review* 56 (December 1962): 947–52. For an important discussion of the role of "nondecisions" in the political process and the research difficulties associated with it, see Raymond E. Wolfinger, "Nondecisions and the Study of Local Politics," *American Political Science Review* 65 (December 1971): 1063–80; Frederick W. Frey's comment entitled "Comment: On Issues and Nonissues in the Study of Power," ibid., pp. 1081–1101; and Wolfinger's response "Rejoinder to Frey's 'Comment,'" ibid., pp. 1102–4. From an interesting assessment of the thorny difficulties involved in researching nondecisions which is the core of his article, Wolfinger makes a rather astonishing leap in his "Rejoinder to Frey" where he concludes that "nondecisions is an *unnecessary* idea" (p. 1104). Frey admits the research problems but is less willing to jettison the concept which he sees as an "absolutely vital area for investigation" (p. 1092). Frey's considerable experience in analyzing political processes outside the American and European contexts may partially explain his continued determination to research these less visible dimensions of politics.

against informant bias? How does one reconcile strongly differing opinions between and among informants? How does one close the gap between reputation for power or influence and the actual possession of power or influence? Reputational analysis also carries a series of built-in self-fulfilling biases. Somewhere in the procedure, respondents are asked to choose from a list of names in the running for elitehood. Thus, it has already been decided that there is an elite and that its members are on that particular list. A slightly broader type of self-fulfilling prophecy is seen in the fact that the indication of reputation for power may in fact lead to the acquisition of power.[58]

The procedural and operational difficulties associated with the elite approach have been confronted and to some degree lessened through contemporary research efforts. A variety of techniques are now available to scholars, although each carries its own peculiar strengths and shortcomings. By being aware of all of these stances and by perhaps employing a combination of them, a researcher may come closer to effective elite identification.[59] It is less likely, however, that he will be as easily able to move beyond elite identification and description to elite political activity and political outcomes. As Edinger and Searing point out:

> We may be unable to obtain sufficiently detailed information on the social background histories of elite group members to allow us to achieve satisfactory explanations and predictions. And we may not find sufficient attitudinal consistency related to social background to do better than investigators employing less quantitative and more intuitive approaches. If we are to do better, both requirements will have to be satisfied.[60]

The Elitist-Pluralist Controversy

One of the great debates that has marked contemporary social science has been the one that has pitted "elitist" against "pluralist." Two key studies exist at the heart of this intellectual confrontation and these are Floyd Hunter's *Community Power Structure* and Robert Dahl's *Who Gov-*

---

[58]For a detailed and sophisticated discussion of the problems of elite identification, see Frederick W. Frey, "The Determination and Location of Elites: A Critical Analysis," paper prepared for delivery at the Sixty-sixth Annual Meeting of the American Political Science Association, Los Angeles, Calif., September 8–12, 1970.

[59]See, for example, Robert Presthus, *Men at the Top* (New York: Oxford University Press, 1964).

[60]Lewis J. Edinger and Donald D. Searing, "Social Background in Elite Analysis: A Methodological Inquiry," *American Political Science Review* 61 (June 1967):445.

erns?[61] The former is a reputational study of Atlanta and posits the existence of an elite; the latter is a decisional analysis of New Haven and denies the existence of an elite while emphasizing a pluralistic "polyarchy." An immense interdisciplinary forest of literature has grown up around this issue in a way that has obscured and retarded as much as it has clarified and enlightened.

The pluralists, who interestingly enough tend to be political scientists, contend that power is diffused and dispersed. The processes of industrialization and modernization have brought about increasing specialization and differentiation which have resulted in the constant formation of new interests and groups. This diversity has meant the continuing fractionation of power, and the competition among various power centers is the essence of the political process. In this sense, it is very relevant that the pluralists often rely on group analysis. In terms of methodological technique, the pluralists have, like Dahl, tended to pursue a decisional path, while elite scholars have more often gone the reputational route of Hunter, a sociologist.

The pluralist perspective also has the moral strength of being far more compatible with modern democratic theory than the elite approach. In the heated debate with elite analysts, this particular consideration has served at times to support the righteousness of the pluralist's position. It has also charged this important intellectual discussion with an unfortunate ideological emotionalism that has hampered theoretical progress. The presentation of the elite approach has suffered the most in this situation as it has constantly been subject to deep distortion by its detractors. Pareto, for example, is accused of exhibiting "a sadistic pleasure in finding faults with mankind" and of employing the "psychology of the disappointed lover."[62] Mosca is claimed to have formulated his approach "as a useful propaganda device with which to criticize all and every intellectual position which advocates democracy and socialism."[63] C. Wright Mills is criticized for his "militancy" and is described as "one of these caretakers of the socialist polemical tradition."[64] Not surprisingly, Geraint Parry writes that "these disputes have become

---

[61]Floyd Hunter, *Community Power Structure* (Chapel Hill: University of North Carolina Press, 1953); Robert A. Dahl, *Who Governs?* (New Haven: Yale University Press, 1961).

[62]Max Ascoli, "Society Through Pareto's Mind," *Social Research* 3 (February 1936):85; and Werner Stark, "In Search of the True Pareto," *British Journal of Sociology* 14 (June 1963):104.

[63]Raymond Barkley, "The Theory of the Elite and the Mythology of Power," *Science and Society* 19 (Spring 1955):106.

[64]Philip Rieff, "Socialism and Sociology," *Partisan Review* (Summer 1956) as reprinted in G. William Domhoff and Hoyt B. Ballard, eds., *C. Wright Mills and the Power Elite* (Boston: Beacon Press, 1968), p. 167.

arguments about political ideology."[65] Differences between the elitist-pluralist perspective have tended to harden along several fronts (e.g., technique, ideology, academic discipline), making this particular controversy an unusually formidable impediment to scientific theory building.

However, there have been compensations. The price for conceptual fuzziness and methodological inelegance has become very high. The scholar is immediately called to account for inattention to theoretical rigor and consistency. This, in turn, has brought noticeable improvement and order into the study of some of the fundamental issues of politics. A serious examination of *both* the elitist and pluralist positions also can suggest new insights and directions in the development of approaches to political study.

The pluralist and elitist positions share a number of similarities. At the core of both positions is a basic concern for the distribution of power. Procedural techniques and conceptual frameworks are also very similar, although they differ slightly from researcher to researcher. The basic difference is one of conclusion regarding the concentration and diffusion of power.[66] The heat of the controversy has tended to obscure these similarities, and it is only now becoming evident that the two positions "are not so starkly opposed as some of the more vocal proponents of each would have us believe."[67] The clouding effect of ideological preferences has been joined by an inordinate emphasis upon community studies resulting in a misty myopia that has hidden some fundamental likenesses. The elitist-pluralist battle has been fought on the limited terrain of American community studies with little attention to the processes of non-American, and especially non-Western societies.[68]

This lack of comparative perspective has slowed the realization, for example, that both elitist and pluralist stances contain the same procedural and conceptual weaknesses. It is far more difficult to apply decisional, reputational, or positional techniques in Asian and African

---

[65]Parry, *Political Elites,* p. 120.

[66]This conclusion is strongly influenced by the attitude the researcher takes into his study. Those who are looking for the concentration of power generally find it. Those who seek the diffusion of power find power diffused.

[67]Robert T. Golembiewski, William A. Welsh, William J. Crotty, *A Methodological Primer for Political Scientists* (Chicago: Rand McNally, 1969), p. 162. This study by Golembiewski, Welsh, and Crotty stands as one of the extraordinarily fine analyses of theory and method in political science.

[68]Those political scientists who have applied the elite approach in studying non-Western societies, for example, have generally implemented a reputational technique. This runs against the strong trend in elite community analysis where the political scientists are those who stress the decisional and attack the reputational.

societies where formal frameworks mean less and where respondents may be less cooperative. It is also more complex to apply the familar conceptual apparatus to less familiar environments. In this kind of setting, the inadequacies of one single stance also become quickly evident. Attempts to relate and integrate seem much more urgent. Elitism and pluralism can be viewed as different ends of the same spectrum, and group and elite analysis combined offer a more promising approach. Not accidentally, the anthropologists have been the ones who have done the most work in combining and integrating the stratification and group approaches. The trend, however, is broadening, and Golembiewski, Welsh, and Crotty have recently made a compelling argument for "a continuous concept of community power" and for "pluralism-elitism conceived as a continuum."[69]

Elite Analysis and Modernization

The elite approach contributes in several ways to an understanding of the patterns and processes of change and modernization. The first advantage it carries in this respect is the attention it accords the attitudes and orientations of political leaders. By permitting in-depth analysis of the attitudes that elite actors maintain towards the issue of modernization, elite study is able to account for the strategies of change that rest at the roots of programs to preserve or transform. Attitudinal study is critical here, for perceptions regarding issues of change directly shape the policies that bear on political development and modernization. This is especially true when the study focuses upon the orientations of those individuals in society who are in the best position to shape, direct, and control the forces of change. The built-in relationship between the elite approach and the political culture approach is particularly valuable to any analysis of modernization (see chapter 3). Ideas of political innovation or political stagnation as entertained by members of the elite profoundly influence a society's capacity to meet the challenge of change.

A second but related strength that elite study offers to an understanding of developmental processes derives from the special position the elite maintains in society. Political experience and expertise reside here and not in "the mass of the population who have in many cases been maintained in subjection and inactivity . . ."[70] The deliberate and conscious methodology of modernization is primarily the business of the elite. An elite may pursue a policy of piecemeal reform and revision

[69]Golembiewski, Welsh, and Crotty, *A Methodological Primer,* pp. 181–82.

[70]Bottomore, *Elites and Society,* p. 89.

in the hopes of staying one step ahead of social explosion; it may resist any change and attempt to isolate and insulate itself and its society; it may institute a program of deep and deliberate social and political transformation. An elite may be divided against itself concerning what development strategy it should adopt; or it may be quite cohesive in this same respect. Certain elites may initiate policies of transformation in certain systems (e.g., the economic system), while supporting repressive programs of preservation in other systems (e.g., the political system). Elite members may agree upon developmental ends, but they may disagree about what means to adopt in pursuing those ends. These kinds of issues are extremely significant to the study of modernization. Indeed, modernization itself is defined by some authors as the passage from one type of elite rule to another type of elite rule.

A slightly different consideration that evolves from the special position that an elite maintains in society and politics concerns the key relation between *control* and *change.* An elite has relatively more control than any group in society because of its authority and its relation to the instruments of coercion and persuasion in society. Although an elite's authority and control may be fleeting commodities, they are essential to successful confrontation with the problem of modernization. The direction and guidance of modernizing programs requires strength and control. To obstruct and thwart these processes demands even more strength and control. Political elites stand high in these qualities, and the stance they decide to assume with this strength merits careful analysis. In an age of constantly increasing challenges of new social and political forces, peoples everywhere subject their leaders to closer and harder scrutiny. Elite analysis represents a systematic scholarly attempt to do the same.

The elite approach can yield the most fruitful results with regard to precisely those societies about which we know least and within which the processes of modernization are most dramatically evident. African, Asian, Middle Eastern, and Latin American societies lend themselves to the elite approach for two basic reasons: (1) they tend to be those societies which are most obviously elitist; and (2) personal and informal politics are relatively more significant here. Elite study is in many ways tailored to this kind of social and political setting. In the Afro-Asian world, social structures are quite rigid, political participation is limited, economic gaps are broad, and human demands are sharp. The depth of the challenge of modernization and the crucial role that elites play in the process is abundantly clear in this situation. By enabling the researcher to understand the basic patterns of power and wealth in these societies, elite analysis offers at the same time new insights into the basic issue of modernization.

Since elite study involves a concentration upon modernization as viewed and addressed by societal leadership, it can account best for *deliberate, reform-oriented* kinds of change. It is especially valuable in explaining strategic social change and in presenting the intricacies of processes generally referred to as "defensive modernization," "reform from above," and "incremental reformism." Since the elite has a vested interest in preserving the system in which it is an elite, as well as in protecting its own position within that system, the elite approach tends to represent an unusually strong means of analyzing reforming change. At the level of modifying change, elite study has much to offer. With regard to the analysis of other forms of change, however, the inadequacies of this approach begin to become evident.

Elite investigation cannot by itself account for the crucial transformational aspects of modernization. Although it can bare the will of the *leadership* concerning the problem of development, it cannot explain the will and capacity of the *society* to meet the challenge. In this sense, even the analysis of a revolutionary elite is not adequate for the explanation of transforming change. Elite study in essence is analysis of a crucial element in society. This kind of analysis, however, does not possess the power of penetration necessary to explain modernization and political development. T. B. Bottomore writes that the success of elites in instituting modernization depends "to a very large extent upon their success in arousing popular enthusiasm, and upon the extent of the support which they can get from major social classes such as the poorer peasants and the industrial workers."[71]

The elite approach, as a theoretical approach, cannot account for the key role of classes and masses. Elite theoreticians have attempted to confront this difficulty in various ways. Most common, of course, is minimizing and belittling the role of non-elite groups in society. If "the masses" can be dismissed as insignificant, then elite study looks very good indeed. Another tactic is to define an elite so broadly and loosely that non-elites become elites. It is not unknown for such groups as the proletariat and middle classes to be defined into the elite whenever it is useful to do so.[72] A slight variation on this theme is to introduce terms such as "counterelite," "strategic elite," and "sublimative elite." Although this helps draw distinctions, it at the same time hints that all groups are part of the elite universe. A final method is to drag elements from other approaches into the elite study whenever elite analysis is

---

[71]Bottomore, *Elites and Society*, p. 102.

[72]T. B. Bottomore, for example, somewhat inconsistently includes the middle class as one of his elite types. See ibid., pp. 89–93.

found lacking. This is, of course, legitimate, but then one is no longer applying the elite approach.

No matter whether the elite scholar decides to use such terms as "counterelites" or "masses,"[73] non-elite groups are residual categories in the elite approach to the study of politics. This profoundly cripples the ability of elite study to analyze and explain the revolution of modernization. Change is not always initiated from above; in fact, one could just as easily make the point that change originates from below. Certainly much change originates in a challenge. And it is in the middle and lower classes in society from which challenges emanate; those who have *least* are more apt to demand social transformation than those who have *most.* Elite study does not concern itself with the attitudes and orientations that lead to the innovation of change at this level.

Therefore, while the elite approach accounts very well for change at one level, it has a strong static bias at another level. This can be seen in terms of the origination and innovation of change as indicated above, and is also evident in the actual implementation of modernizing policy. Social and political transformation involve mass participation, comprehensive institutionalization, national commitment, and the continually broadening distribution of wealth and power in society. It is much more than a game of musical chairs in which leaders exchange places and alternate programs designed to revise and reform. The elite theorist cannot adequately account for this kind of change with his theoretical stance. The comprehensive analysis of social and political transformation requires an investigation of the middle and lower strata of society that is at least as thorough as the one applied to the elite. The elite approach to the study of politics is most obviously inadequate both from a theoretical and a practical perspective in an age of revolutionary change.

---

[73]The cavalier attitude that many elite scholars display towards non-elites is reflected in this term "mass." This is a very convenient way of lumping everyone together who is not part of the elite. A mass is a lump that exists somewhere below the elite.

CHAPTER VI

Class Analysis

Since the days of Aristotle, class analysis has represented an important theoretical approach to the study of the social and political systems. Stratification by class has been utilized by prominent scholars such as Karl Marx, Adam Smith, Max Weber, Joseph Schumpeter, Thorstein Veblen, T. H. Marshall, and Pitrim Sorokin in order to explain patterns of economic competition, political conflict, and social change. In modern American political science, however, class analysis has yet to receive the attention and acceptance that have marked the traditional formal-legal and contemporary structural-functional approaches. The reaction against traditional formal and institutional study has tended to take the shape of the group and elite approaches which to a large degree continue to displace or disguise class analysis.

Obstacles and Objections

There are several reasons why the class approach is a latecomer to the list of systematically developed approaches to the study of comparative political processes. In the first place, American political theory, on both the popular and academic levels, has traditionally assumed that classes have played an insignificant role in American society. Overt class appeals and symbols are relatively rare in the United States. Illustrative of this circumstance is the fact that unlike most major industrialized countries the United States does not have a working class political party. Democratic beliefs are sustained on the image of a classless society or one in which a large middle class dominates. Pluralist and group interpretations abound, especially among political scientists. As a result, the class approach has not received the serious attention of political scholars in the United States.

A second reason for the retarded development of class analysis has been its close identification with the work of Karl Marx. During an important period of contemporary American scholarship, the linkage carried overtones of pro-Communism and un-Americanism, and those theorists who spoke in class terms were suspected of ideological treason.[1] In the early and middle 1950s, therefore, when comparative political study was in the initial throes of transformation, few scholars chose to introduce class analysis. Those who were so inclined deflected their scholarship into the spongy terrain of "sector," "segment," or "stratum" analysis.[2]

Largely due to the work of Marx, the class concept has become intimately intertwined with economic phenomena. Political scientists were searching for a subject matter uniquely their own and as a result desired to focus their attention upon that which was most obviously political. First they settled upon governmental institutions and later upon groups such as legislatures and parties as the cores of their analysis. Class considerations were not regarded as central to political scholarship.

A fourth consideration that has contributed to scholarly resistance to class analysis is rooted in the behavioral movement. In their drive for scientific generalization and objectivity, the advocates of behavioralism found the class approach lacking in two major respects. The class concept was first viewed as carrying too much ideological and heavily value-laden baggage. "Class" was also considered to be virtually impossible to confront and measure with any substantial degree of precision or accuracy. The growth of the class approach was, therefore, stunted during one of the major contemporary developments in political science.

Finally, the class approach has been difficult to apply in the broad

---

[1]Vernon V. Aspaturian writes that "one of the great advantages of the Soviet analytical system is that it has been allowed to establish a virtual monopoly on class analysis." According to Aspaturian: "What happened is that Marxists effectively united a valid and reputable system of social analysis with a disreputable and feared prognosis, and as a result of guilt by association, the respectability of class analysis was ideologically tarnished." See Vernon V. Aspaturian, *Process and Power in Soviet Foreign Policy* (Boston: Little, Brown, 1971), p. 269.

[2]See, for example, John J. Johnson, *Political Change in Latin America: The Emergence of the Middle Sectors* (Stanford: Stanford University Press, 1958). In the Preface to this study, the author writes: "As the alternatives to 'classes' and 'strata' the terms 'middle sectors,' 'middle groups,' 'middle segments,' 'middle components,' 'middle elements,' used interchangeably, were settled upon to convey the idea of 'middleness' without paralleling any fixed criteria of 'middleness' employed in areas outside Latin America." See pp. viii–ix.

context of comparative political analysis. A foliage of myths has grown up around the approach that portrays it as inapplicable not only to liberal democratic societies such as the United States but also to the Third World societies of Asia, Africa, the Middle East, and Latin America. Part of the reason for this attitude resides in the fact that the classical and more orthodox class formulations have been developed within and applied to a limited number of Western societies. Because of this, a number of critics have argued that class analysis is unable to confront the broad range of contexts necessary for the generation of theory that will carry cross-cultural significance.

Despite these five interrelated obstacles, the class approach to the study of comparative politics has very recently been the focus of increasing scholarly attention. With the deep preoccupation that contemporary social scientists are exhibiting towards the issues of modernization and political development, and the increasingly evident limitations of both elite and group analysis in this regard, there has been a recent return to class as the central theoretical concept. This trend has included conceptual and theoretical reassessment and research,[3] general historical and multinational comparative studies,[4] and empirical analyses of particular Asian, African, Middle Eastern, and Latin American societies.[5] The movement to resurrect and refine the class approach is

[3]The outstanding contributions include Ralf Dahrendorf, *Class and Class Conflict in Industrial Society*, rev. Eng. ed. (Stanford: Stanford University Press, 1959); Stanislaw Ossowski, *Class Structure in the Social Consciousness*, trans. Sheila Patterson (London: Routledge and Kegan Paul, 1963); Milton M. Gordon, *Social Class in American Sociology* (New York: McGraw-Hill, 1958); and T. B. Bottomore's two studies, *Elites and Society* (New York: Basic Books, 1964) and *Classes in Modern Society* (New York: Pantheon Books, 1966).

[4]Stimulating examples are Gerhard Lenski, *Power and Privilege: A Theory of Social Stratification* (New York: McGraw-Hill, 1966); and Barrington Moore, Jr., *Social Origins of Dictatorship and Democracy: Lord and Peasant in the Making of the Modern World* (Boston: Beacon Press, 1966).

[5]Among the writings of this category, see especially the following: Lloyd A. Fallers, "Social Stratification and Economic Processes in Africa," in Reinhard Bendix and Seymour Martin Lipset, eds., *Class, Status, and Power*, 2nd ed. (New York: Free Press, 1966), pp. 141–49; Richard L. Sklar, "Political Science and National Integration—A Radical Approach," *Journal of Modern African Studies* 5 (May 1967): 1–11; Kenneth W. Grundy, "The 'Class Struggle' in Africa: An Examination of Conflicting Theories," *Journal of Modern African Studies* 2 (November 1964): 379–93; Robert L. Hardgrave, Jr., "Caste: Fission and Fusion," *Economic and Political Weekly* (July 1968): 1065–70; Wolfram Eberhard, "Social Mobility and Stratification in China," in Bendix and Lipset, eds., *Class, Status, and Power*, pp. 171–82; James A. Bill, "Class Analysis and the Dialectics of Modernization in the Middle East," *International Journal of Middle East Studies* 3 (October 1972): 417–34; James F. Petras, "Class Structure and its Effects on Political Development," *Social Research* 36 (Summer 1969): 206–30; Frank E. Myers, "Social Class and Political Change in Western Industrial Systems," *Comparative Politics* 2 (April 1970): 389–412; Manfred Halpern, *The Politics of Social Change in the Middle East and North Africa* (Princeton: Princeton University Press, 1963), pp. 41–112; and the articles by Richard N. Adams and Anthony Leeds in Dwight B. Heath and Richard N. Adams, eds., *Contemporary Cultures and Societies of Latin America* (New York: Random House, 1965), pp. 257–87, 379–404.

significant to comparative political analysis and the drive to draw meaningful linkages between political systems and the challenge of change.

Class, Society, and Politics

According to the class approach, society-wide stratification is the fundamental reality of social and political life. This stratification system not only includes all members of a society, but also forms the basic determinant of conflict and change. Classes are aggregations that must be defined in relation to one another, and conflict is the essential characteristic that marks these relations.

The basic units of analysis in the class approach are aggregates of individuals who hold similar positions with regard to the possession of values such as power, wealth, authority, or prestige. These classes always relate to one another in hierarchical patterns of superordination and subordination. The conflict that naturally develops out of the relationships between the units linked in this hierarchical inequality generates the dynamics that result in social and political change.

The class approach raises the following kinds of questions concerning society and politics. What are the basic characteristics of classes and how is class membership determined? How do classes relate to one another and what impact do these relations have upon the social structure? What is the relation between the class structure and the political system? What are the essential patterns of cooperation and conflict that mark class linkages? How does class interaction affect the basic issue of continuity and change? How and when does class conflict lead to revolution? What is the relation between elites, leaders, groups, and classes?

Although class scholars disagree concerning the particular basis of stratification, generally they recognize the political system as the locus of decision making ultimately shaping the class structure. The role of the political system in molding the class structure and the impact of the class structure in turn upon the political system are important areas in which class analysts generate hypotheses. The relation between politics and class is one of the most critical points of investigation for this approach.

The centrality of conflict to class analysis is such that the approach is sometimes referred to as "the theory of class struggle."[6] One leading social theorist discusses the class approach as a "coercion theory of society" and summarizes the latter in terms of the following four tenets:

[6]Roy C. Macridis, *The Study of Comparative Government* (New York: Random House, 1955), p. 47.

(1) Every society is at every point subject to processes of change; social change is ubiquitous.
(2) Every society displays at every point dissensus and conflict; social conflict is ubiquitous.
(3) Every element in a society renders a contribution to its disintegration and change.
(4) Every society is based on the coercion of some of its members by others.[7]

Class scholars have provided a number of differing emphases and variations of class structural types. In the case of most non-Western and Third World societies, class configurations are drawn and studied according to the analyst's particular point of emphasis. The class approach, therefore, has tended to develop in accord with the problems addressed by the investigator as well as in accord with the empirical findings gleaned from the studies. Figure 4 provides a diagrammatic view of four basic class structures as they have been presented in the literature by scholars of various Third World or "less-developed" societies. These graphic representations are obviously simplified and somewhat distorted from reality. Further, they do not represent an exhaustive categorization. They do, however, provide a pronounced view of various important ways in which practitioners of the class approach have envisioned the structures and relations they have analyzed. They also indicate the differing emphases that can be introduced in the analysis of class structure.

The Pyramidal Class Structure Scholars of Third World political systems have most often described the layout of classes in these societies in terms of a triangular or pyramidal structure. As diagram (a) in figure 4 indicates, this structural type emphasizes both the ordering and size of classes. The base of the pyramid represents the lower classes while the upper class exists at the very apex. Class membership gradually decreases towards the top of the triangle. From top to bottom, however, the slope takes the form of a broadening flare. Strictly speaking, the pyramidal design refers to a class structure in which a single individual is located at the pinnacle. It is most applicable, therefore, to monarchical societies where one individual sits at the apex of the social and political system. Pyramids truncated near the top would most accurately describe structures of societies where oligarchical elites rule.

The pyramidal structural type is one in which those with most wealth, prestige, authority, or power are located at the top in small numbers. Those who have the least of any of these values are the many

---

[7]Dahrendorf, *Class and Class Conflict,* p. 162.

located at the bottom of the triangle. The relative size and ordering of classes which are revealed in this kind of diagrammatic form make it logically possible for numerous variations on this form to exist. One common example that prevails in many Western industrial societies is the diamond-shaped structure. Here, the middle class dominates the society while both upper and lower classes are relatively small.

The Hierarchical Class Structure Diagram (b) of figure 4 depicts a simplified version of a hierarchical class alignment. Like the pyramidal form, the hierarchical structure indicates the relative size and ordering of particular classes. Unlike the pyramidal formulation, however, this structural type does not portray the class system as an integrated, sloping whole. It is rather a rectangular alignment that stresses distinctions and differentiations between and among classes. The most common and intricate variation of this kind of structure is the one developed in community sociology where six different boxes or classes are vertically aligned and referred to as the upper-upper, lower-upper, upper-middle, lower-middle, upper-lower, and lower-lower classes.

Both the pyramidal and hierarchical arrangements are popular in contemporary social science literature. The hierarchical structural type has tended to emphasize detailed description and analysis of each class in and of itself. A profile is drawn for each class in the structure. The pyramidal view has provided a more integrated picture and assessment of the class structure as a whole. Both structural types have in slightly different ways ordered classes along a vertical continuum depending upon their members' possession of such key values as power and wealth.

The Overlapping Class Structure In an effort to overcome the tendency to arrange and analyze classes in terms of compressed geological layers, scholars have relatively recently attempted to design conceptual structures that will take into account the fact that classes do interlock and overlap with one another. The most significant attempt thus far in this regard has been a formulation by Gerhard Lenski, a modification of which is reproduced in diagram (c) of figure 4.[8] According to Lenski, this is a graphic representation of the class structure in a typical agrarian society.

Diagram (c) stresses the interrelationship between classes, with special emphasis upon the fact that classes cannot be sharply separated by slashing horizontal lines. An element of uncertainty is always involved, for example, concerning the status of upper-lower and lower-middle

[8]Lenski, *Power and Privilege*, p. 284.

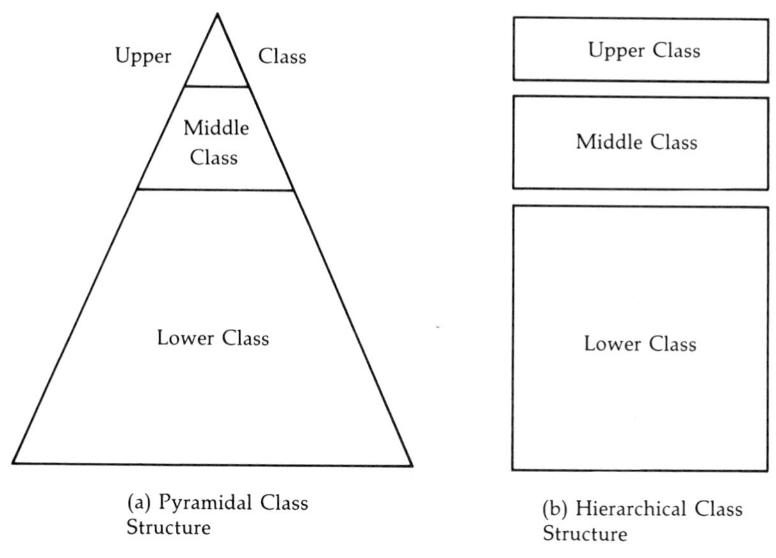

(a) Pyramidal Class Structure

(b) Hierarchical Class Structure

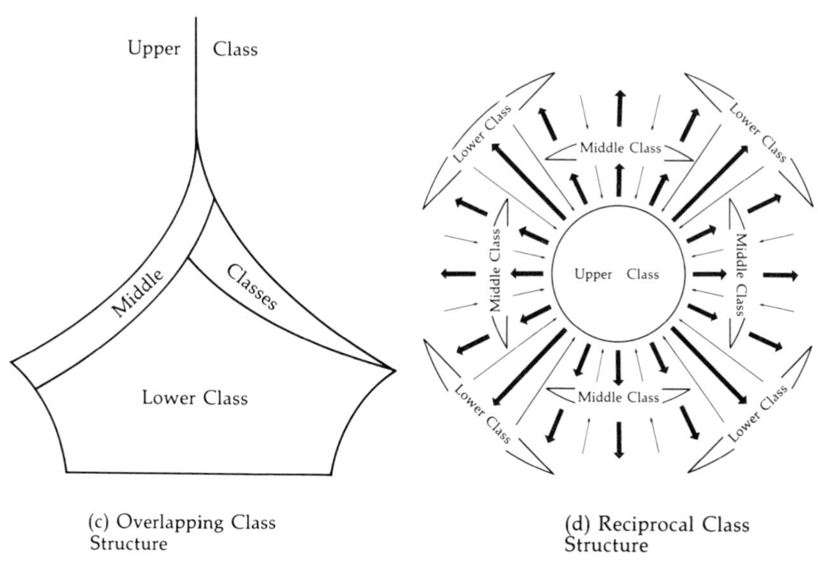

(c) Overlapping Class Structure

(d) Reciprocal Class Structure

FIGURE 4 Four Diagrammatic Views of Class Structure

class membership. Lenski's formulation, therefore, emphasizes the fact that classes interlock and overlap one another. Diagram (c) also is more representative of the actual degree of inequality that separates the upper from the lower classes. The hierarchical and pyramidal views of class structure greatly minimize and distort this crucial gap.

The Reciprocal Class Structure Diagram (d) of figure 4 presents a circular arrangement in which the upper class is located at the core of the circle while the lower classes exist around the circumference.[9] Although this conceptual characterization does not attempt to indicate relative class size, it does focus attention upon the complex interclass patterns and processes.

The emphasis in this particular structural form is upon the reciprocal pressures that mark interclass relations. These relations are two directional in the sense that classes in less advantageous positions in the structure are often able to exert influence upon those in more advantageous positions. At the same time, however, the classes remain in general hierarchy since the power or influence flow is always heavier from upper to lower classes. In diagram (d), therefore, the heavier arrows all point towards the circumference of the outer circle. Class relations may be reciprocal in nature, but this reciprocity must be uneven and unequal.

Reciprocal class analysis permits the study of complex interclass patterns rather than emphasizing the description of particular class units. The deepest focus is upon tilted relations of reciprocity that serve to bind the classes to one another while at the same time building elasticity into the class structure itself. Even in the rigidly defined context of Indian social structure the caste system involves relationships of mutual obligation and reciprocity—but not of equality. Indeed, the caste system presupposes ideally the interdependent relationship of occupational castes functioning according to prescribed patterns of behavior, providing at once economic security and a clearly defined status and role.[10]

As these four illustrations indicate, the manner and method of applying the class approach vary considerably. These simplified diagrammatic examples stress also the differing dimensions of class structure that can be emphasized in applying this particular approach to the study of comparative politics. Although class analysis must necessarily consider the ordering of the key units, this might be done in various ways.

---

[9]For the theoretical presentation of this structural form, see J.A. Bill, "Class Analysis and the Dialectics of Modernization." For the empirical grounding of this model, see James A. Bill, *The Politics of Iran: Groups, Classes, and Modernization* (Columbus, Ohio: Merrill, 1972).

[10]Robert L. Hardgrave, Jr., *The Nadars of Tamilnad: The Political Culture of a Community in Change* (Berkeley: University of California Press, 1969), p. 5.

Emphasis may be placed upon the class units themselves or upon the patterns that relate these units one to the other. Considerations such as class size, class shape, and class strength are also relevant factors in the study of class structure. Perhaps the crucial issue, however, and one that has yet to be considered, concerns the basic standard that is used to order and relate classes. On what basis are these pyramidal, rectangular, and circular continua organized? In other words, how are classes defined and what are their fundamental characteristics?

The Class Concept Defined

The development of class analysis as a theoretical approach to the study of politics and society has closely paralleled the changing understanding of the essence of the class concept itself. Since the time when Marx first introduced his formulations, a number of significant theoretical attempts to define and redefine this key concept have been made. An examination of these exercises and the reasoning that surrounds them will help to expose the core of the class approach.[11]

"Class" and the Means of Production

The term "class" is immediately associated with the work of Karl Marx, and although the latter may not have been the originator of class analysis, he must stand as the man who gave it meaning, depth, and appeal. Despite this, in all of Marx's writing he never provides an explicit definition of the concept so basic to his theory. The closest he comes is Chapter 52 of *Capital* where he begins to discuss "class" only to break off after a few paragraphs.[12] The writings of Marx, however, do provide various insights into his conception of class, and two excellent commentaries by Ralf Dahrendorf and Stanislaw Ossowski explore this matter in depth.[13] The latter has documented the numerous views that Marx held concerning class structure and has demonstrated convincingly that

---

[11]Portions of this section have appeared in the following two articles: James A. Bill, "Class Analysis and the Challenge of Change," *Comparative Political Studies* Volume 2, Number 3 (October 1969) pp. 389–400, used by permission of the publisher, Sage Publications, Inc., and James A. Bill, "Class Analysis and the Dialectics of Modernization in the Middle East," *International Journal of Middle East Studies* 3 (October, 1972): 417–34, used by permission.

[12]Karl Marx, *Capital,* trans. Ernest Untermann (Chicago: Charles H. Kerr and Co., 1909), III, pp. 1031–1032.

[13]See Dahrendorf, *Class and Class Conflict,* and Ossowski, *Class Structure.*

the structure was in fact addressed in a number of quite distinct ways. Few sensitive theorists, however, have criticized Marx for lack of rigor in his theory building since he was also a polemicist deeply involved in the business of revolution. For Marx, "class" was more significant in terms of political strategy than in terms of conceptual clarity.

In Marx's view, the class concept was basically defined and determined by its relationship to the means of production in society. In Marxian class analysis, the economic system is the prime system. Marx's most explicit statements concerning class reveal this as well as the fact that although the economic factor is primary, the social, political, and subjective ramifications are never to be overlooked or underrated.[14] Marx's concept of class structure was fundamentally dichotomous, although evidence can be found to support the argument that Marx recognized a hierarchy of classes.[15] Marx concentrated his theory and writing upon an inevitable confrontation between classes which stand in basic opposition to one another. The outcome of this conflict explains the dynamics of change through history. The Marxian analysis of class offered a new and comprehensive approach to the study of the development of man and society and had its own profound impact on world history. At the same time, it introduced conceptual and theoretical equipment that offered much to the study of comparative politics and social change. In these senses, Marx deserves the credit for popularizing class as a tool of analysis.

The Marxian use of the class concept carries with it some very relevant and useful characteristics which later writers have often discarded, distorted, or ignored. In the first place, Marx was concerned mainly with forces, trends, and relations. Not in the least interested in static description, Marx saw in class the basic force of movement of the deepest and most general kind. This emphasis upon the fundamental relationship between class and the processes of revolutionary change was a major contribution. Class indicated conflict, and this became the driving dynamic of change. In short, Karl Marx presented class as the basic concept for analyzing a changing society through time.

Marx's theories were understandably shaped to a great extent by the society and age in which he lived—early nineteenth century Europe during the harsh stages of industrialization. Much of what he said and implied then will not stand with regard to agriculturally oriented and tribally based Afro-Asian societies or modern Western post-industrial societies. Marx's own writings concerning what he termed "Asiatic

---

[14]See, for example, Karl Marx, *The Eighteenth Brumaire of Louis Bonaparte* (New York: International Publishers, n.d.), esp. p. 109.

[15]See Ossowski, *Class Structure,* pp. 69–88.

societies" reveal a conspicuous absence of class analysis. In his occasional references to China, India, and Russia, Marx did not discuss the class relations of these societies. Instead, he tended to stress the importance and power of the state and bureaucratic organization as if these abstractions *were* the ruling class. According to Karl Wittfogel: "This was a strange formulation for a man who ordinarily was eager to define social classes and who denounced as a mystifying 'reification' the use of such notions as 'commodity' and 'the state', when the underlying human (class) relations were left unexplained."[16] In his *New York Daily Tribune* articles, Marx viewed Asiatic societies primarily as they affect and are influenced by the industrializing West. Western class relations were stressed even here.[17]

The ultimate emphasis upon the economic in defining and determining class is one of the major theoretical criticisms of Marxian class analysis. This preoccupation has tended to restrict and constrict the concept, making it less applicable to societies where other power bases or relations may be more vital. In Asian and Middle Eastern societies, for example, political influence, personal manipulation, kinship loyalties, bargaining techniques, saintly ancestry, and traditional education, in addition to wealth, may have decisive impact upon stratification. The critical relations often involve modes of maneuver rather than modes of production.

A conceptual framework based on economics also oversimplifies the class structure. This has resulted in the brushing aside of several key classes whose appearance and growth was not a basic part of the theory. At the same time, the phenomenon of mobility was largely ignored, and interclass movements which have been crucial to the viability of certain political systems were seldom discussed within the Marxian approach.[18]

---

[16]Karl Wittfogel, *Oriental Despotism: A Comparative Study of Total Power* (New Haven: Yale University Press, 1957), p. 380. For an enlightening discussion of Marx's analysis of Asiatic societies, see pp. 374–82.

[17]See, for example, the articles on India and China reproduced in Henry M. Christman, ed., *The American Journalism of Marx and Engels* (New York: New American Library, 1966), pp. 83–109, 185–210.

[18]One of the best indications of the difficulties that Marxian class analysis holds for contemporary sociopolitical study concerns the approaches taken by recent socialists and revisionist theoreticians. Eastern European scholars, in particular, have recently paid a great deal of attention to the class concept. In 1963, President Gomulka warned Polish intellectuals to cease describing society in terms of Western "bourgeois" sociology of stratification and to make use instead of Marx's analytic definition of class. Despite this attention, however, there has been little done with regard to the reconceptualization of the class concept. Activity has been concentrated in the area of theoretical surveys of the literature on class studies referring to the appearance of new classes in society. Soviet scholars have been even less daring in their re-evaluation. Rather than re-define Marx's basic concept, they have decided to stretch it to meet the demands of change. Thus, practically all potential revolutionary groups and classes are being considered "working

Class and Status

Since the appearance of Robert and Helen Lynd's *Middletown* in 1929, American social scientists have become increasingly involved in community studies that have focused attention on the existence of stratification and class. The name usually associated with this kind of study has been W. Lloyd Warner and the school of sociologists that he represents.

In 1941, Warner and a group of associates produced their first major study of "Yankee City."[19] This study had a great impact upon American sociology, and, together with the other Warner projects, it has been reviewed and criticized for a quarter of a century. The pattern for most of the criticism, however, was set by C. Wright Mills whose classic review in the *American Sociological Review* in 1942 not only presented an unrivaled analysis of the study but also served to distinguish some of the factors essential to a relevant and meaningful conceptualization of class.[20]

The first Warner-directed community study was the fundamental one, and in it the conceptual framework was outlined. Warner's conceptual chapter, however, made no attempt to define the class concept which in the end proved to be the one most basic to the approach. The original assumption was that the basic determinant of class was economic, but Chapter Five states that this was not the case, for "other evidences began to accumulate which made it difficult to accept a simple economic hypothesis."[21] Class is therefore defined as "two or more orders of people who are believed to be, and are accordingly ranked by members of the community, in socially superior and inferior posi-

---

classes." Terms such as "semi-proletariat," "incipient proletariat" and "commercial-clerical proletariat" reveal the attempt to include the professional and salaried middle classes within the working class. Soviet sociologists have come to equate "physical" and "intellectual" labor and point out that "white-collar people are not in any way different from workers." See L. A. Gordon and L. A. Fridman, "Distinctive Aspects of the Working Class in the Economically Underdeveloped Countries of Asia and Africa," *Soviet Sociology* 2 (Winter 1963): 46–63; and M. N. Rutkevich, "Elimination of Class Differences and the Place of Non-Manual Workers in the Social Structure of Soviet Society," *Soviet Sociology* 3 (Fall 1964): 3–13. Important modifications of the Marxian concept of class have been made in Maoist theory. See John B. Starr, "Conceptual Foundations of MaoTse-Tung's Theory of Continuous Revolution," *Asian Survey* 11 (June, 1971): 610–28.

[19]W. Lloyd Warner and Paul S. Lunt, *The Social Life of a Modern Community,* Yankee City Series, Vol. I, (New Haven: Yale University Press, 1941). This was the first and most important study of the series in terms of intellectual impact and conceptual explicitness.

[20]C. Wright Mills, "Review of W. L. Warner and P. S. Lunt's 'The Social Life of a Modern Community,' " in *American Sociological Review* 7 (April 1942): 263–71. Another excellent review of the Warner approach is Seymour M. Lipset and Reinhard Bendix, "Social Status and Social Structure," Parts I and II, *British Journal of Sociology* 2 (June and September 1951): 150–68, 230–54.

[21]Warner and Lunt, *Social Life of a Modern Community,* p. 81.

tions."[22] According to Warner, class is linked to status and determined by what people of the community think or say. The fact that the residents see class in many different terms and determine it according to many diverse criteria became evident in the research.

The studies of this school of sociologists tend to consist of masses of data which when pooled together result in the arrangement of the members of a community into one of six slots of a class ladder running from upper-upper to lower-lower class. This kind of arrangement is an important variety of the hierarchical class type portrayed in figure 3, diagram (b).

The Warner approach was a pioneering effort in many ways, and it served to give meaning and impetus to class analysis in America. It also contributed obliquely to conceptualization by taking a big step away from Marx and indicating that class could be seen in other than an economic basis of reference. Perhaps its greatest contribution, however, was an unintended one, for in endeavoring to study America in terms of class, it encountered conceptual difficulties which others could consider and then offer constructive criticisms and useful alternatives.

The inadequacies of the community approach stem from the very definition that is assigned to class. Although the community sociologists see it primarily in terms of status, they also distinguish it in terms of property, wealth, family, and geography. There is considerable confusion concerning which of these characteristics prevail at any particular time and how they relate to one another and especially to the key variable of status. Perhaps the greatest weakness of the Warner school, however, inheres in the term *description.* The community sociologists, by and large, have been less interested in analysis than in description and detail. Much of their energy has been expended in gathering and sorting facts and very little in defining relations. On these grounds, Mills criticizes them most severely, pointing to "the lack of an eye for interrelations" and the masses of facts about which one can in the end ask "So what?"[23] Much of the reason for this absence of analysis lies in the fact that "there is no set of questions in terms of which the definitions used are framed,"[24] and thus the final result can only be a configurative description.

Class and Authority

In fundamental theoretical reaction against the schools of descriptive community stratification, a 1959 study appeared and called for a return

---

[22]Ibid., p. 82.

[23]Mills, "Review of Warner and Lunt," pp. 270–71.

[24]Ibid., p. 265.

to the class concept as used by Karl Marx and, ultimately, for a redefinition that would improve upon the Marxian formulations. In *Class and Class Conflict in Industrial Society,*[25] German sociologist Ralf Dahrendorf presents a theoretical attempt to reappraise the class concept as it has been used in the literature and to reshape it as an important tool of comparative analysis.

Besides clarifying and relating many of the key concepts and contributions in the field of class analysis, Dahrendorf presents two major contributions of his own: the difference between class as an analytic concept and stratum as a descriptive concept; and the displacement of Marx's crucial economic determinant by what Dahrendorf terms "authority relations." Throughout *Class and Class Conflict,* the author argues that the confusion of class and stratum has resulted in the virtual disappearance in the West of class as an analytic conceptual tool.[26] Dahrendorf writes: "However one may interpret, extend, or improve Marx, classes in his sense are clearly not layers in a hierarchical system of strata differentiated by gradual distinctions."[27]

Dahrendorf defines classes as "conflict groups that are generated by the differential distribution of authority in imperatively coordinated associations."[28] The key to this definition is found in his conception of authority as a legitimate relation of superordination and subordination which can rest on many bases—the ownership of property or modes of production being only one. Stratification on the basis of authority has also been stressed by W. Wesolowski, who writes that "if there is any functional necessity for stratification, it is the necessity of stratification according to the criterion of authority and not according to the criterion of material advantage or prestige."[29]

Although the Dahrendorf conceptualization is a major contribution to the literature on class, it also carries a number of conceptual shortcomings. Perhaps due to his preoccupation with industrial associations, Dahrendorf views class in terms of interest groups and even defines them in these terms. He explicitly makes the point that he is concerned not with class as seen in terms of society or society's segments, but with class in terms of "imperatively coordinated" associations. He states that

---

[25]Dahrendorf, *Class and Class Conflict.*

[26]See, especially, ibid., pp. ix, 19, 63, 76, 107–9, 139–40.

[27]Ibid., p. 76.

[28]Ibid., p. 204. For Dahrendorf's most explicit statements concerning the class concept, see also pp. 138, 148–152, 173, 204, 238, 247.

[29]W. Wesolowski, "Some Notes on the Functional Theory of Stratification," in Bendix and Lipset, eds., *Class, Status, and Power,* p. 69.

"social classes are always conflict groups"[30] and that "interest groups are the real agents of group conflict."[31] It becomes extraordinarily difficult to understand the distinction between group and class, with the most probable difference being that class is one species of group.[32] We are told little beyond this and are led to assume that the emphasis is more on group than on class. The confusion becomes most apparent when Dahrendorf attempts to apply these concepts in an empirical study of changing class structure.[33] This confusion of group and class is carried even further in the treatment of *conflict* group and class. Both conflict groups and classes are defined in terms of authority relations, and this leads to the inevitable conclusion that wherever there are authority patterns there are also conflict groups *and* classes.

In an important point related to the emphasis placed on certain associations, Dahrendorf rests his definition of class solely upon authority relations. As we have indicated above, this is an important contribution. The Dahrendorf conceptualization, however, remains rather limited and specialized in nature. For Dahrendorf, authority is "legitimate power" which is ultimately and primarily related to "imperatively coordinated associations." Also, authority is said to concern "social positions or roles," whereas power "is essentially tied to the personality of individuals." While power "is merely a factual relation, authority is a legitimate relation."[34] This conceptualization does not consider superordinate-subordinate relations that exist outside associations (much less "imperatively coordinated" associations). It also contributes little to the analysis of societies where "factual" relations are more significant than "legitimate" relations and where personalities are at least as important as formalized positions. As such, this formulation is only of indirect relevance to those societies where legitimacy is often yet to be established and where personalism reigns supreme within the class structure.

Dahrendorf himself does not always seem certain that he wants to limit his conceptualization to this degree. He writes, for example, that "the fundamental inequality of social structure, and the lasting determi-

---

[30]Dahrendorf, *Class and Class Conflict,* p. 238.

[31]Ibid., p. 181.

[32]For Dahrendorf's position on classes as species of groups, see ibid., pp. 26, 152, 171, 213, 306.

[33]See Dahrendorf, "Recent Changes in the Class Structure of European Societies," *Daedalus* 93 (Winter 1964): 225–70. A sample of the conceptual chaos exhibited in this article is seen when the author remarks that he is interested in examining the relations of the four "groups" that make up the "class" structure and when he terms these groups [classes?] "the ruling groups," "the service class," "the ruled or subjected groups," and "the intellectuals."

[34]Dahrendorf, *Class and Class Conflict* pp. 166–67.

nant of social conflict, is the inequality of *power and authority* which inevitably accompanies social organization."[35] Here and in scattered other places in the study, the author links power and authority—a somewhat surprising fact considering the pains that were previously taken to differentiate the two. In this formulation, the *key* relations defining class obviously involve authority and not power.

Class and Power

The general view concerning the difference between power and authority is that authority is somehow a "legitimate," "formal," "legal," "rightful," or "approved" power.[36] It is "the institutional counterpart of power."[37] Scholars who have stressed authority patterns rather than power patterns have tended to be specialists in Western, industrial society and politics. In such societies, the role of formal institutions and associations looms especially large, and questions of boundary maintenance, legality, functional specificity, and authoritative allocations are of immediate relevance. As we have seen in the group chapter, however, in many areas of the world social and political systems are built upon informal and dissentious relations. With some of these distinctions in mind, not surprisingly the class-authority linkage has been recently loosened and replaced by a broader concept.

In 1959, Leonard Reissman made an explicit plea to define class in terms of power when he attempted to view Max Weber's work in this way: "Interestingly enough, this emphasis upon power, upon which the meaning of Weber's theory of stratification depended, has been almost totally overlooked by many sociologists. Few theories and fewer research designs have done anything with Weber's system, nor has either picked up the cue of power as the central focus for the study of class."[38] Although American sociology has tended to stress prestige and economics in defining class, a closer examination reveals that the power dimension was always recognized, if de-emphasized.[39] Such prominent scholars as S. N. Eisenstadt, Seymour Martin Lipset, Hans L. Zetterberg,

---

[35]Ibid., p. 64. Italics added.

[36]See, for example, Carl J. Friedrich, ed., *Authority* (Cambridge: Harvard University Press, 1958).

[37]Talcott Parsons, "On the Concept of Political Power," in Bendix and Lipset, eds., *Class, Status, and Power,* p. 249.

[38]Leonard Reissman, *Class in American Society* (Glencoe, Ill.: Free Press, 1959), p. 58.

[39]After presenting all three dimensions, both Milton M. Gordon and Kurt Mayer underplay and ignore the power dimension. See Gordon, *Social Class in American Sociology;* and Mayer, "The Theory of Social Classes," in *Transactions of the Second World Congress of Sociology,* Vol. II, (London: International Sociological Association, 1954), 321–35.

Gerhard Lenski, Manfred Halpern, and Richard N. Adams have stressed stratification in terms of power.[40]

Class conceived in terms of power is perhaps better equipped to account for the complexities and subtleties that occur in many stratification systems. Complicated bargaining techniques and exchange transactions that promote and obstruct vertical mobility patterns are cases in point. The power emphasis also brings the social and political dimensions of stratification into the analysis alongside the economic and psychological considerations. These kinds of factors give the class approach greater analytic flexibility, and also increase its relevance to the study of Afro-Asian and Latin American political systems.

The power focus strikes at the veil of ethnocentricity that surrounds traditional class analysis, thereby broadening the contexts of comparability and the empirical base for theorizing. It also introduces, however, a number of new conceptual problems. The most serious of these is the fact that the power concept has a widely known history of definitional haze and controversy. "Power" has over the years stubbornly resisted efforts to infuse it with methodological measurement and theoretical precision.[41] It remains, however, the latest link in the intellectual chain designed to refine and strengthen the class approach to the study of politics.

Groups, Elites, and Classes

The group, elite, and class approaches are closely intertwined and interrelated. In each case, the basic unit of analysis is an aggregate of individuals possessing a particularly defined position in the political process. This unit and the position it occupies are considered to be the crucial variables in explaining the operation of the political system. Few scholars, however, have attempted to distinguish between and among these basic concepts. As a result, the approaches themselves are constantly confused with one another, and, in the work of some practitioners, they

---

[40]See S. N. Eisenstadt, "Changes in Patterns of Stratification Attendant on Attainment of Political Independence," *Transactions of the Third World Congress of Sociology* (London: International Sociological Association, 1956), pp. 32–41; Seymour Lipset and Hans Zetterberg, "A Theory of Social Mobility," in Bendix and Lipset, eds., *Class, Status, and Power,* pp. 561–73; Lenski, *Power and Privilege;* Halpern, *Politics of Social Change;* and Richard Adams, *The Second Sowing: Power and Secondary Development in Latin America* (San Francisco: Chandler, 1967).

[41]For a fine collection of leading theoretical analyses of the power concept, see Roderick Bell, David V. Edwards, and R. Harrison Wagner, eds., *Political Power: A Reader in Theory and Research* (New York: Free Press, 1969).

disintegrate into incomprehensible morasses of inconsistent terminology.

Those scholars who have attempted to distinguish and sort out these approaches have helped build some conceptual clarity and consistency into the three approaches. This not only has strengthened the respective conceptual frameworks, but also has paved the way for the integration of the approaches. An eclectic utilization of all three approaches has become a promising method of confronting social problems and political issues. Any successful integration of approaches, however, presupposes a careful and detailed dissection and differentiation of each of the elements involved. In other words, a sound *synthesis* of approaches rests upon a prior *analysis* of the approaches in question.

Class and Group

Class analysis is more easily distinguished from the group approach than from elite study. While a group is an aggregation of individuals who interact in pursuance of a common goal or shared interest, a class is a much more narrowly focused concept. The latter represents a collection of individuals who share relatively equally in one of the fundamental or central distributive values, i.e., power, wealth, or prestige. Although the unit class is marked by relative *equality* within its own membership, its relations with other similar units (classes) are characterized by relative *inequality.* Classes are only defined in terms of other classes and the distinguishing yardstick always involves power, wealth, prestige, or some combination thereof. If it can be demonstrated, however, that a class is a unit whose members interact and pursue a common goal, then class can be considered one type of group.

The class approach is preeminently stratification analysis. Interclass relations are dominated by division and conflict which in turn promote a changing class structure, and ultimately a changing political system. In contrast, stratification is not a critical variable in group analysis, as the latter envisions a universe of aggregates that compete and cooperate along many lines and in every possible direction. In the class approach, conflict, coercion, dissent, imbalance, and change are the dominant characteristics. In the group approach, cooperation, collaboration, consensus, balance, and continuity tend to dominate.

A class is a collectivity that is always of basic and direct import to social and political analysis. It is determined by such ingredients as power, wealth, and prestige, and is used primarily to account for such basic issues as conflict and change. An individual may belong to many groups, but he holds membership in only one class. Class analysis, therefore, is quite distinct from group analysis. The differences derive essentially from the specialized characteristics that inhere in the conceptualization of class.

Class and Elite

It is considerably more difficult to separate rigorously the class and elite approaches[42] than it is to distinguish between class and group analyses. The major reason, of course, is that the class and elite approaches overlap one another to a greater degree. The state of intellectual disorder that reigns in this regard is attested to by the manner in which the central concepts of both approaches are interchanged and confused. The literature is filled with the indiscriminate usage of concepts such as ruling classes and governing elites, upper classes and ruling elites, and elite classes and intraclass elites. The class and elite approaches have seldom been systematically and analytically distinguished from one another.[43]

Class analysis and the elite approach share a number of significant characteristics. Both approaches emphasize the fundamental reality of stratification. Stratification is a structured inequality that divides those who have most from those who have least of a particular value. In both forms of analysis, this is the orienting premise. The second similarity between the two approaches concerns the particular values on the basis of which the stratification system is formed. Power, authority, wealth, and prestige are the central stratifying determinants in both approaches. If a more specific distinction is involved here, it would be that the power variable tends to be emphasized in elite analysis, while wealth and prestige have been most often stressed in stratification by class.[44] Finally, both approaches focus most sharply upon the phenomena of conflict. Conflict follows directly from division and inequality and promotes the dynamic of change.

The class and elite approaches to the study of politics are divided by one fundamental difference. This distinction is in turn responsible for a number of the sharply different conclusions that develop from these two approaches. Elite study is based upon only one stratifying seam, and the analysis focuses essentially upon only one side of that seam.

---

[42]For preliminary distinctions between the elite and class approaches, see chapter five in this volume.

[43]A major exception is the work of T. B. Bottomore. See his *Elites and Society,* pp. 18–41.

[44]In discussing the variety of class analysis applied to American political processes, Celia S. Heller writes that "The future historian of knowledge may be puzzled that the stratification studies of the most industrial country of our time concentrated so heavily on status to the neglect of power." See Celia S. Heller, *Structured Social Inequality: A Reader in Comparative Social Stratification* (London: Macmillan & Co., Collier-Macmillan, 1969), p. 115.

Intrinsic to the elite approach is the fact that analysis is tilted in one direction, i.e., towards the uppermost reaches or peak of the particular stratified unit.[45] The core of theoretical attention is limited to those who have the most, while those who have less must by the very nature of the approach remain a residual category.

The class approach, in contrast, exhibits no intellectual preoccupation with any particular unit or segment of the stratified structure. In class study, analysis usually focuses on more than one line of stratification. Class analysis is society-wide analysis, and the lowest echelons are as much the subject of study as are the highest. The "masses," in the vocabulary of elite scholarship, are broken up and analyzed directly as "classes" in this approach.

Besides being broader in scope, the class approach is also concerned with a level of analysis that is in some ways more fundamental than the level of elite investigation. T. B. Bottomore writes, for example, that "an entirely misleading view of political life is created if we concentrate our attention upon the competition between elites, and fail to examine the conflicts between classes and the ways in which elites are connected with the various social classes."[46] Elites are rooted and grounded in classes. Studies of the origins of elite membership must rely, for example, upon a discussion and recognition of classes.

Among the important consequences that flow from the distinctions dividing class and elite analyses are two of special relevance. The first consequence derives from the different manner of conceiving the relations between the rulers and the ruled. For elite scholars, the rulers are portrayed as a well-organized minority who act in a coherent fashion within the political system. The ruled, on the other hand, are residually viewed as an unorganized globular mass. The latter rests at the periphery of politics where it is monotonously manipulated and mauled by the elite. Class analysts contrast rulers with the ruled and portray the latter as aggregates of individuals who, if not organized, certainly possess the potential to organize. In this sense, the ruled as well as the rulers play an active and important role in politics. Celia S. Heller perceptively points out that these two differing perspectives "are also the bases of contrasting views of the future."[47] Elite scholars often tend to be pessimistic about change because the non-elite force that might occasion it "is a mass of politically uninterested beings, short-sighted concerning events outside their immediate experiences."[48] Class scholarship, however, often reflects an optimistic view of the future as the lower classes

---

[45]Ralf Dahrendorf, therefore, refers to the elite approach as a "one-class model." See Dahrendorf, *Class and Class Conflict,* p. 199.

[46]Bottomore, *Elites and Society,* p. 118.

[47]Heller, *Structural Social Inequality,* p. 113.

[48]Ibid.

are viewed as forces that contain a very real potential to demand and propel change.

Directly related to this first general point is the differing perspective that both approaches develop towards the issue of change. Partially due to the fact that elite study tends to ignore any in-depth investigation of the non-elite, the latter becomes by default a passive conglomeration that scarcely figures in the dynamics of politics. Processes of development and modernization are discussed, therefore, exclusively from the vantage point of those who rule. The class approach, on the other hand, is able to confront the issue of change from below as well as from above. Revolution that originates and bubbles up from below is one of the issues most often discussed by class analysts. The capacity to understand and explain the fundamental problem of change within the perspective of each approach is seriously affected by these kinds of distinctions. As we will see in the final section of this chapter, the elite and class approaches differ quite substantially in terms of their ability to confront effectively the issue of modernization.

The group, elite, and class approaches constitute one of the most easily combined series of approaches available for the study of comparative politics. The integration of these three analytic orientations is a relatively uncomplicated intellectual procedure as the approaches tend to dovetail with one another. This particular combination of approaches has been implicitly applied in a number of recent major contributions analyzing broad comparative political processes.[49] Besides this, increasing studies of somewhat narrower empirical focus also rely heavily upon integrated group, elite, and class analysis.[50] Too few investigations, however, have explicitly, systematically, and consistently defined and refined the conceptual and theoretical apparatus involved.

Class Analysis Evaluated

The class approach carries the following five strengths for the analysis of comparative political processes: (1) the class concept is preeminently an analytic and relational concept; (2) class study operates at a fundamental level of analysis; (3) the approach is peculiarly suited to account for conflictual and competitive relations; (4) class analysis has powerful

---

[49]See, for example, Barrington Moore, Jr., *Social Origins;* Samuel P. Huntington, *Political Order in Changing Societies;* and S. N. Eisenstadt, *The Political Systems of Empires: The Rise and Fall of the Historical Bureaucratic Societies* (New York: Free Press, 1963).

[50]Examples include Richard L. Sklar, *Nigerian Political Parties: Power in an Emergent African Nation* (Princeton: Princeton University Press, 1963); Carlos A. Astiz, *Pressure Groups and Power Elites in Peruvian Politics* (Ithaca, N.Y., and London: Cornell University Press, 1969); James F. Petras, *Politics and Social Forces in Chilean Development* (Berkeley: University of California Press, 1969); and James A. Bill, *The Politics of Iran.*

comparative value; and (5) the class approach is shaped specifically to address the revolutionary and transforming dimensions of change.

Class, which is the core concept in this approach, is a relational term, essentially analytic rather than descriptive. Class analysts attempt to raise "why" questions, and the emphasis of the approach is upon linkages and relations. A class by itself is devoid of meaning but must always be defined in relation to another class. Ralf Dahrendorf summarizes this point when he contrasts class as an analytic concept and stratum as a descriptive concept. According to Dahrendorf, "*class* is always a category for the purposes of the analysis of the dynamics of social conflict and its structural roots, and as such it has to be separated strictly from *stratum* as a category for purposes of describing hierarchical systems at a given point of time."[51]

Class study treats a level of analysis that is in many ways most basic. In our terms, the class is the most important inclusive unit within the social structure of a society. All individuals are initially born into a particular class. This is quite different from the situation of interest groups, for example, where membership is determined voluntarily. It is important in this context that an individual can belong simultaneously to any number of groups, but he can belong to only one class. Finally, since classes compose much of the backbone of the social structure, they serve as linchpins for the analysis of the related social, political, and economic systems.

The class approach shares with the elite approach a focus upon conflict. It is in this respect peculiarly suited to the analysis of social and political patterns that lead to and result from competition and tension. Class analysis is intellectually slanted in the direction of addressing problems of inequality, dissent, and disequilibrium. Of all the approaches to political study, this orientation is best suited to account for conflict, coercion, and violence. As such, it is generally contrasted with functional and systems analyses which are heavily criticized for their stability bias. Even the elite approach provides a somewhat modified view of conflict relations by its emphasis upon the methodology of balance and accommodation engaged in by the political leadership. Thus, in a world where phenomena such as conflict, inequality, and violence are increasingly considered to be central and typical in the political process, the class perspective continues to gain acceptance.[52]

---

[51]Dahrendorf, *Class and Class Conflict.* p. 76.

[52]This trend is accompanied by a recent surge of dialectical analyses. See, for example, Manfred Halpern, *The Dialectics of Transformation in Politics, Personality, and History* (Princeton University Press, forthcoming); and Kenneth E. Boulding, *A Primer on Social Dynamics* (New York: The Free Press, 1970).

Since one of the underlying assumptions of class analysis is that all societies are divided into classes, the approach has the broadest possible applicability. Cross-societal comparative study is consistent with this approach and, indeed, is even encouraged by the approach. The deep concern with such issues as conflict and violence occurring dramatically in a wide variety of contexts throughout the world is a major reason for comparative efforts. Although certain practitioners of class analysis do not always proceed comparatively, this is not because of any weakness inherent to the approach. Usually, it is due to the scholar's proclivity to begin study through a detailed and in-depth analysis of one context. This permits him to refine his conceptual and theoretical apparatus and at the same time to develop a dynamic investigation of the political system under scrutiny. From here, he may choose to move into more truly comparative terrain. Most class approaches are still confined to the first stage of this process.

Perhaps the most crucial advantage of the class approach is its capacity to confront revolutionary change and the transforming dimensions of the process of modernization. In terms of its systematic development, the class approach has historically been linked to the phenomenon of revolutionary change. This, of course, is due primarily to the theoretical investigations of Karl Marx. Class analysis is intrinsically designed to explain societal transformation. The issues of conflict and violence are key characteristics in class interaction and often lead to the destruction of the ongoing class structure. Because of the linkage between the class structure and the political system, revolution in the one arena means revolution in the other context as well. Through the dialectical manner in which classes are linked to one another, the class approach contains a dynamic perspective. This dynamism can help account for radical change for a number of reasons. These reasons are what distinguish the elite and class approaches in their applicability to developmental analysis.

Sociopolitical transformation usually bubbles up from below. Many times it is occasioned by the gaps and divisions that divide collectivities one from the other. Class divisions which occur about such fundamental issues as power, wealth, and prestige are particularly vital and sensitive areas of contention. The patterns of change that develop out of pressures and eruptions from below can be discussed within the context of class analysis. They cannot be logically handled through the analytic lens of the elite scholar.

The class approach also has the capacity to address the process of "revolution from above." In this situation, the ruling class institutes peaceful programs of social and political transformation and thereby avoids much of the destructive violence that potentially exists within the class dialectic. Unlike the elite approach, which can only bare the intentions of the leadership concerning modernization, class analysis can also come to grips with the ideas and capabilities of the society at large in this regard. Many empirical class studies, therefore, focus their attention upon the relations between political change and the workers, peasants, or professional middle class.

Class conflict does not necessarily imply revolutionary change. Whether or not it does is a significant issue demanding empirical investigation. Under what circumstances differing levels and intensities of change occur out of class interaction is itself a question of fundamental importance. This sensitivity within the class approach to the entire problem of change is part of an even broader advantage of the approach. Class analysis has, by and large, been developed to address many of the most fundamental issues that confront political man. These include the issues of continuity and change, as well as the conflict and competition that accompany the process of allocating such values as power, wealth, and prestige.

The first difficulty that marks the class approach is one common to many approaches. Conceptual confusion reigns. The class concept itself is particularly susceptible to this form of theoretical debilitation, and has a wide range of confused and confusing facets. There are the subjective as opposed to the objective definitions, the descriptive versus the analytic interpretations, the normative as opposed to the empirical definitions, and the prestige versus the economic interpretations. The class concept is sometimes interchanged with and sometimes differentiated from such concepts as caste, estate, stratum, sector, group, and elite. Celia Heller writes that the lack of any standardized vocabulary is a malady especially pronounced in stratification studies. And she concludes in this regard that "there is no solution in sight for this Tower of Babel."[53] Conceptual difficulty is compounded in class study because of the overwhelming impact of one formulation, i.e., the Marxist approach. Recent class scholarship, no matter how successful it may have been in improving upon Marxian class analysis, must still contend with the fact that many scholars and observers continue to equate the class approach with the Marxian approach. Besides the problems that this carries for the development of refined conceptual frameworks, it also has strong ideological implications.

Class analysis remains laden with ideological baggage. As such, it gives off normative and emotional signals that cause people to embrace it or condemn it on grounds other than serious intellectual judgment. The class approach continues to be closely associated with Marxism,

---

[53]Heller, *Structured Social Inequality,* p. 487.

communism, and socialism, despite the fact that numerous practitioners of the approach have explicitly differentiated their variation of the approach from the Marxian conception. Communicating the approach is extremely difficult since it requires dispelling strong preconceptions. As the approach becomes more prevalent, this difficulty will become less serious. The towering figure of Marx, however, continues to cast a shadow over class study.

One of the most serious problems of class analysis involves the question of researchability. Research techniques and methodology remain relatively primitive with regard to the class approach for three major reasons. (1) The state of chaos that marks the conceptual framework discourages cooperative and comparative efforts to tighten technique. If little or no agreement exists on what the significant variables are, then there is little basis for precision in techniques. (2) The relations usually considered to be critical to the approach include such conceptually controversial terms as power, authority, and prestige. Relatively little progress has been made, in any systematic or sophisticated sense, with regard to the operationalization and measurement of such concepts. (3) Because of its broad-ranging character, class analysis demands an incredible amount of information and data. It is usually only feasible, therefore, for the researcher to collect data pertaining mainly to one class or to a particular segment thereof. Society-wide study requires society-wide data.

Class scholars usually rely heavily upon written sources and historical study. When carrying out field research, they tend to proceed via structured and unstructured interviewing, participant observation, and, occasionally, questionnaires. Ironically, precisely those class analysts who have been most sophisticated in their techniques have been those who have produced the more sterile, descriptive studies. The community sociologists are the major case in point. Yet, class scholarship must reflect more rigor and precision. Otherwise, it will be at best an approach that addresses interesting questions in a manner almost completely dependent upon the intuitive talents of the researcher involved. At worst, it will be a hodgepodge of confusing and contradictory concepts that trail away into a descriptive jungle in which stratification is documented by assertion.

CHAPTER VII

Functionalism and Systems Analysis

No two approaches have been more influential in contemporary comparative politics than functionalism and systems analysis, and surely no others have been more controversial. These approaches were systematically developed in political science during the 1950s and 1960s, when the discipline was shaken by the behavioral movement. Much of the terminology and conceptual equipment that infused these approaches was new and different to the analysis of comparative politics.

The Structural-Functional Approach

The use of jargon in political science, or in the social sciences generally, has been a source of deep frustration to those—both inside and outside the discipline—who seek to follow the literature. Jargon arises in response to the need for precision in any field of knowledge. It provides, for the initiated, shorthand notations for whole concepts or basic elements of a scientific paradigm. If it is esoteric in excluding the layman, it nevertheless seeks to provide precision in meaning for those within the discipline. The purpose of jargon is more effective and efficient communication. The development of jargon within a discipline may be a measure of its growth as a science. The use of jargon, however, necessarily reduces the scope of communication to those familiar with its specialized concepts and to those who share a particular paradigm.

As has been frequently noted, political science is pre-paradigmatic or is at least confronted with a number of contending paradigms. In political science, jargon, while seeking precision, frequently only compounds confusion. In quest of rigor, but lacking a scientific paradigm, social scientists do not always use jargon in the same way, and, worse, some social scientists are not even consistent in their own usage at different times. The issue of jargon is especially germane to the conceptual frameworks constructed about structural-functional and systems analysis.

Perspective and Conceptual Framework

From its beginnings in the late nineteenth century, the functional approach in the social sciences has been caught up in terminological confusion. "Too often," Robert Merton has written, "a single term has been used to symbolize different concepts, just as the same concept has been symbolized by different terms. Clarity of analysis and adequacy of communication are both victims of this frivolous use of words."[1]

The word *function* is used with a variety of meanings: occasion, use, aim, consequence, activity, purpose, effect, motive, and so on. Its most precise usage is in mathematics, "where it refers to a variable considered in relation to one or more other variables in terms of which it may be expressed or on the value of which its own value depends."[2] In this sense, for example, the rapidly expanding population of the developing areas is primarily a *function* of declining death rates. From this notion, the social sciences use the phrases "functional interdependence" and "functional relations."

The origins of functionalism in the social sciences are linked most directly to organicism and, specifically, to homeostatic physiology.[3] The term *function,* in this usage, is adapted from the biological sciences, where it refers to the "vital or organic processes considered in the respects in which they contribute to the maintenance of the organism."[4]

The premise of functional (or structural-functional) analysis "is nothing less than to provide a consistent and integrated theory from which can be derived explanatory hypotheses relevant to all aspects" of a given social system. The approach is characterized by certain common features: "first, an emphasis on the whole system as the unit of analysis; second, postulation of particular functions as requisite to the mainte-

---

[1]Robert K. Merton, *Social Theory and Social Structure,* rev. ed. (New York: Free Press, 1957), p. 20. Italics omitted.

[2]Ibid., p. 21.

[3]A. James Gregor, "Political Science and the Uses of Functional Analysis," *American Political Science Review* 52 (June 1968): 427.

[4]Quoted in Merton, *Social Theory and Social Structure,* p. 21.

nance of the whole system; third, concern to demonstrate the functional interdependence of diverse structures within the whole system."[5] The principal objective of functional analysis is to determine the contribution which a social item (a structure or process) makes to the persistence of the system in which it occurs, that is, the role it plays in maintaining the system within specified limits.

The logic of functional analysis, following Merton, involves the following sequence of steps:

> First of all, certain functional requirements of the organism [or the social system] are established, requirements which must be satisfied if the organism is to survive, or to operate with some degree of effectiveness. Second, there is a concrete and detailed description of the arrangements (structures and processes) through which these requirements are typically met in 'normal' cases. Third, if some of the typical mechanisms for meeting these requirements are destroyed, or are found to be functioning inadequately, the observer is sensitized to the need for detecting compensating mechanisms (if any) which fulfill the necessary function. Fourth, and implicit in all that precedes, there is a detailed account of the structure *for which* the functional requirements hold, as well as a detailed account of the arrangements *through which* the function is fulfilled.[6]

Marion Levy states the problem of functional analysis in ordinary language: What must be done if a society is to persist? How must what must be done be done?[7]

While functionalism has been one of the dominant modes of analysis in the social sciences, it has suffered continuous attack on charges that it is "illogical, value-laden, and incapable of explaining anything."[8] Functionalism has been criticized as verbally obscure; methodologically ambiguous; teleological; conservative and ethnocentric; incapable of dealing adequately with change; empirically untestable; and lacking in both explanatory and predictive power.

---

[5]William Flanigan and Edwin Fogelman, "Functional Analysis," in James C. Charlesworth, ed., *Contemporary Political Analysis* (New York: Free Press, 1967), p. 76.

[6]Merton, *Social Theory and Social Structure,* p. 49.

[7]Marion J. Levy, Jr., "Some Aspects of 'Structural-Functional' Analysis and Political Science," in Roland Young, ed., *Approaches to the Study of Politics* (Evanston: Northwestern University Press, 1958), p. 53. Also see Levy, "Functional Analysis," in *The International Encyclopedia of the Social Sciences* (New York: Macmillan and Free Press, 1968), Vol. 6, pp. 21–29. The model is developed in Levy, *The Structure of Society* (Princeton: Princeton University Press, 1952), and in *Modernization and the Structure of Societies* (Princeton: Princeton University Press, 1966).

[8]Francesca M. Cancian, "Varieties of Functional Analysis," in *The International Encyclopedia of the Social Sciences,* Vol. 6, p. 29.

Historically, writes Carl Hempel, "functional analysis is a modification of teleological explanation, i.e., of explanation not by reference to causes which 'bring about' the event in question, but by reference to ends which determine its course."[9] The final cause is presumed to determine the behavior of the system and to "explain" a given social item. Here function closely approximates purpose. This teleological perspective forms "the image of deliberate purposive behavior or of systems working in accordance with a preconceived design." There is no empirical criterion, however, for the attribution of purpose, and to do so "tends to encourage the illusion that a profound type of understanding is achieved."[10]

The roots of functional analysis are found in the work of Emile Durkheim, but the British anthropologist Radcliffe-Brown made its formulation as an approach explicit. The concept of social function is based, in his words, "on an analogy between social life and organic life."[11] It is, as Radcliffe-Brown well knew, a venerable analogy. It is also an analogy which Chalmers Johnson has termed "uncritical."[12]

For Radcliffe-Brown, individual human beings are "the essential units" of analysis and are connected by networks of social relations into an integrated whole. "The function of any recurrent activity . . . is the part it plays in the social life as a whole and therefore the contribution it makes to the maintenance of the structural continuity."[13] Malinowski, with his own variety of functionalism, shared this theoretical perspective. He sought "the explanation of anthropological facts at all levels of development by their function, by the part which they play within the integral system of culture, by the manner in which they are related to each other within the system. . . ."[14]

---

[9]Carl G. Hempel, "The Logic of Functional Analysis," in Llewellyn Gross, ed., *Symposium on Sociological Theory* (Evanston: Row, Peterson, 1959), p. 277.

[10]Ibid., p. 300.

[11]A. R. Radcliffe-Brown, *Structure and Function in Primitive Society* (London: Cohen and West, 1952), p. 178.

[12]Chalmers Johnson, *Revolutionary Change* (Boston: Little, Brown, 1966), p. 49. See also Robert A. Nisbet, "Reflections on a Metaphor," in *Social Change and History* (New York: Oxford University Press, 1969), pp. 240–304. There he writes, "Generalization is beyond question what we seek from the empirical and concrete. But is is generalization *from* the empirical, the concrete, and the historical; not generalization achieved through their dismissal; not generalization drawn from metaphor and analogy." (pp. 303–4.)

[13]A. R. Radcliffe-Brown, "On the Concept of Function in Social Science," *American Anthropologist* 37 (1935): 395–96, quoted in Merton, *Social Theory and Social Structure,* p. 22.

[14]Bronislaw Malinowski, "Anthropology," *Encyclopedia Britannica,* First Supplementary Volume (London and New York: 1926), pp. 132–3, quoted in Merton, *Social Theory and Social Structure,* p. 22. For a fine discussion of the role that leading anthropologists have played in the development of the functional approach, see Maurice Mandelbaum, "Functionalism in Social Anthropology," in Sidney Morgenbesser et al., eds., *Philosophy, Science, and Method* (New York: St. Martin's Press, 1969), pp. 306–32.

The functional analysis of Radcliffe-Brown, Malinowski, and other early anthropologists has been described as "a dead horse" and of an extreme form which no longer fairly characterizes contemporary functionalism.[15] Robert Merton, in his classic study of functional analysis, identifies three postulates associated with classical functionalism:

> first, that standardized social activities or cultural items are functional for the *entire* social or cultural system; second, that *all* such social and cultural items fulfill sociological functions; and third, that these are consequently indispensable.[16]

Merton argues, however, that these postulates are in fact unnecessary to the functional orientation. Nevertheless, even the most sophisticated functionalists remain vulnerable to the problems arising from these three interconnected postulates.

The first postulate, that of the functional unity of society, is explicit in the work of Radcliffe-Brown: "The function of a particular social usage is the contribution it makes to the total social life as the functioning of the total social system." This implies, he says, the "functional unity" of the social system. Functional unity is defined as "a condition in which all parts of the social system work together with a sufficient degree of harmony or internal consistency, *i.e.,* without producing persistent conflicts which can neither be resolved nor regulated."[17]

In identifying "system-relevant" functions, few analysts specify the reciprocal relations among these functions. Despite the assumption that the functions are necessarily interrelated, the linkage is rarely articulated. The degree of integration is an empirical variable and is subject to verification. All societies are not equally well-integrated. Changes may occur in the degree of integration within a society over time as well as in the variation among different societies. Functions themselves may also vary in relative significance for system maintenance both over time and in different systems.[18] Beyond this, the postu-

---

[15]Pierre L. Van den Berghe, "Dialectic and Functionalism: Toward a Theoretical Synthesis," *American Sociological Review* 28 (October 1963): 695. Van den Berghe, in attempting a theoretical synthesis between functionalism and dialectics, argues for the postulate of dynamic equilibrium as "the real cornerstone" of the functional approach. He presents "an expanded model of equilibrium" so as to allow for "the possibility of maladjustive change, of vicious circles of malintegration, and of abrupt 'social mutations' through revolution." (pp. 697–98.)

[16]Merton, *Social Theory and Social Structure,* p. 25.

[17]Radcliffe-Brown, "On the Concept of Function," p. 397, quoted in Merton, *Social Theory and Social Structure,* pp. 25–26.

[18]Robert T. Golembiewski, William A. Welsh, and William J. Crotty, *A Methodological Primer for Political Scientists* (Chicago: Rand McNally, 1969), p. 253.

late of functional unity may divert the analyst's attention from the possible disparate consequences of a particular social item for diverse groups within the society or for individuals within these groups.[19] In order to deal with the multiple consequences any given item may have, Merton distinguishes between *functions* and *dysfunctions.* Functions, for Merton, are those "observed consequences which make for the adaptation or adjustment of a given system." Dysfunctions are those which lessen adaptation or adjustment.[20]

At any given instant, an item may have both functional and dysfunctional consequences. It is always necessary to distinguish the object: functional or dysfunctional in relation to what? What may be functional for the society as a whole may be dysfunctional for subsystems within the society. The unity of a total society cannot be taken as an assumption. Functional analysis requires the specification of the units for which a given social item is functional, and the analysis must allow for the possibility of diverse consequences. A given social item may be either functional or dysfunctional, or may be functional at one level and dysfunctional at another.[21]

The second postulate, universal functionalism, holds that all standardized social or cultural forms have positive functions.[22] Malinowski states this in its most extreme form: "The functional view of culture insists . . . upon the principle that in every type of civilization, every custom, material object, idea and belief fulfills some vital function.[23] The basic notion here is that whatever *is* is useful and serves some vital purpose in the maintenance and integration of the social system—in short, that it is *functional.*

A particular item, however, may be either functional or dysfunctional, or, at the same time, have both functional and dysfunctional consequences. As the same item may have multiple functions, all may not be intended, or, for that matter, even known. Merton distinguishes between manifest and latent functions. Manifest functions are those intended and recognized by participants within the system. Latent func-

---

[19]Merton, *Social Theory and Social Structure,* pp. 26–28.

[20]Ibid., p. 51. Levy reserves the term *eufunction* for the more specific meaning of system maintenance. He defines function neutrally as "a condition, or states of affairs resultant from the operation . . . of a structure through time." "Some Aspects . . .," p. xv. Most social scientists have preferred, however, to use the term *function* as a system relevant effect of structure. See Robert T. Holt, "A Proposed Structural-Functional Framework," in Charlesworth, *Contemporary Political Analysis,* p. 88.

[21]Merton, *Social Theory and Social Structure,* p. 30.

[22]Ibid.

[23]Malinowski, "Anthropology," quoted in Merton, *Social Theory and Social Structure,* p. 30.

tions are those which are neither intended nor recognized.[24] The concept of latent function sensitizes the analyst to the varied and disparate consequences of a function and directs his attention toward a range of consequences beyond the avowed "purpose" of a given function.[25] Marion Levy further distinguishes between those functions which may be unintended but recognized and those intended but unrecognized. "These concepts focus attention on the level of explicitness and sensitivity of the members of a given system to the structures in terms of which they operate."[26]

The third postulate, indispensability, follows directly from the second, holding that whatever *is* is not merely functional, but also necessary. Thus, Malinowski says that each cultural item, in fulfilling some vital function, "represents an indispensable part within a working whole."[27]

A function is value-neutral. An item may be functional to the maintenance of a system, but is not necessarily, in normative terms, good or preferred. Preference is the product of a socially conditioned perspective. What is functional to a repressive political system will surely not be valued by the analyst merely because it is functional. The *is,* however, has all too often been confused with the *ought.* The emphasis on system maintenance and adaptation has carried a conservative bias, a justification and rationalization of the status quo. This reflects, in part, the conservative origins of sociology as a discipline, but the conservatism of functionalism lies less in the nature of the approach itself than in its practitioners who may endow the analytical model with normative value. Alexis de Tocqueville warned against the confusion of the familiar with the necessary: "what we call necessary institutions are often no more than institutions to which we have grown accustomed."[28]

The functional model tends to stress continuity over change; at a certain level, stability is assumed for analytic purposes.[29] A model of society in terms of integration and order may provide the criterion, in the form of an ideal type, by which conflict and change may be exam-

---

[24]Merton, *Social Theory and Social Structure,* p. 51.

[25]Ibid., p. 68. See Merton's classic analysis of the latent functions of the political machine, pp. 78–82.

[26]Levy, "Functional Analysis," p. 25.

[27]Malinowski, "Anthropology," quoted in Merton, *Social Theory and Social Structure,* p. 32.

[28]Cited in Merton, *Social Theory and Social Structure,* p. 37. Merton points to the *radical* potential of functional analysis and states that "the fact that functionalism can be seen by some as inherently conservative and by others as inherently radical suggests that it may be *inherently* neither one nor the other." (pp. 38–39.)

[29]Oran Young, *Systems of Political Science* (Englewood Cliffs, N.J.: Prentice-Hall, 1968), p. 36.

ined.[30] The analysis of conflict and change as *deviations* from the "norm" leads in practice, however, to the frequent assumption that integration and order are in fact *normal* and that whatever contributes to the maintenance of a given system is not only functional, but *good.*

Functional Indispensability

Kenneth Sherrill[31] has explored some of the problems of functional indispensability in his analysis of Almond and Verba's *The Civic Culture.* Almond and Verba posit the existence of an ideal set of orientations toward politics, or a political culture, which they term a "civic culture." This culture is "mixed" in that it is characterized by a particular combination of three citizenship orientations: the participant, the subject, and the parochial. Each citizen is also characterized individually by such a mixture.[32] Almond and Verba select the United States and Great Britain as "representing relatively successful experiments in democratic government. An analysis of these two cases will tell us," they say, "what kinds of attitudes are associated with stably functioning democratic systems, the quantitative incidence of these attitudes, and their distribution among different groups in the population."[33]

Not surprisingly, four hundred pages after deciding to use the United States and Great Britain as their standards, Almond and Verba find that these two nations most closely approximate what they have called the "civic culture."[34] This, or course, is considered the most desirable mixture of people and orientations. From the assumption that the two nations are successful stable democracies characterized by a cultural "mix" at a particular time (the survey was conducted in 1959–1960), functional value is then given to the peculiar character of the mix. If the United States and Britain have a certain proportion of people with subject and parochial orientations, that is, with low levels of political knowledge, efficacy, and participation, then the maintenance of such patterns becomes "necessary" for the stability and persistence of these

---

[30]Harold Kaplan, "The Parsonian Image of Social Structure and Its Relevance for Political Science," *Journal of Politics* 30 (November 1968): 893–95.

[31]Kenneth S. Sherrill, "Political Modernization as an Attitudinal Syndrome," paper presented at the annual meeting of the American Political Science Association, New York, 1966. See also Sherrill, " 'Political Modernization' and the United States" (Ph.D. diss., University of North Carolina, 1967), and "The Attitudes of Modernity," *Comparative Politics* 1 (January 1969): 184–210.

[32]Gabriel A. Almond and Sidney Verba, *The Civic Culture* (Princeton: Princeton University Press, 1963), p. 20.

[33]Ibid., p. 37.

[34]Ibid., pp. 440, 455.

systems.[35] In other words, Almond and Verba assume that the "civic culture" is the *only* cultural mix consistent with democratic society, when, in fact, all that they have shown is that the particular mix is associated with those societies identified as most democratic.

Sherrill identifies another serious problem in the apparent assumption that the three types of citizens—participants, subjects and parochials—are randomly distributed within the population. The case studies of subjects and parochials presented by Almond and Verba would suggest otherwise. Deprivations are cumulative: Parochials tend to be disproportionately poor, uneducated, rural, and, in the United States, black, Mexican-American, and Appalachian white. "If maintaining the mix means maintaining the pattern of life to be found in the rural south of the United States," Sherrill argues, "then the value of the mix must be weighed against other, and perhaps higher, social values."[36]

In assuming universal and indispensable functional qualities for all aspects of the system, Almond and Verba unwittingly rationalize poverty and social injustice in the name of democratic stability. It appears that their norm is stability, not democracy. In the concluding chapter, they argue that

> if politics becomes intense, and if it remains intense because of some salient issue, the inconsistency between attitude and behavior will become unstable. But any relatively permanent resolution of the inconsistency is likely to have unfortunate consequences. If behavior is brought into line with attitudes, the amount of attempted control of elites by nonelites will create governmental ineffectiveness and instability. On the other hand, if attitudes change to match behavior, the resulting sense of impotence and noninvolvement will have damaging consequences for the democratic quality of the political system.[37]

This fear of mass political participation is also embedded in the pluralist notion that apathy is functional to democratic stability. Empirical research establishes that there are large portions of the populations of even the most participant political systems, like the United States, which are uninvolved, uninformed, and apathetic about politics. Such

---

[35]Sherrill notes, however, that "the question remains as to why it is necessary to have certain people in the system who are subjects or parochials, even though their ideal 'citizen' combines his participant orientation with these other two orientations," "Political Modernization as an Attitudinal Syndrome," p. 5.

[36]Ibid., p. 6. Also see Satish Arora, "Pre-Empted Future? Notes on Theories of Political Development," *Behavioral Sciences and Community Development* (India) 2 (September 1968): 111–15.

[37]Almond and Verba, *The Civic Culture,* p. 483.

apathy is then regarded as contributing to democratic stability by insuring that political conflict involves neither large numbers of people nor those who operate with an intensity unmediated by the "bargaining culture" produced by the pluralistic pattern of crosscutting social cleavages. In the best-selling introductory text, *The Politics of American Democracy,* Irish and Prothro write, "Many people express undemocratic principles in response to questioning but are too apathetic to act on their undemocratic opinions in concrete situations. And in most cases, fortunately for the democratic system, those with the most undemocratic principles are also those who are least likely to act."[38] "Too many good citizens," they contend, "could actually be bad for the system."[39]

The postulate of indispensability, assuming that each element within a system performs some vital function for system survival, goes far beyond the minimum requirements of functional analysis. Merton argues, however, that "there are certain *functions* which are indispensable in the sense that, unless they are performed, the society (or group or individual) will not persist."[40] This is the concept of *functional requisites,* those "imperatives" which must be fulfilled if the system is to persist. Closely related to the concept of functional requisites is that of the *functional prerequisites,* those functions which must be fulfilled or pre-exist before a given system can come into being. Despite the fact that "embedded in every functional analysis is some conception, tacit or expressed, of the functional requirements of the system," Merton observes that the functional requisite remains "one of the cloudiest and empirically most debatable concepts in functional theory."[41]

Levy insists that his requisites for the persistence of a society are not derived merely by definition, but are the minimal implications of the existence of a society in its setting. They are not empty deductions, but empirical relationships to be independently *discovered.* Talcott Parsons,

---

[38]Marian D. Irish and James W. Prothro, *The Politics of American Democracy,* 3rd ed. (Englewood Cliffs, N.J.: Prentice-Hall, 1965), p. 69. James Prothro and Charles Grigg express the view again: "Apathy can play a constructive role if it leads those who reject the techniques called for by the democratic creed to inactivity or to acceptance of decisions they themselves would not have made." "Social Coordination by the Educated Minority," *Political Research: Organization and Design* (now *American Behavioral Scientist*) 3 (January 1960): 8.

[39]Irish and Prothro, *Politics of American Democracy,* p. 78. For a critique of the preoccupation with stability and the notion that "apathy may reflect the health of a democracy," see Graeme Duncan and Steven Lukes, "The New Democracy," *Political Studies* 11 (1963): 156–77, reprinted in Charles A. McCoy and John Playford, eds., *Apolitical Politics* (New York: Thomas Y. Crowell, 1967), pp. 160–84.

[40]Merton, *Social Theory and Social Structure,* p. 33.

[41]Ibid., p. 52.

the most prominent functionalist in American sociology,[42] argues, however, that social scientists are not yet ready for a precise theoretical formulation of social systems. This admits that the functional requisites on either the general or particular level cannot then be determined.

Parsons "seems prepared to grant that functionalism is, at its best, a programmatic guide to research."[43] For Parsons, functionalism is a theory building strategy, a "theoretical device" for raising significant questions and generating suggestive hypotheses. It is *useful,* Parsons advises, to conceive of a social entity or process as a *system* of behavior, having the teleological properties of self-regulation. Insofar as this involves merely the view that the parts of society are interrelated in patterns of behavior about which it is possible to formulate testable hypotheses, then functionalism, as Kingsley Davis contends, is synonymous with sociological analysis.[44] Parsons and the proponents of the functional approach, however, are clearly saying more than this.

Parsons, in his model of the social system, constructs an ideal type. He posits four requisite functions, or "functional imperatives," for any system: (1) pattern maintenance, (2) goal attainment, (3) adaptation, and (4) integration.[45] "He is not making an empirical statement but is proposing that it would be fruitful to categorize and interpret social structures in terms of their contributions to these functions."[46] But despite Parson's caution, he, as so many functionalists, fails to preserve the distinction between the ideal type and empirical reality. "In this way," Harold Kaplan writes, "Parsons' ideal type is transformed into an allegedly accurate portrayal of observable systems."[47]

Flanigan and Fogelman argue that "there are no grounds for supposing that one set and only one set of functions are requisite. The analyst

---

[42]See especially Talcott Parsons, *The Social System* (New York: Free Press, 1951); Parsons and Edward Shils, eds., *Toward a General Theory of Action* (Cambridge: Harvard University Press, 1951); Parsons and Neil Smelser, *Economy and Society* (New York: Free Press, 1959). For a discussion of Parsons' work, see William C. Mitchell, *Sociological Analysis and Politics: The Theories of Talcott Parsons* (Englewood Cliffs, N.J.: Prentice-Hall, 1967) and Max Black, ed., *The Social Theories of Talcott Parsons* (Englewood Cliffs, N.J.: Prentice-Hall, 1962).

[43]Gregor, "Political Science and the Uses of Functional Analysis," p. 435.

[44]"The Myth of Functional Analysis as a Special Method in Sociology and Anthropology," *American Sociological Review* 24 (December 1959): 757.

[45]See Karl Deutsch, "Integration and the Social System: Implications of Functional Analysis," in Philip E. Jacob and James V. Toscano, eds., *The Integration of Political Communities* (New York: Lippincott, 1964), pp. 179–208. William C. Mitchell posits four requisite functions which closely approximate those of Parsons in *The American Polity* (New York: Free Press, 1962). One of the earliest applications of requisite analysis in comparative politics was by David E. Apter in *The Gold Coast in Transition* (Princeton: Princeton University Press, 1955).

[46]Cancian, "Varieties of Functional Analysis," p. 34.

[47]Harold Kaplan, "The Parsonian Image of Social Structure," p. 897.

can define his 'requisite functions' as he pleases, and he can be equally imaginative in locating which structures perform what functions."[48] This raises some severe problems in the failure to distinguish empirical and normative criteria. The analyst may well see as *necessary* those items which constitute for him "good" system adjustment. "The danger is particularly prominent because any 'requisite' is difficult to test, if indeed it does not defy testing."[49]

Functionalism in Comparative Political Analysis

The work of Gabriel Almond involves what he calls "the functional approach to comparative politics." As described by Almond in *The Politics of Developing Areas,* all political systems have four characteristics in common and in terms of which they may be compared. First of all, "political systems, including the simplest ones, have political structure. . . . Second, the same functions are performed in all political systems, even though these functions may be performed with different frequencies, and by different kinds of structures. . . . Third, all political structure, no matter how specialized, whether it is found in primitive or in modern societies, is multifunctional. . . . Fourth, all political systems are mixed systems in the cultural sense. There are no 'all-modern' cultures and structures, in the sense of rationality, and no all-primitive ones, in the sense of traditionality."[50] All political systems, in this sense, are transitional.[51]

Although Almond nowhere offers a specific definition of *function,* he postulates seven functional requisites which must be fulfilled by any political system. On the political or "input" side are political socialization and recruitment, interest articulation, interest aggregation, and political communication. On the governmental or "output" side are rule-making, rule-application, and rule-adjudication.[52] The functions

---

[48]Flanigan and Fogelman, "Functional Analysis," p. 80.

[49]Golembiewski et al., *A Methodological Primer for Political Scientists,* p. 254.

[50]Gabriel A. Almond "Introduction: A Functional Approach to Comparative Politics," in Gabriel A. Almond and James S. Coleman, eds., *The Politics of Developing Areas* (Princeton: Princeton University Press, 1960), p. 11.

[51]Ibid., p. 24.

[52]Ibid., p. 17. Almond speaks of "functions" as being equivalent with the traditional notion of "powers," as in the classical separation of powers between the legislative, executive, and judicial, to which Almond's output functions explicitly correspond (pp. 4, 17). Also see Gabriel A. Almond and G. Bingham Powell, Jr., *Comparative Politics: A Developmental Approach* (Boston: Little, Brown, 1966), pp. 10–12. For a discussion of the personal context in which these categories were formulated, see Almond's introductory essay, "Propensities and Opportunities," in *Political Development: Essays in Heuristic Theory* (Boston: Little, Brown, 1970), pp. 17–19.

are not of an equivalent nature, in that political communication is a mechanism by which the other functions are performed—output, as well as input, not to mention feedback.

"An adequate analysis of a political system must locate and characterize all of these functions," Almond states, "and not simply those functions performed by the specialized political structure."[53] Nowhere, however, does Almond make it clear just why *these* six functions, and not others, are necessary or whether they are sufficient for system maintenance. Almond is deeply sensitive to the parochialism of traditional comparative politics. His "functional categories" were developed for the purpose of comparing whole political systems—Western and non-Western; modern, transitional, and traditional. The functions, however, are highly ethnocentric in their derivation. "The problem essentially was to ask a series of questions based on the distinctive political activities existing in Western complex systems. In other words, we derived our functional categories from the political systems in which structural specialization and functional differentiation have taken place to the greatest extent."[54] This requisite assumption provides the Procrustean bed to which all systems are fitted. The validity of the assumption cannot be tested: "The same functions may be performed with different frequencies, and by different kinds of structures."[55] Thus, each of the seven functions must be fulfilled, by definition, if the system is to be maintained. Since a given system to be analyzed obviously "exists," then the functions *are* being performed. The problem is to locate the structures, whether institutionalized or intermittent: "If the functions are there, then the structures must be . . ."[56]

The functions are offered as a "preliminary" proposal, [57] and are modified in the development of Almond's work. In *Comparative Politics: A Developmental Approach,* Almond and Powell distinguish between three levels of functions, described as "activities."[58] On one level are *capability functions* (regulative, extractive, distributive, and responsive) which determine the performance of the system in its environment. At the second level, the *conversion functions* (interest articulation, interest aggregation, and political communication; rule-making, rule-application, and rule-adjudication) are internal to the system and involve the input-output flow as the system meets demands with authoritative

[53]Gabriel Almond in Almond and Coleman, *The Politics of Developing Areas,* p. 12.

[54]Ibid., p. 16.

[55]Ibid., p. 11.

[56]Ibid., p. 12.

[57]Ibid.

[58]Almond and Powell, *Comparative Politics.* p. 14.

decisions. The third level is that of the *system maintenance and adaptation functions,* specifically political socialization and recruitment. "The theory of the political system will consist of the discovery of the relations between these different levels of functioning—capabilities, conversion functions, and system maintenance and adaptation functions—and of the relation of the functions at each level."[59]

The broader framework is, in part, a response to the less dynamic character of the earlier formulation. Almond seeks "to explore developmental patterns, to explain how political systems change and why they change."[60] His political system is one of interdependence, but not necessarily of harmony. He offers a kind of "probabilistic functionalism,"[61] but as the framework has expanded, the functional categories seem to have become open-ended. There are presumably other, yet unspecified requisite functions. Almond's use of the term *function* is hardly precise, but his basic problem—the thorny issue of functional requisites—is shared with Parsons, Levy, and all those who would employ functional analysis.

Political analysis has employed a diversity of requisite functions—"very nearly a unique set for each study." Flanigan and Fogelman contend that "until precise criteria are established for the identification of functions and a theoretically sophisticated argument is made for a particular set of functions," functionalism, as an approach, will be severely limited.[62]

Closely associated with the identification of requisite functions is the assertion that certain structures are "indispensable for fulfilling each of these functions." Merton contends that the assumption of structural requisites is not only contrary to fact, but diverts attention from the possibility that alternative social structures may serve the functions necessary for the persistence of the system. Functional needs are permissive rather than determinant of special social structures: *"just as the same item may have multiple functions, so may the same function be diversely fulfilled by alternative items."* Merton here seeks to sensitize the analyst to the existence of functional alternatives, equivalents, or substitutes.[63]

Different structures may serve the same requisite, and different requisites may be fulfilled by the same structure. The relations between structures and functions may vary not only between systems, but also over time within a given system. The empirical determination as to

---

[59]Ibid., pp. 29–30.

[60]Ibid., pp. 13.

[61]Ibid., p. 12.

[62]Flanigan and Fogelman, "Functional Analysis," p. 81.

[63]Merton, *Social Theory and Social Structure,* pp. 33–34. Italics added.

whether or not a given item has functional equivalents can be made only under specified conditions. Hempel argues that "in most, if not all, concrete cases it would be impossible to specify with any precision the range of alternative behavior patterns, institutions, custom, or the like that would suffice to meet a given functional prerequisite or need. And even if that range could be characterized, there is no satisfactory method in sight for dividing it into some finite number of cases and assigning a probability to each of these."[64]

Functionalism, Explanation, and Change

Carl Hempel argues that "functional analysis no more enables us to predict than it enables us to explain the occurrence of a particular one of the items by which a given functional requirement can be met."[65] From the postulation of certain functional requisites, the inference is then made as a categorical assertion that the requisites will be satisfied in some way. This assumes self-regulation on the part of the system, that is, within certain limits of tolerance or adaptability, the system will satisfy the various functional requirements for its persistence by developing the appropriate traits so as to effectively meet any system challenge.[66] In this sense, the system is homeostatic. It is a teleological, or goal-directed system, and its basic goal is self-maintenance.

Hempel points out, however, that "a formulation proposed as a hypothesis of self-regulation can serve as a basis for explanation or prediction only if it is a reasonably definite statement that permits of objective empirical test. . . . Unfortunately, . . . the formulations offered in the context of concrete functional analyses quite often fall short of these general standards." The kind of system or its limit of tolerance within which the functional requirements are satisfied is not adequately indicated.[67] Ralf Dahrendorf argues that "instead of abstracting a limited number of variables and postulating their relevance for explanation of a particular problem, [functionalism] represents a huge and allegedly all-embracing superstructure of concepts that do not describe, proposi-

---

[64]Hempel, "Logic of Functional Analysis," p. 286. Hempel writes, "The information typically provided by a functional analysis of an item *i* affords neither deductively nor inductively adequate grounds for expecting *i* rather than one of its alternatives. The impression that a functional analysis does provide such grounds, and thus explains the occurrence of *i*, is no doubt at least partly due to the benefit of hindsight: when we seek to explain an item *i*, we presumably know already that *i* has occurred." (p. 286).

[65]Ibid., p. 288.

[66]Ibid., p. 290.

[67]Ibid., pp. 291–92. Also see Gregor, "Political Science and the Uses of Functional Analysis," pp. 432–33.

tions that do not explain, and models from which nothing follows."[68]

Part of the difficulty is that the key terms of functional analysis are rarely given operational definitions and thus cannot be put to an objective test.[69] One of the most serious problems lies in the meaning of "maintenance," "persistence," or "survival." In biology, as Hempel notes, "survival" of an organism has a fairly clear meaning, but social systems are another matter altogether. There is always the danger of tautology: Requisites are postulated upon which the survival of the system depends, but as the system under analysis has obviously "survived," then it is assumed that the functional requisites are fulfilled.[70] In functional analysis, the definition of system requisites must be supplemented by empirically testable specification of the "normal" or "healthy" state of the system, with clear delineation of the limits of tolerance beyond which the system can be regarded as no longer persisting.[71]

The concept of integration, as noted earlier, is just as problematic as that of survival. As all societies, over both time and space, will necessarily vary in degree of integration, no society is likely to be perfectly integrated—including those tribal societies from which the early anthropologists, like Malinowski, derived their vision of harmony.[72] The concepts of adjustment and adaptation involve similar problems of specification. In the absence of empirical criteria, the concepts have no definite meaning. Tautologically, *any* system response might be construed as an adjustment. Subjectively, adjustment might become whatever the analyst regards as "good" for the system in terms of his own values.[73]

The functional approach may account for the adaptive and modifying dimensions of change, but it cannot adequately confront radical and transforming change. The functional vocabulary reflects in depth this bias, as can be seen in the terminology of the "functional imperatives" of Talcott Parsons. Words such as maintenance, adaptation, and integration occur throughout the functionalist literature. As the challenge of modernization unleashes forces of change throughout the world, the structural-functional approach, at best, permits us to understand change only in terms of system maintenance and preservation. Intrasystemic fluctuations are viewed in the context of homeostasis and equilibrium.

---

[68]Ralf Dahrendorf, "Out of Utopia: Toward a Reorientation of Sociological Analysis," *American Journal of Sociology* 64 (September 1958): 119.

[69]Hempel, "Logic of Functional Analysis," p. 293.

[70]See Cancian, "Varieties of Functional Analysis," pp. 35–36.

[71]Hempel, "Logic of Functional Analysis," p. 294.

[72]See Cancian, "Varieties of Functional Analysis," p. 36.

[73]Hempel, "Logic of Functional Analysis," p. 295.

Except in the case of genuinely self-regulating systems, the explanatory power of functional analysis is severely limited, and its predictive significance practically nil.[74] The task of functionalism in the social sciences is to determine the respects and the degrees to which various systems are self-regulating. Failing this, functionalism cannot be regarded as theory, Hempel contends, "but rather as a program for research guided by certain heuristic maxims or 'working hypotheses.' "[75]

Functional analysis, as an analogy, provides an analytic and heuristic model. It offers taxonomic frameworks and classificatory schemes for collecting and coding research material. This was the conception behind the Little, Brown Series in Comparative Politics. By following a common approach in the analysis of individual countries, utilizing Almond's functional schema, it then becomes possible to compare these countries "systematically and cumulatively." Each country, rather than being treated in more traditional, *sui generis* fashion, would be examined in terms of common functional categories.[76] Because "it provides a set of standardized categories that can be applied successfully over widely disparate political systems," functional analysis has been particularly useful in the study of comparative political systems.[77] It does not, however, provide a body of theory, and it has neither explanatory nor predictive power.

Systems Analysis

The systems approach in political science is closely related to functionalism, both based on a conception of political phenomena as a "system of interrelated and reciprocally regulated patterns of action and orientation, patterns that cluster together in equilibrium and that . . . have certain needs for maintenance and survival."[78] Gabriel Almond, in his

---

[74]Ibid., p. 296.

[75]Ibid., pp. 301–2.

[76]The series, edited by Almond, Coleman, and Pye, include volumes on England, the Philippines, the Republic of South Africa, the USSR, Israel, Japan, Germany, France, North Africa, and India. That Almond's functions have never been rigorously operationalized, however, has meant that from volume to volume, their treatment has varied. The editors, in the foreword to the series, recognize the inevitable difficulties of their task. While expressing gratitude to their colleagues for willingness "to organize their discussions around a common set of functional topics in the interest of furthering comparisons," the editors urge each author "to adapt the common framework to the special problems of the country he is discussing and to express his own theoretical point of view."

[77]Oran Young, *Systems of Political Science* (Englewood Cliffs, N.J.: Prentice-Hall, 1968), p. 33. Also see Gregor, "Political Science and the Uses of Functional Analysis," pp. 430–34.

[78]Howard A. Scarrow, *Comparative Political Analysis: An Introduction* (New York: Harper and Row, 1969), p. 59.

functional approach, utilizes the concept of the political system instead of the more traditional "state," limited by its legal and institutional connotations.[79] Almond distinguishes the political system in terms of a particular set of interactional properties: comprehensiveness, interdependence, and existence of boundaries.[80] In the work of David Easton, however, the systems approach is most fully articulated.

Systems in Comparative Political Study

Easton, in *The Political System,* published in 1953, offered a major critique of the condition of political science as a discipline. In this deeply influential book, Easton argued for the use of the systems concept "as an analytical tool designed to identify those integrally related aspects of concrete social reality that can be called political."[81] Over the succeeding decade, the development of Easton's systems approach drew heavily on the communications science of cybernetics and on general systems theory, an ambitious attempt to provide an analytical framework for the study of all phenomena, physical and social, as behaving systems.[82]

Easton wishes to construct an empirically oriented general theory of politics, and to that end, he seeks to define the kinds of functions characteristic of any political system through a systematic framework for political analysis. He examines "the basic processes through which a political system, regardless of its genetic or specific type, is able to persist as a system of behavior in a world either of stability or of change."[83]

Easton's analysis rests on four premises:

1. *System.* It is useful to view political life as a system of behavior.

---

[79]Almond, *The Politics of Developing Areas,* p. 4.

[80]Ibid., pp. 7–9. See S. E. Finer, "Almond's Concept of 'The Political System': A Textual Critique," *Government and Opposition* 4 (Winter 1969–70): 3–21; and Almond's rejoinder, "Determinacy-Choice, Stability-Change: Some Thoughts on a Contemporary Polemic in Political Theory," in the same issue, pp. 22–40.

[81]David Easton, *The Political System* (New York: Knopf, 1953), p. 61.

[82]Easton, *A Framework for Political Analysis* (Englewood Cliffs, N.J.: Prentice-Hall, 1965), p. xi. For a discussion of general systems theory and an extensive bibliography, see Ludwig von Bertalanffy, *General System Theory* (New York: Braziller, 1968). For cybernetics, see Norbert Weiner, *Cybernetics,* 2nd ed. (New York: John Wiley and Sons, 1961) and *The Human Use of Human Beings* (Boston: Houghton, Mifflin, 1950); W. Ross Ashby, *An Introduction to Cybernetics* (New York: John Wiley and Sons, 1956) and *Design for a Brain* (New York: John Wiley and Sons, 1952). Karl Deutsch has made an important application of cybernetics to political science in *The Nerves of Government: Models of Political Communication and Control* (New York: Free Press, 1963).

[83]Easton, *A Framework for Political Analysis,* p. x.

2. *Environment.* A system is distinguishable from the environment in which it exists and open to influences from it.
3. *Response.* Variations in the structures and processes within a system may usefully be interpreted as constructive or positive alternative efforts by members of a system to regulate or cope with stress flowing from environmental as well as internal sources.
4. *Feedback.* The capacity of a system to persist in the face of stress is a function of the presence and nature of the information and other influences that return to its actors and decision-makers.[84]

As conceived by Easton, systems analysis

> takes its departure from the notion of political life as a boundary-maintaining set of interactions imbedded in and surrounded by other social systems to the influence of which it is constantly exposed. As such, it is helpful to interpret political phenomena as constituting an open system, one that must cope with the problems generated by its exposure to influences from these environmental systems. If a system of this kind is to persist through time, it must obtain adequate feedback about its past performances, and it must be able to take measures that regulate its future behavior. Regulation may call for simple adaptation to a changing setting in the light of fixed goals. But it may also include efforts to modify old goals or transform them entirely. Simple adaptation may not be enough. To persist it may be necessary for a system to have the capacity to transform its own internal structure and processes.[85] (see figure 5.)

The pattern of analysis involves the examination of the following variables:

> first, the nature of the inputs;
> second, the variable conditions under which they will constitute a stressful disturbance on the system;
> third, the environmental and systemic conditions that generate such stressful conditions;
> fourth, the typical ways in which systems have sought to cope with stress;
> fifth, the role of information feedback; and, finally,
> sixth, the part that outputs play in these conversion and coping processes.[86]

---

[84]Ibid., pp. 25–26.
[85]Ibid., p. 25.
[86]Ibid., p. 132.

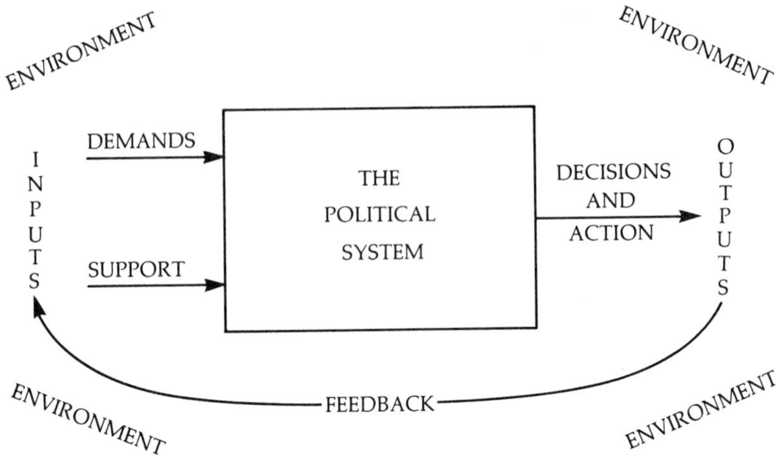

FIGURE 5 A Model of the Political System, (Redrawn from Easton, *A Framework for Political Analysis,* p. 112)

Easton emphasizes the analytic character of systems: "all systems are constructs of the mind."[87] What constitutes a system is determined by definition and is not given in nature. Nothing is gained theoretically by designating some systems as "natural," for the point at which a system of interrelated variables ceases to be a system and emerges as only a random collection remains indeterminant.[88] All systems involve variables which are, more or less, interrelated. Easton suggests that "any set of variables selected for description and explanation may be considered a system of behavior." The problem is "to decide whether the set of activities is an interesting one" insofar as it is relevant and advances our theoretical understanding. The criteria for the determination of what is to be included within the political system is purely instrumental. "Logically, therefore, we are free to include within a political system any range of actions at all; substantively, in the light of the objectives of research with regard to political life, we are limited by our conception of what is significant and relevant for an understanding of why people act in the way that they do in political situations."[89]

Political systems are analytical constructs in yet another way. They involve an abstraction of the political from the reality of the larger

[87]Ibid., p. 27.

[88]Ibid., pp. 29–30.

[89]Ibid., pp. 30–31.

matrix of human behavior. The political system is made up of roles, not of individuals, and is defined in terms of the political aspects of social action. It cannot be concretely separated. Any action may be at once both political and non-political in various aspects. Prayer would seem to be a solely religious act, but when it occurs in a public school, it enters the political system. Voting, on the other hand, is a political act, yet it may have specifically non-political aspects, as, for example, in a case where voting reflects a desire for social acceptance rather than political preference. Thus, in this sense, the political system is not a physical entity, but it is, as a pattern of interaction, empirically observable.[90]

Offering these caveats, Easton himself then breathes life into his political system in such a way as to endow it with teleological character. It is "a goal-setting, self-transforming, and creatively adaptive system."[91] The analytic construct takes on a certain concreteness. Easton speaks of the "life processes of political systems"[92] and argues that "the primary goal of political analysis is to understand how political systems manage to *persist* through time."[93] He gives little attention to their transformation or "death."

Easton assumes that "there are certain basic political activities and processes characteristic of all political systems even though the structural forms through which they manifest themselves may and do vary considerably in each place and each age."[94] The requisite function of any political system, and the criteria by which its boundaries are defined, is "the authoritative allocation of values for a society,"[95] that is, the process of how binding decisions are made and implemented for a society. *Values* refer to those things, material goods or symbolic rewards, which people want. They are, by definition, scarce. *Allocations* are those decisions and related activities that distribute, grant, or deny values in the society. Allocations are *authoritative* when decisions are accepted as legitimate and binding, for whatever reason—threat of force, self-interest, or recognition of legitimacy. The requirement that such allocations be *for a society* distinguishes those decisions made for the inclusive social system from those in subsystems which may resolve conflict through authoritative allocations of values, but for a limited

---

[90]See ibid., pp. 35–45.

[91]Ibid., p. 132.

[92]Ibid., p. 99.

[93]Ibid., p. 55. Italics added. In *A Systems Analysis of Political Life,* Easton says that "the question that gives coherence and purpose to a rigorous analysis of political life as a system of behavior is . . . How do any and all political systems manage to persist in a world of both stability and change?" (New York: Wiley, 1965), p. 17.

[94]Easton, *A Framework for Political Analysis,* p. 49.

[95]Ibid., p. 50.

membership, as in a family, church, association, or local body of government. The set of activities related to authoritative allocations for the society as a whole Easton terms "the political system."

In all societies, scarcity leads to conflict and the demands for conflict resolution. Where disputes over the allocation of values cannot be "resolved independently and where they are also perceived to be excessively disruptive of the prevailing ideas of order and justice, every society provides for processes through which special structures either aid in achieving some regulation of the differences or impose a settlement."[96] Insofar as the authority is regarded as legitimate, the imposed settlement, ultimately backed by the threat of physical coercion, will be accepted as binding by most members of the society, even by those who may be adversely affected by the decision.[97]

The boundaries of the political system are determined by whether the interactions are predominantly oriented toward the authoritative allocation of values for a society. What remains outside the political system constitutes the environment, to which the political system is open and responsive. The elements of the differentiated environment—the ecological, biological, personality, and social systems—are taken as "given" and represent the independent variables or parameters of the political system.[98]

The Problem of Demands and Supports

Changes in the environment relevant to the political system are conceptualized by Easton as *inputs,* summary variables of demands and support. Demands represent the politicization of raw wants or preferences. As these preferences are articulated, they are "put into" the political system as demands that the authorities respond to these self-conscious needs, that the government do something. The volume and variety of demands are regulated by certain structures—interest groups, parties, opinion leaders, or the mass media—which aggregate and articulate the often diffuse and undifferentiated demands made on authorities. By drawing the disparate variety of demands together in a workable and simplified program for action, the system can presumably respond more effectively. Beyond these structural regulators, many cultural restraints serve to modify potential demands arising from the environment. While the sphere of every political system has increasingly expanded, certain

[96]Ibid., p. 53.

[97]Ibid., p. 54.

[98]See ibid., pp. 59–75.

kinds of wants may still be regarded as inappropriate for political settlement.[99]

One of the most effective sources of demand regulation is in the differential access which members may have to the political system. All members are not likely to enjoy meaningful access and are not "equally likely to give voice to a demand."[100] The members of a political system will differ widely in their political capital—money, status, prestige, and numbers. With limited resources, the authorities of any political system will respond most effectively to those demands from members with political capital, upon whom they are ultimately dependent for support. In this sense, the mode of analysis reflects an elitist orientation: emphasis is almost entirely on politically relevant members of the system.[101] The model suggests a game of extortion, and, indeed, no political system operates on solely altruistic lines. But Easton's model never really comes to terms with what implicitly underlies the whole process. If ultimately authority is backed by a "monopoly of the legitimate use of physical force,"[102] all members of the political system are at least potentially equal. In a Hobbesian sense, violence gives to each member political capital to which the system must be responsive—either through repression or in meeting the demands which may be expressed, as in a ghetto riot, by violence.

Three levels of support may be distinguished: the authorities, the regime (or constitutional order), and the political community. Support for each object may vary independently, but strong associative relationships normally involve a "spillover" effect, by which support for one object is transferred to the others. Political opposition is characterized as "negative support." Persistence depends on "the maintenance of a minimum level of attachment for each of the three identified political objects. Where the input of support falls below this minimum, the persistence of any kind of system will be endangered."[103] "A system may seek to instill in its members a high level of *diffuse support* in order that regardless of what happens the members will continue to be bound to it by strong ties of loyalty and affection." This form of support is independent of specific rewards and is normally the product of a political socialization stressing partriotism and loyalty to leaders, constitu-

---

[99]Ibid., pp. 122–23.

[100]Ibid., p. 122.

[101]See Oran Young, *Systems of Political Science*, pp. 46–48.

[102]Max Weber, "Politics as a Vocation," in H. H. Gerth and C. Wright Mills, eds., *From Max Weber: Essays in Sociology* (New York: Oxford University Press, 1958), p. 78.

[103]Easton, *A Systems Analysis of Political Life*, p. 220.

tion, and country. "No system," Easton writes, "could endure for very long if it did not seek to build up a reservoir of support."[104]

Diffuse support may provide elasticity, but under what conditions does such support "come to the rescue" of the system?[105] In the long run, every system falls back on *specific support,* generated by "the satisfaction a member feels when he perceives his demands as having been met."[106] *Outputs* represent system response to existing or anticipated demands and are distinguished from their consequences or *outcomes.* Authorities may attempt to change the environment or to modify the political system itself in seeking to fulfill demands. Alternatively, effective response may be bypassed in favor of symbolic outputs—such as empty rhetoric, promises, and flag-waving, or in the diversionary tactics of fear and scapegoatism. This might be in the creation of fear of an external threat or of internal subversion. Failing all else, authorities may fall back on the negative output of coercion to ensure system persistence and their continued power.

No political system can meet all of the demands of all of its members all of the time. The support by members serves as "credit" on which the system operates, but "if the authorities are unable or unwilling to meet the demands of the members in some determinable proportions," discontent would soon mount and system support, built up through previous outputs, would decline.

Demands, independent of their impact or support, may impose stress on the system in terms of sheer volume. It may be that there are simply too many demands, with a variety, content, and intensity which overwhelm the system in what Easton calls "input overload." No system has an infinite capacity to accept and process demands, but the threshold of capability varies with each kind of system, its structure and culture.[107]

The capacity of a system to respond effectively to stress is derived from the central process of *feedback,* information about the state of the system and its environment, which is communicated back to the authorities. Feedback is critical to system persistence, for "only on the basis of knowledge about what has taken place or about the current state of affairs with respect to demand and support would the authorities be able to respond by adjusting, modifying, or correcting previous decisions, including the failure to make a decision."[108] Effective feedback, with maximum accuracy and minimum delay, by no means guarantees

---

[104]Easton, *A Framework for Political Analysis,* p. 125.

[105]See Reid R. Reading, "Is Easton's System-Persistence Framework Useful? A Research Note," *Journal of Politics* 34 (February 1972): 258–67.

[106]Easton, *A Framework for Political Analysis,* p. 125.

[107]Ibid., pp. 119–21.

[108]Ibid., p. 129.

effective response. Output failure may threaten any system. "Even if the authorities do obtain accurate information, lack of will to use it, lack of resources to put it to use, inadequate wisdom and skills in doing so may all contribute as much to an inability to meet a decline in support as the absence of such information feedback itself."[109]

Easton provides a model of "a vast conversion process" in which "the inputs of demand and support are acted upon in such a way that it is possible for the system to persist and to produce outputs meeting the demands of at least some of the members and retaining the support of most."[110] The strains and imbalances which result from rising demands and crumbling support are catalysts of system change.

Systems Analysis, Stability, and Change

Disturbances, both from the environment and from within the system itself, may impose stress on the political system, threatening its capacity to persist. The persistence of a given political system, Easton argues, requires the presence of certain *essential variables*—"the allocation of values for society and the relative frequency of compliance with them"[111]—which operate within a "normal range." If these variables are displaced beyond a critical range by stress, the system collapses. "Systems analysis directs our attention toward the processes that all types of political systems share and that make it possible for them to cope, however successfully, with stresses that threaten to destroy the capacity of a society to sustain any political system at all."[112] It is by no means clear, however, whether such system change involves radical alteration *within* a single, persisting system or whether it involves the creation of an entirely new political system. The fact is that for all Easton's concern for systemic change, the processes of change—revolutionary or evolutionary—are never fully discussed.

Non-persistence, for Easton, "suggests the complete breakdown and evaporation of a political system."[113] This may mean physical annihilation or disintegrative anarchy. The disappearance of political systems may be momentary—as a result of civil war, revolution, or military defeat. While Easton says that a political system may recover its integrity, the problem remains as to whether it is the *same* system. If the

---

[109]Ibid., p. 130.

[110]Ibid., p. 131.

[111]Easton, *A Systems Analysis of Political Life,* p. 24.

[112]Easton, *A Framework for Political Analysis,* p. 79.

[113]Ibid., p. 83.

political community, as defined by geographic population, remains the same, perhaps the radical change might be viewed as involving the system's persistence. The matter would not be so simple in the case of disintegration or amalgamation of states, as in the breakup of the Austro-Hungarian Empire or of Pakistan or in the creation of Malaysia or Yugoslavia. Even less clear analytically is the situation posed by rival systems, as in South Vietnam, where two governments claim control over the "hearts and minds" of the people—one by day and one by night.

Persistence, in Easton's view, is more than self-maintenance, a concept "heavily charged with the idea of stability."[114] Persistence demands resilience in the face of stress. If a system is to survive, it must have the capacity to cope effectively with disturbances, either from the environment or from within the system. The political system must be able either to manipulate its environment so as to relieve stress or have the capacity to make "substantial and significant changes" or even fundamental modifications of its "scope, membership, structure and processes, goals, or rules of behavior."[115] Thus, the system is homeostatic or self-regulating, "even to the point of self-transformation."[116] Perhaps, as Eugene Miller suggests, "the remarkable capacity to persist which Easton finds in political systems is due largely . . . to his manner of defining persistence."[117]

A Comparative Critique

Systems analysis, in its close relationship with structural-functional analysis, is confronted by many of the same problems that plague functionalism. Easton's model, for all his attempts otherwise, involves what Herbert Spiro has called an "excessive preoccupation with stability."[118] This need not necessarily be so. Morton Kaplan has argued that "if we can construct a theory for a system or type of system, as a system of equilibrium, we can then inquire how individual variations in the parameters will produce deviant or unstable behavior."[119] The view of

---

[114] Easton, *A Framework for Political Analysis,* p. 88.

[115] Ibid., pp. 86–87.

[116] Ibid., p. 87; also see p. 95.

[117] Eugene F. Miller, "David Easton's Political Theory" *Political Science Reviewer* 1 (Fall 1971): p. 231.

[118] Herbert Spiro, "An Evaluation of Systems Theory," in Charlesworth, ed., *Contemporary Political Analysis,* p. 173.

[119] Morton Kaplan, "Systems Theory," in Charlesworth, ed., *Contemporary Political Analysis,* p. 151.

change or conflict as *deviant* behavior, however usually involves a normative bias toward stability. This is revealed in the very question Easton regards as the most fundamental: how systems *persist.* Easton's concern with persistence and stress involves a remarkable insensitivity to values, to the purpose of politics in terms of *who gets what.* This lack of emphasis on distribution and goal attainment is reflected in the discussion of roles, where, as Oran Young points out, "the flow of analysis is directed toward the contribution of various role patterns to the persistence of the system, rather than toward the contribution of the system to the well-being of the role holders."[120]

In systems analysis, as in functional analysis, conflict is regarded as a source of stress, a threat to system persistence. Stability becomes the highest value, the primary goal of system behavior, with political consensus as its base. Beyond the conservatism the model may suggest, serious analytical problems arise from the stability orientation. In emphasizing "the functions of social conflict," Lewis Coser argues that certain forms of conflict, rather than being necessarily dysfunctional, may make important and vital contributions to the maintenance of the whole system. In a series of propositions, distilled from the work of Georg Simmel, Coser holds that conflict serves to establish and reinforce the identity of groups within the system and that reciprocal antagonisms serve to maintain the total system by establishing a balance between the various groups and component parts of the system.[121]

However one may evaluate the utility of Easton's systems analysis, "the simple fact of the matter is that this outlook has become a part of modern political science."[122] The concept of the political system is by no means new. Thomas Hobbes, in 1651, had written in those terms. "Anyone who attempts to study politics scientifically," according to Herbert Spiro, "must at least implicitly think of politics as though it were functioning as some sort of system. That is, he must assume that more or less regular relationships can be discerned among various aspects of politics and between phenomena he describes as political and certain other phenomena not so described."[123]

What Easton has done is to make these relationships explicit and self-conscious. Easton provides a framework as a useful way of analyzing the political world and of ordering the diffuse data of political life. It is a "conceptual framework around which the more complex structure

[120]Oran Young, *Systems of Political Science,* p. 47.

[121]Lewis Coser, *The Functions of Social Conflict* (New York: Free Press, 1956), pp. 34–35.

[122]James R. Klonoski, review of *A Systems Analysis of Political Life* in *The Western Political Quarterly* 20 (September 1967): 738.

[123]Spiro, "An Evaluation of Systems Theory," p. 164.

of a theory may possibly, in the slowness of time, be added."[124] In his aspiration to general theory, however, Easton has constructed a model perhaps so ethereal that it is, lacking more explicit operationalization, unlikely to yield empirically testable hypotheses and theories. As a consequence, in contrast to the work of Gabriel Almond, it has had little direct influence on empirical research in comparative politics. The deliberate degree of abstraction frees the model from the specificity of any particular type of system and thereby facilitates broad comparison, but it does so at the expense of content.[125] "The whole framework," writes Klonoski, "has a sense of remoteness and abstraction from the facts and values of politics." The gap between theory and reality is not effectively bridged in such a way as to explain why things happen as they do.[126]

The structural elements of the system are never explicitly articulated, and the "black box," representing the authority structures of government—the traditional object of closest analytical concern—remains shrouded in mystery. "While suggesting certain structural components of a political system as a whole (the political community, the regime and the authorities)," Easton does not provide the "concepts needed to analyze the concrete subsystems of a system."[127]

The systems approach has sensitized the political analyst to the complex interrelationships of political life with the whole social system of which it is itself a part. It has drawn attention to political phenomena as constituting an interrelated system of behavior and, consequently, has brought a renewed emphasis on the analysis of the *whole* political system, as distinct from the study of its discrete parts or contributing elements. Systems analysis, as in the case of functionalism, is most immediately valuable, however, as a framework for classification and analysis of large and diffuse aggregates of data.[128] By providing explicit and standardized criteria by which political phenomena can be examined, genuine comparison becomes possible. Herein lies the enormous contribution of both Gabriel Almond and David Easton to the study of comparative politics. Whatever weaknesses their schemata may entail, they have lifted comparative politics from the intuitive and *sui generis* to a level of self-conscious theory and systematic analysis.

---

[124]Easton, *A Systems Analysis of Political Life,* p. 12.

[125]See Oran Young, *Systems of Political Science,* p. 46.

[126]Klonoski, review of *A Systems Analysis of Political Life,* pp. 738–39.

[127]Bertram M. Gross, review of *A Systems Analysis of Political Life* in *The American Political Science Review* 61 (March 1967): 157.

[128]See Oran Young, *Systems of Political Science,* p. 23.

CHAPTER VIII

Comparative Politics and Theory Building

Having analyzed separately a number of theoretical approaches, it is now possible to assess the general state of theory building in the study of comparative politics. A comparative examination of the various approaches reveals a surprising similarity in terms of stages of theoretical advance. Although certain approaches may reflect slightly more progress in some arenas, they often lag behind other approaches in quite different respects. No single approach therefore, possesses a marked advantage in the overall process of theory construction.

An Overview

The group approach has been extremely successful in raising relevant questions, and has had great therapeutic value by undercutting traditional formal study. At the difficult stage of conceptualization, the political culture approach perhaps enjoys a slight edge over the other orientations. As the most recent systematic approach, it has not yet become embroiled in the inevitable controversy of competing definitions and conflicting conceptual frameworks.[1] The most sophisticated and widely adopted classificatory schemes have been those developed

[1]This is explained also, perhaps, by the fact that very few political scientists in the area of comparative politics have made basic conceptual contributions to this approach.

by the structural-functional and systems analysts. In terms of researchability, the elite approach has taken relatively large strides forward. Finally, class analysis has been most useful in addressing the transforming dimensions of modernization and political development.

In general terms, comparative political analysis remains bogged down at the critical early stages of theory building, i.e., at the levels of conceptualization and classification. According to Giovanni Sartori, a major difficulty in advancing the discipline is that political science "has been conducive to indefiniteness, to undelimited and largely undefined conceptualizations."[2] Each approach examined in this study carries serious conceptual weaknesses.[3] The concepts basic to each approach are either left undefined or are defined vaguely, inconsistently, and/or illogically. The difficulties of this situation are compounded by the continued introduction of competing conceptualizations and by the crystallization of keen rivalry between and among such ideas.

One of the key pillars underlying the advance of physical science has been "the tacit desire among scientists to assure that in a given argument they are in fact discussing the same concepts."[4] The great theoreticians in the physical sciences stress the necessity for deep communication and cooperation between scholars.[5] A precondition for this is that each individual be able to understand the other's language. Conceptual fuzziness cripples such communication, and promotes muddled classification and vague theory. The situation is accurately summarized by Sartori: "The empirical problem is that we badly need information which is sufficiently precise to be meaningfully comparable. Hence we need a filing system provided by discriminating, i.e., taxonomic, conceptual containers."[6]

The literature in comparative politics reflects a proliferation of taxonomies and typologies. Gabriel Almond's classification of associational, institutional, nonassociational, and anomic interest groups is an example drawn from the group approach. Harold Lasswell's version of elite study includes a basic typology of elites based on eight values—power, wealth, respect, well-being, rectitude, skill, enlightenment, and

---

[2]Giovanni Sartori, "Concept Misformation in Comparative Politics," *The American Political Science Review* 64 (1970): 1035.

[3]This is true, of course, even of the political culture approach. It is, in a sense, ironic that traditional formal and institutional approaches had relatively explicit and consistent conceptual frameworks.

[4]Gerald Holton and Duane H. D. Roller, *Foundations of Modern Physical Science* (Reading, Mass.: Addison-Wesley, 1958), p. 218.

[5]See, for example, J. Robert Oppenheimer, *The Open Mind* (New York: Simon and Schuster, 1955).

[6]Sartori, "Concept Misformation," p. 1052.

affection. An elaborate schema of class types is presented by Gerhard Lenski, who discusses political, property, occupation, educational, ethnic-racial, age, and sex power classes. Besides power classes, Lenski's frame of reference includes privilege and prestige classes. One of the most influential classificatory schemes in comparative social and political study is Talcott Parson's four functional imperatives that are presented as critical to the existence of any system. These requisite functions—pattern maintenance, goal attainment, adaptation, and integration—are a key part of the structural-functional and systems approaches. Finally, a typology central to the political culture approach is Almond and Verba's presentation of parochial, subject, and participant cultures.

Since conceptualization and classification are intimately related to one another,[7] the difficulties in concept formation have fed directly into the process of classifying. Fuzzy conceptualization means ambiguous classification. Even such significant classificatory schemes as those explicitly mentioned above, therefore, have seldom generated meaningful sets of hypotheses. At best, they have supported a number of cautious generalizations largely in the form of tendency statements.

Attempts at theory building in comparative politics have resulted, at best, in a number of empirical generalizations concerning such issues as patterns of decision making, power and authority relations, and processes of modernization. These kinds of generalizations, which tend to develop very sporadically out of the still weak conceptual frameworks and classificatory schemes referred to above, have very rarely been put to the empirical test. As a result, scholars have strung together various statements at a low level of generality that have seldom been picked up and tested in different contexts by other scholars. Besides the fact that some scholars may find the work of others trivial and uninteresting, they are also deterred from replicating and testing due to their own preoccupations at the level of conceptualization and classification.

Theorizing in comparative politics remains embedded in its preliminary stages for a number of impressive reasons. One of the most important of these is an intellectual dogmatism that expresses itself at various levels of the theoretical enterprise—dogmatism in the sense that some scholars tend to portray certain theoretical approaches, conceptual frameworks, classificatory schemes, and research techniques as positive truth. Unyielding commitments are made to particular intellectual stances, and theoretical perspectives are frozen into objects of attack and defense. This situation runs in direct contradiction to the testimony of numerous great scientists who describe openness as being the single

[7]See Sartori's article "Concept Misformation."

most essential ingredient in scientific inquiry. Social scientists often seem to be less sensitive to this consideration than physical scientists. The history of the behavioral movement in political science is an especially appropriate case in point, since it centered upon the methods and techniques of the discipline itself.[8]

Inflexibility reigns at both extremes of the continuum of opinions concerning approaches and theory in comparative political analysis. Many competent scholars have tended to cluster at these extremes. At one pole are located those individuals who define theory only in deductive, axiomatic, and highly formal terms. These thinkers speak and write about "the scientific method" and often stress sophisticated quantitative research techniques and the preeminence of precise measurement. In Sartori's terms, these are the "overconscious" thinkers.[9] This group of theorists could learn a great deal by examining more closely the philosophy and methods of the physical scientists whom they seek to emulate. Physicists, for example, are fond of quoting P. W. Bridgman, who in his *Reflections of a Physicist,* writes: "I like to say that there is no scientific method as such, but that the most vital feature of the scientist's procedure has been merely to do his utmost with his mind, *no holds barred.*"[10] Hunches, guesses, and intuition are considered an integral, and, indeed, crucial part of scientific inquiry.[11]

Inductive theory building, which is the formulation of generalizations that are more comprehensive than the facts upon which they are initially based, is an important and recognized methodology in the physical sciences. Sir Isaac Newton in his *Optics* states the following: "As in Mathematics, so in Natural Philosophy, the investigation of difficult things by the Method of Analysis, ought ever to precede the Method of Composition. This Analysis consists in making Experiments and Observations, and in drawing general Conclusions from them by Induction, and admitting of no Objections against the Conclusions, but such as are taken from Experiments, or other certain Truths. For Hypotheses are not to be regarded in experimental Philosophy. And although the arguing from Experiments and Observations by Induction be no Demonstration of general Conclusions; yet it is the best way of arguing which the Nature of Things admits of . . ."[12] Even Albert Einstein,

---

[8]See chapter 1.

[9]Sartori, "Concept Misformation," p. 1033.

[10]P. W. Bridgman, *Reflections of a Physicist* (New York: Philosophical Library, 1950), p. 370.

[11]See Richard Feynman's important lecture entitled "Seeking New Laws" in Feynman, *The Character of Physical Law* (Cambridge, Mass.: M.I.T. Press, 1965), pp. 149–73.

[12]Sir Isaac Newton, *Optics,* Book III, Part I.

whose formulations are far removed from inductive and observational procedures, has written in his autobiographical notes that: "I really could have gotten a sound mathematical education [at the Polytechnic Institute in Zurich]. However, I worked most of the time in the physical laboratory, fascinated by the direct contact with experience."[13] Contemporary American physics is divided into the experimentalists, phenomenologists, or empirical theorists on the one hand and the axiomatic, deductive theorists on the other hand. It is estimated that over 90 percent of these physicists are engaged in inductive procedures of theory building.[14]

Despite this, the deductive element is also critical to theory construction. Only a deductive method can stand the test of rigorous logic in the sense that induction does not strictly admit of falsification. Karl R. Popper writes that "no matter how many instances of white swans we may have observed, this does not justify the conclusion that *all* swans are white."[15] The great French mathematician and physicist, Pierre Duhem, therefore, has attacked Newton who "asserted that in a sound physics every proposition should be drawn from phenomena and generalized by induction."[16] According to Duhem: "The teaching of physics by the purely inductive method such as Newton defined it is a chimera. Whoever claims to grasp this mirage is deluding himself and deluding his students. He is giving them, as facts seen, facts merely foreseen; as precise observations, rough reports; as performable procedures, merely ideal experiments; as experimental laws, propositions whose terms cannot be taken as real without contradiction. The physics he expounds is false and falsified."[17]

As indicated in chapter 1, scientific inquiry is marked by a pendulum-like swing between inductive and deductive intellectual procedures. There is constant movement back and forth from specific to general and vice versa. The methodology of induction belongs most properly to the realm of discovery, problemation, and observation, while deduction is indispensable to the operations of testing and confirming. In the early stages of theory building, therefore, the process of induction tends to dominate. The background of ideas and impressions against which the-

[13]Quoted in Holton and Roller, *Foundations of Modern Physical Science,* pp. 253–54.

[14]Edmond Berger, physicist, Argonne Laboratories, personal interview, November 14, 1971.

[15]Sir Karl R. Popper, *The Logic of Scientific Inquiry* (New York: Harper Torchbook, 1965), p. 27. This book provides an excellent account of the logical strengths that deductive methods have over inductive methods.

[16]Pierre Duhem, *The Aim and Structure of Physical Theory,* trans. Philip P. Wiener (Princeton: Princeton University Press, 1954), p. 191.

[17]Ibid., pp. 203–4.

ory is formulated has been inductively constructed over a number of years. This, of course, goes far to explain why theorists in comparative politics rely most heavily upon an inductive methodology of research.

Located at the other extreme among political analysts are the "unconscious" thinkers,[18] who are largely unaware of the procedures and methodology which they adopt as practicing scientists. They tend to react against theory building and seldom embark even upon the practice of explicit conceptualization and systematic classification. Empirical research and observation take place relatively indiscriminately and haphazardly, and intuitive judgements prevail. Occasionally, these scholars will make major contributions, but they can do little to further the cause of explanation. According to Sartori: ". . . the profession as a whole is grievously impaired by methodological unawareness. The more we advance technically, the more we leave a vast, uncharted territory behind our backs."[19] This comment suggests a major related complicating factor. Many contemporary scholars of comparative politics confuse science with technique and theory with method.[20]

In reaction to the nineteenth century scientist Lord Kelvin's statements that measurement and numbers are the crucial elements in science, two American physicists write that "a stand like Kelvin's (which at present appears to be having a formidable influence on some thinkers in the social studies) does justice neither to the complexity nor to the fertility of the human mind, and certainly not to the needs of contemporary physical science itself—neither to scientists nor to science. Quite apart from the practical impossibility of demanding of one's mind that at all times it identify such concepts as 'electron' only with the measurable aspects of that construct, there are specifically two main objections: first, this position mistakes how scientists as individuals do their work and, second, it mistakes how science as a system grows out of the contributions of individuals."[21] The internationally distinguished theoretical physicist, Richard P. Feynman, has also attempted to explode the myth "that you should not talk about what you cannot measure."[22] Robert M. Hutchins has criticized the "misinterpreters of science" whose slogan is, "If you can't count it, it doesn't count." According to Hutchins, "the most striking feature of social science today is the total absence of theory. Its greatest modern achievement is

---

[18]Sartori, "Concept Misformation," p. 1033.

[19]Ibid.

[20]These confusions are rife in all branches of political science. Comparative politics is relatively well off in this regard.

[21]Holton and Roller, *Foundations of Modern Physical Science,* p. 229.

[22]Feynman, *The Character of Physical Law,* p. 164.

the public opinion poll. Social scientists can count, but cannot comprehend."[23]

Despite the fact that quantification does not equate with science, it is nonetheless an important part of the theory building process. Mathematics permits science to treat numerous variables in complex settings with precision and parsimony.[24] It is written "that the work of the physical scientist is based on a faith as ancient as it is astonishing, namely, that the phenomena of nature which we observe are describable in terms of axioms or postulates that are mathematical, and that such observations are explained when we find mathematical expressions relating them."[25] Quantification and research techniques, however, are reliant upon problemation, conceptualization, and classification. Skill in manipulating data is no substitute for selecting key issues and developing sound conceptual frameworks. In an extensive discussion of this point, Sartori writes "that long before having data which can speak for themselves the fundamental articulation of language and of thinking is obtained logically—by cumulative conceptual refinement and chains of coordinated definitions—not by measurement. Measurement of what? We cannot measure unless we know first what it is that we are measuring. Nor can the degrees of something tell us what a thing is."[26]

In comparative political analysis there has been a proclivity either to ignore methodology and theory building or to leap over conceptual and theoretical terrain directly into statistical and quantitative techniques. The occupants of these two polar positions then intellectually snipe at one another using as ammunition such terms as "unscientific" and "traditional" as opposed to "scientism" and "faddism." Caught in the crossfire are those thinkers who toil away in the area of concept formation, taxonomy construction, and middle range generalization. Besides their exposed positions within the more general debate, they often compete with one another over concepts and approaches. Under these circumstances, it is not surprising that theoretical progress has been slow.

Reinforcing the difficulties outlined above is, of course, the difficulty of the subject matter under investigation. As we indicated in the opening chapter of this study, the infinite possibilities that inhere in the nature of social behavior and the constantly changing state of political

---

[23]Robert M. Hutchins et al., *Science, Scientists, and Politics* (Santa Barbara, Calif.: Center for the Study of Democratic Institutions, 1963), p. 3.

[24]See Richard Feynman's discussion entitled "The Relation of Mathematics to Physics" in Feynman, *The Character of Physical Law,* pp. 35–58.

[25]Holton and Roller, *Foundations of Modern Physical Science,* p. 223.

[26]Sartori, "Concept Misformation," p. 1038.

processes make generalization, explanation, and prediction difficult and hazardous. J. Robert Oppenheimer writes that "in politics there is little that can correspond to the scientist's repetition of an experiment. An experiment that fails in its purpose may be as good or better than one that succeeds, because it may well be more instructive. A political decision cannot be taken twice. All the factors that are relevant to it will conjoin only once."[27] Oppenheimer goes on, however, to argue that key elements in scientific inquiry are important and helpful to the study of society and politics. Careful observation, logical analysis, organization, consistency, objectivity, rigor, and generalization are certainly within the bounds of possibility for comparative political study. Rigorous methodology and systematic inquiry, however, do not guarantee significant results. The changing complexities of man and politics remain difficult to understand and explain.

Despite all the limitations, difficulties, and impediments to theorizing in the study of comparative politics, a number of notable and successful strides have been taken forward. In the first instance, recent years have witnessed a mellowing of the dogmatism that has tended to dominate social science over the last two decades during the heyday of behavioralism. The issue of scientific discovery and theory building remains of central concern, but differing methods and approaches to this process are more readily recognized and tolerated. It is increasingly admitted, for example, that the inductive-deductive controversy fails to recognize the intimate and intricate manner in which both intellectual operations are interrelated. Although some theorists may prefer to concentrate on more inductive methodology, others seek to focus their attention upon the deductive dimensions of theoretical research. The Newton-Duhem controversy outlined above, which has had its counterpart in the social sciences, has been replaced increasingly by the more accurate realization that both methods are crucial.

Scientists such as Henri Poincare, W. I. B. Beveridge, W. D. Bancroft, and Charles Nicolle classify scientists into two broad types according to which method of thinking they emphasize.[28] Beveridge writes that "at one extreme is the speculative worker whose method is to try to arrive at the solution by use of imagination and intuition and then test his hypothesis by experiment of observation. The other extreme is the

---

[27] J. Robert Oppenheimer, *The Open Mind* (New York: Simon and Schuster, 1955), pp. 109–10.

[28] Poincare was a French mathematician, Beveridge a British animal pathologist, Bancroft an American chemist, and Nicolle a French biologist. Poincare described scientists who stress deductive methods as "intuitive" and those who proceeded inductively as "logical." Bancroft used the terms "guessers" and "accumulators." Beveridge preferred the terminology "speculative" and "systematic." See W. I. B. Beveridge, *The Art of Scientific Investigation* (New York: Norton, 1957), pp. 139–59.

systematic worker who progresses slowly by carefully reasoned stages and who collects most of the data before arriving at the solution."[29] In comparative political analysis, one must recognize not only that both intellectual procedures are intertwined but also that scholars emphasizing either method are essential to the advance of the discipline.

A second and related strength in the development of comparative political inquiry is the deepening and continuing commitment to an understanding and refinement of the intellectual procedures and methodological processes by which comparative thinkers go about their work.[30] An important part of this process is the drive to be more explicit, rigorous, systematic, and precise in the observation and explanation of political relations. By the thoughtful refining and reshaping of the intellectual tools that are necessary to the analytic tasks at hand, scholars of comparative politics are better preparing themselves for their work. Social scientists in general are now taking a more informed and realistic look at the methodology of the physical sciences. Both the initial euphoria with which a number of political scholars embraced the style of physical science and the contempt with which others dismissed the relevance of such science to their own investigations have now begun to disappear. The result is more cooperation and communication between and among scientists of different fields. The study of physics no less than politics has undergone a number of searching periods of assessment and reassessment concerning theory and method.[31] The core

---

[29]Ibid., p. 159.

[30]The recent and burgeoning literature on the role of theory and method in comparative political study attests to this point. Particularly distinguished examples include books such as Richard L. Merritt's *Systematic Approaches to Comparative Politics* (Chicago: Rand McNally, 1970), and articles such as Philip H. Melanson and Lauriston R. King, "Theory in Comparative Politics: A Critical Appraisal," *Comparative Political Studies* 4 (July 1971): 205–31. Melanson and King write that "inquiry guided by some degree of scientific consciousness, as well as some appreciation for its philosophical foundations, will enhance the reliability of political knowledge because the properties of theory have a stronger capacity to define circumstances where predictions are possible." (p. 225).

[31]With the development of the theory of relativity, the field of physics was shaken into a fundamental reassessment of theory and method. The key studies that formed the early core of this theoretical examination were P. W. Bridgman's two books, *The Logic of Modern Physics* (New York: Macmillan, 1932) and *The Nature of Physical Science* (Princeton: Princeton University Press, 1936). Bridgman's reformulations of scientific method carried a heavy empirical tinge and were labelled "operationalism." Bridgman himself defines "operationalism" in a way that clearly reflects the concern felt within the physical sciences for sensitizing themselves to their theory building procedures. In *The Nature of Physical Theory,* Bridgman defines operationalism as "the technique by which analysis makes itself conscious of what it actually does in any situation . . ." (p. 7). Among the studies on the methodology of scientific investigation and theory building that developed in reaction to Bridgman's works are the following: Henry Margenau, *The Nature of Physical Reality,* 1st ed. (New York: McGraw-Hill, 1950); and A. Cornelius Benjamin, *Operationism* (Springfield, Ill.: Thomas, 1955).

of an interest in the philosophy of science and empirical theory that now exists in the field of comparative political study represents a strong commitment to the systematic quest for political knowledge.

The art of theory building is now recognized as an integrated process that includes problemation, observation, conceptualization, and classification as essential ingredients. In all of the approaches analyzed in this volume vigorous activity continues at these levels. Innovative and systematic conceptual frameworks and classificatory schemes by scholars such as Gabriel A. Almond, David E. Apter, Leonard Binder, Harry Eckstein, Alfred Diamant, and Samuel P. Huntington have had a positive impact upon the study of comparative politics and, indeed, upon the study of political science. Scholars increasingly travel abroad to do research that is infused and strengthened by a concern for theory. As they continually return with revised conceptualizations and classifications, with challenging hypotheses and theoretical statements, and with fresh data and new questions, comparative political analysis will open new doors to discovery and explanation.

At the same time that theoretical approaches are constantly being sharpened and remolded, they are also being applied more discriminately and rigorously. Comparative scholars choose their approaches more and more on the basis of: (1) a sound understanding of the inherent strengths and weaknesses of each approach; and (2) the relevance of the approach to the major problem under investigation. Theoretical approaches are also being fused and integrated in a consistent and systematic manner. In this way, they complement and strengthen one another, thereby broadening their applicability while increasing their explanatory power.

In a recent reassessment of the state of theory in political science, Karl W. Deutsch summarizes the situation well when he concludes that "much has been learned but our main tasks still are waiting to be done."[32] In the area of comparative politics, more has recently been learned than in any other field of political study. Ironically, comparative analysis is where most tasks remain to be done. The further one travels along the road to theory, the more aware one is of the vast distances that lie ahead.

---

[32]Karl W. Deutsch, "On Political Theory and Political Action," *The American Political Science Review* 55 (March 1971): 24.

Selected Bibliography

Chapter I: The Systematic Study of Comparative Politics

The Study of Comparative Politics

Almond, Gabriel A. and G. Bingham Powell, Jr., *Comparative Politics: A Developmental Approach.* Boston: Little, Brown, 1966.

Beer, Samuel H. and Adam B. Ulam. *Patterns of Government: The Major Political Systems of Europe.* 3rd ed. New York: Random House, 1973.

Blondel, Jean. *An Introduction to Comparative Government.* New York: Praeger, 1969.

Brown, Bernard E. *New Directions in Comparative Politics.* London: Asia Publishing House, 1962.

Carter, Gwendolyn M. and John H. Herz. *Major Foreign Powers.* 5th ed. New York: Harcourt, Brace and World, 1967.

Dragnich, Alex N. *Major European Governments.* Rev. ed. Homewood, Illinois: Dorsey Press, 1966.

Eckstein, Harry. "A Perspective on Comparative Politics, Past and Present," in Harry Eckstein and David Apter, eds., *Comparative Politics: A Reader.* New York: Free Press, 1963, pp. 3–32.

Finer, Herman. *The Major Governments of Modern Europe.* Evanston, Ill.: Row, Peterson, 1962.

———. *The Theory and Practice of Modern Government.* 4th ed. London: Methuen, 1961.

Friedrich, Carl J. *Constitutional Government and Democracy.* 4th ed. Waltham, Mass.: Blaisdell, 1968.

Groth, Alexander J. *Comparative Politics: A Distributive Approach.* New York: Macmillan, 1971.

Hawley, Claud E. and Lewis A. Dexter. "Research and Methodology: Recent Political Science Research in American Universities." *American Political Science Review* 46 (1952):470–85.

Heckscher, Gunnar. *The Study of Comparative Government and Politics.* New York: Macmillan, 1957.

Hudson, Bradford, and Howard E. Page. "The Behavioral Sciences: Challenge and Partial Response." *American Behavioral Scientist* 6 (1963).

Jensen, Richard. "History and the Political Scientist," in Seymour Martin Lipset, ed., *Politics and the Social Sciences.* New York: Oxford University Press, 1969, pp. 1–28.

LaPalombara, Joseph. "Macrotheories and Microapplications in Comparative Politics: A Widening Chasm." *Comparative Politics* 1 (1968):52–78.

Lasswell, Harold D. "The Future of the Comparative Method." *Comparative Politics* 1 (1968):3–18.

Loewenstein, Karl. "Report on the Research Panel on Comparative Government." *American Political Science Review* 38 (1944):540–8.

MacKenzie, W. J. M. *Politics and Social Science.* Baltimore: Penguin Books, 1967.

Macridis, Roy C. "Comparative Politics and the Study of Government: The Search for Focus." *Comparative Politics* 1 (1968):79–90.

———. *The Study of Comparative Government.* Garden City, New York: Doubleday, 1955.

Macridis, Roy C. and Robert E. Ward, eds. *Modern Political Systems: Europe.* 3rd ed. Englewood Cliffs, N.J.: Prentice-Hall, 1972.

Merritt, Richard L. and Stein Rokkan, eds. *Comparing Nations: The Use of Quantitative Data in Cross-National Research.* New Haven, Conn.: Yale University Press, 1966.

Neumann, Robert. *European and Comparative Government.* 3rd ed. New York: McGraw-Hill, 1960.

Rustow, Dankwart. "Modernization and Comparative Politics: Prospects in Research and Theory." *Comparative Politics* 1 (1968):37–51.

Scarrow, Howard A. *Comparative Political Analysis: An Introduction.* New York: Harper and Row, 1969.

Somit, Albert and Joseph Tanenhaus. *American Political Science: A Profile of a Discipline.* New York: Atherton Press, 1964.

Wilson, Woodrow. *The State: Elements of Historical and Practical Politics.* Boston: C. Heath, 1889.

Wolin, Sheldon S. "Political Theory as a Vocation." *American Political Science Review* 63 (1969):1062–82.

Theory and Theory Building

Beveridge, W. I. B. *The Art of Scientific Investigation.* New York: Norton, 1957.

Blalock, Hubert M., Jr. *Theory Construction: From Verbal to Mathematical Formulations.* Englewood Cliffs, N.J.: Prentice-Hall, 1969.

Blalock, Hubert M. and Ann B. Blalock, eds. *Methodology in Social Research.* New York: McGraw-Hill, 1968.

Bondi, H. *Assumption and Myth in Physical Theory.* Cambridge: University Press, 1967.

Bowen, Don R. *Political Behavior of the American Public.* Columbus, Ohio: Merrill, 1968.

Bridgman, P. W. *The Logic of Modern Physics.* New York: Macmillan, 1932.

———. *The Nature of Physical Science.* Princeton: Princeton University Press, 1936.

Brodbeck, May. "Models, Meaning, and Theories," in Llewellyn Gross, ed., *Symposium on Sociological Theory.* New York: Harper and Row, 1959.

Campbell, Norman R. "The Structure of Theories," in Herbert Feigl and May Brodbeck, eds., *Readings in the Philosophy of Science.* New York: Appleton-Century-Crofts, 1953, pp. 288–308.

Catlin, George E. G. *The Science and Method of Politics.* New York: Knopf, 1927.

———. *A Study of the Principles of Politics.* New York: Macmillan, 1930.

Caws, Peter. *The Philosophy of Science: A Systematic Account.* Princeton: Van Nostrand, 1965.

Charlesworth, James C., ed. *Contemporary Political Analysis.* New York: Free Press, 1967.

Conant, James B. *Science and Common Sense.* New Haven: Yale University Press, 1951.

Deutsch, Karl W. "On Political Theory and Political Action." *American Political Science Review* 55 (1971):11–27.

Easton, David. "The Current Meaning of 'Behavioralism,' " in James C. Charlesworth, ed., *Contemporary Political Analysis.* New York: Free Press, 1967, pp. 11–31.

———. "The New Revolution in Political Science." *American Political Science Review* 63 (1969):1052–61.

———. *The Political System.* New York: Knopf, 1953.

Easton, David, ed. *Varieties of Political Theory.* Englewood Cliffs, N.J.: Prentice-Hall, 1966.

Eckstein, Harry. "Authority Relations and Governmental Performance: A Theoretical Framework." *Comparative Political Studies* 2 (1969):269–325.

Eldersveld, Samuel et al. "Research in Political Behavior," in S. Sidney Ulmer, ed., *Introductory Readings in Political Behavior.* Chicago: Rand McNally, 1961.

Eulau, Heinz. *The Behavioral Persuasion in Politics.* New York: Random House, 1963.

Feynman, Richard. *The Character of Physical Law.* Cambridge, Mass.: M.I.T. Press, 1965.

Frank, Philipp. *Philosophy of Science.* Englewood Cliffs, N.J.: Prentice-Hall, 1957.

Glaser, Barney G. and Anselm L. Strauss. *The Discovery of Grounded Theory.* Chicago: Aldine, 1967.

Golembiewski, Robert T., William A. Welsh and William J. Crotty. *A Methodological Primer for Political Science.* Chicago: Rand McNally, 1969.

Graham, George. *Methodological Foundations for Political Analysis.* Waltham, Mass.: Xerox, 1971.

Grayson-Smith, Hugh. *The Changing Concepts of Science.* Englewood Cliffs, N.J.: Prentice-Hall, 1967.

Gregor, A. James. *An Introduction to Metapolitics: A Brief Inquiry into the Conceptual Language of Political Science.* New York: Free Press, 1971.

Gunnell, John G. "Deduction, Explanation, and Social Scientific Inquiry." *American Political Science Review* 63 (1969):1233–46.

Hadamard, Jacques. *The Psychology of Invention in the Mathematical Field.* Princeton: Princeton University Press, 1945.

Hanson, Norwood R. *Patterns of Discovery.* Cambridge: University Press, 1965.

Hempel, Carl G. *Aspects of Scientific Explanation.* New York: Free Press, 1965.

Holt, Robert T. and John E. Turner, eds. *The Methodology of Comparative Research.* New York: Free Press, 1970.

Holton, Gerald and Duane H. D. Roller. *Foundations of Modern Physical Science.* Reading, Mass.: Addison-Wesley, 1958.

Kerlinger, Fred N. *Foundations of Behavioral Research: Educational and Psychological Inquiry.* New York: Holt, Rinehart and Winston, 1964.

Kuhn, Thomas. *The Structure of Scientific Revolutions.* Chicago: University of Chicago Press, 1962.

Lijphart, Arend. "Comparative Politics and the Comparative Method." *American Political Science Review* 65 (1971):682–93.

Mayer, Lawrence C. *Comparative Political Inquiry: A Methodological Survey.* Homewood, Ill.: Dorsey Press, 1972.

Meehan, Eugene. *The Theory and Method of Political Analysis.* Homewood, Ill.: Dorsey Press, 1965.

Melanson, Philip H. and Lauriston R. King. "Theory in Comparative Politics: A Critical Appraisal." *Comparative Political Studies* 4 (1971):205–31.

Merrill, Sally A. "On the Logic of Comparative Analysis." *Comparative Political Studies* 3 (1971):489–500.

Merritt, Richard L. *Systematic Approaches to Comparative Politics.* Chicago: Rand McNally, 1970.

Moore, Barrington. *Political Power and Social Theory.* New York: Harper Torchbook, 1962.

Popper, Sir Karl R. *The Logic of Scientific Inquiry.* New York: Harper Torchbook, 1965.

Przeworski, Adam and Henry Teune. *The Logic of Comparative Social Inquiry.* New York: John Wiley Interscience, 1970.

Rudner, Richard S. *Philosophy of Social Science.* Englewood Cliffs, N.J.: Prentice-Hall, 1966.

Ryan, Alan. *The Philosophy of the Social Sciences.* New York: Pantheon Books, 1970.

Saidla, Leo E. and Warren E. Gibbs, eds. *Science and the Scientific Mind.* New York: McGraw-Hill, 1930.

Sartori, Giovanni. "Concept Misformation in Comparative Politics." *The American Political Science Review* 64 (1970):1033–53.

Stinchcombe, Arthur L. *Constructing Social Theories.* New York: Harcourt, Brace and World, 1968.

Thomson, Sir George. *The Inspiration of Science.* London: Oxford University Press, 1961.

Thorson, Thomas Landon. *Biopolitics.* New York: Holt, Rinehart and Winston, 1970.

Verba, Sidney. "Some Dilemmas in Comparative Research." *World Politics* 20 (1967): 111–27.

Willer, David and Murray Webster, Jr. "Theoretical Concepts and Observables." *American Sociological Review* 35 (1970):748–57.

Young, Oran. *Systems of Political Science,* Englewood Cliffs, N.J.: Prentice-Hall, 1968.

Chapter II: Modernization and Political Development

Almond, Gabriel, and James S. Coleman, eds. *The Politics of Developing Areas.* Princeton: Princeton University Press, 1960.

Almond Gabriel, and G. Bingham Powell, Jr., *Comparative Politics: A Developmental Approach.* Boston: Little, Brown, 1966.

Apter, David E. *The Politics of Modernization.* Chicago: University of Chicago Press, 1965.

Arora, Satish. "Pre-Empted Future? Notes on Theories of Political Development." *Behavioral Sciences and Community Development* (India) 2 (1968): pp. 85–120.

Bendix, Rinehard. "Tradition and Modernity Reconsidered," *Comparative Studies in History and Society* 9 (1967):294–346.

Binder, Leonard. *Iran: Political Development in a Changing Society.* (Berkeley: University of California Press, 1962).

Binder, Leonard, James S. Coleman, Joseph LaPalombara, Lucian W. Pye, Sidney Verba, and Myron Weiner. *Crises and Sequences in Political Development.* Princeton: Princeton University Press, 1971.

Black, C. E. *The Dynamics of Modernization.* New York: Harper and Row, 1966.

Coleman, James S., ed. *Education and Political Development.* Princeton: Princeton University Press, 1965.

Diamant, Alfred. "Political Development: Approaches to Theory and Strategy," in John Montgomery and William Siffin, eds. *Approaches to Development: Politics, Administration, and Change.* New York: McGraw-Hill, 1966, pp. 14–47.

———. "The Nature of Political Development," in Jason L. Finkle and Richard W. Gable, eds. *Political Development and Social Change.* 1st ed. New York: John Wiley and Sons, 1966, pp. 91–96.

Deutsch, Karl. "Social Mobilization and Political Development." *American Political Science Review* 55 (1961): 493–511.

Eisenstadt, S. N. *Modernization: Protest and Change,* Englewood Cliffs, N.J.: Prentice-Hall, 1966.

Field, G. Lowell. *Comparative Political Development: The Precedent of the West.* Ithaca: Cornell University Press, 1967.

Finkle, Jason L. and Richard W. Gable, eds. *Political Development and Social Change.* 2nd ed. New York: John Wiley and Sons, 1971.

Frank, A. G. *Latin America: Underdevelopment or Revolution.* New York: Monthly Review Press, 1969.

Geertz, Clifford, ed. *Old Societies and New States.* New York: Free Press, 1963.

Halpern, Manfred. "The Rate and Costs of Political Development." *Annals* 358 (1965): 20–28.

Holt, Robert T. and John E. Turner, *The Political Basis of Economic Development.* Princeton: Van Nostrand, 1966.

Horowitz, Irving Louis. *Three Worlds of Development.* New York: Oxford University Press, 1966.

Huntington, Samuel P. "The Change to Change: Modernization, Development, and Politics." *Comparative Politics* 3 (1971):283–322.

———. *Political Order in Changing Societies,* New Haven: Yale University Press, 1968.

Ilchman, Warren. *The Political Economy of Change.* Berkeley: University of California Press, 1970.

Inkeles, Alex. "Participant Citizenship in Six Developing Countries." *American Political Science Review* 63 (1969):1120–41.

Kautsky, John H. *The Political Consequences of Modernization.* New York: John Wiley and Sons, 1972.

LaPalombara, Joseph, ed. *Bureaucracy and Political Development.* Princeton: Princeton University Press, 1963.

LaPalombara, Joseph, and Myron Weiner, eds. *Political Parties and Political Development.* Princeton: Princeton University Press, 1966.

Lerner, Daniel. *The Passing of Traditional Society: Modernizing the Middle East.* New York: Free Press, 1958.

Levy, Marion J., Jr. *Modernization and the Structure of Societies.* Princeton: Princeton University Press, 1966.

Montgomery, John, and William Siffin, eds. *Approaches to Development: Politics, Administration, and Change.* New York: McGraw-Hill, 1966.

Neubauer, Deane. "Some Conditions of Democracy." *American Political Science Review* 61 (1967):1002–9.

Nie, Norman H., G. Bingham Powell, Jr., and Kenneth Prewitt. "Social Structure and Political Participation: Developmental Relationships." *American Political Science Review* 63 (1969): 361–78, 63 (September 1969):808–32.

Nisbet, Robert A. *Social Change and History.* New York: Oxford University Press, 1969.

Organski, A. F. K. *The Stages of Political Development.* New York: Knopf, 1965.

Pye, Lucian W. *Aspects of Political Development.* Boston: Little, Brown, 1966.

Pye, Lucian W. *Politics, Personality and Nation-Building: Burma's Search for Identity.* New Haven: Yale University Press, 1962.

Pye, Lucian W., ed. *Communications and Political Development.* Princeton: Princeton University Press, 1963.

Pye, Lucian W. and Sidney Verba, eds. *Political Culture and Political Development.* Princeton: Princeton University Press, 1965.

Riggs, Fred W. *Administration in Developing Countries: The Theory of Prismatic Society.* Boston: Houghton Mifflin, 1964.

———. "The Dialectics of Development Conflict." *Comparative Political Studies* 1 (1968):197–226.

Rostow, Walt W. *Politics and the Stages of Growth.* Cambridge: Cambridge University Press, 1971.

Rudolph, Lloyd and Susanne. *The Modernity of Tradition: Political Development in India.* Chicago: University of Chicago Press, 1967.

Rustow, Dankwart A. *A World of Nations: Problems of Political Modernization.* Washington: Brookings Institution, 1967.

Sherrill, Kenneth. "The Attitudes of Modernity." *Comparative Politics* 1 (1969): 184–210.

Shils, Edward. *Political Development in the New States.* The Hague: Mouton, 1966.

Ward, Robert E. and Dankwart A. Rustow, eds. *Political Modernization in Japan and Turkey.* Princeton: Princeton University Press, 1964.

Weiner, Myron. "Political Integration and Political Development." *Annals* 358 (1963):52–64.

Weiner, Myron, ed. *Modernization: The Dynamics of Growth.* New York: Basic Books, 1966.

Welch, Claude E., Jr., ed. *Political Modernization.* 2nd ed. Belmont, Calif.: Wadsworth, 1971.

Wriggins, W. Howard. *The Ruler's Imperative: Strategies for Political Survival in Asia and Africa.* New York: Columbia University Press, 1969.

Chapter III: Political Culture and Socialization

Almond, Gabriel, and Sidney Verba. *The Civic Culture.* Princeton: Princeton University Press, 1963.

Banfield, Edward C. *The Moral Basis of a Backward Society.* Glencoe, Ill.: Free Press, 1958.

Dawson, Richard E. and Kenneth Prewitt. *Political Socialization.* Boston: Little, Brown, 1969.

Dennis, Jack. "Major Problems of Political Socialization Research." *Midwest Journal of Political Science* 12 (1968):85–114.

Easton, David, and Jack Dennis. *Children in the Political System: Origins of Political Legitimacy.* New York: McGraw-Hill, 1969.

Fagen, Richard. *The Transformation of Political Culture in Cuba.* Stanford: Stanford University Press, 1969.

Greenstein, Fred. *Children and Politics.* New Haven: Yale University Press, 1965.

———. "Political Socialization," *The International Encyclopedia of the Social Sciences.* New York: Macmillan and Free Press, 1968. Vol. 14, pp. 551–55.

Hardgrave, Robert L., Jr. *The Nadars of Tamilnad: The Political Culture of a Community in Change.* Berkeley: University of California Press, 1969.

Hess, Robert D., and Judith V. Torney. *The Development of Political Attitudes in Children.* Chicago: Aldine, 1967.

Hirsch, Herbert. *Poverty and Politicization: Political Socialization in an American Sub-Culture.* New York: Free Press, 1971.

Hyman, Herbert. *Political Socialization: A Study in the Psychology of Political Behavior,* New York: Free Press, 1959.

Jaros, Dean, Herbert Hirsch, and Frederic J. Fleron, Jr., "The Malevolent Leader: Political Socialization in an American Sub-Culture." *American Political Science Review* 62 (1968):564–75.

Lane, Robert. *Political Ideology.* New York: Free Press, 1962.

Langton, Kenneth P. *Political Socialization.* New York: Oxford University Press, 1969.

Leighton, Alexander. *My Name is Legion: Foundations for a Theory of Man in Relation to Culture.* New York: Basic Books, 1959.

LeVine, Robert. "Political Socialization and Culture Change," in Clifford Geertz, ed., *Old Societies and New States.* New York: Free Press, 1963, pp. 280–303.

Pye, Lucian. "Political Culture," in *The International Encyclopedia of the Social Sciences.* New York: Macmillan and Free Press, 1968. Vol. 12, pp. 218–25.

———. *Politics, Personality, and Nation-Building: Burma's Search for Identity.* New Haven: Yale University Press, 1962.

———. *The Spirit of Chinese Politics: A Psychocultural Study of the Authority Crisis in Political Development.* Cambridge: M.I.T. Press, 1968.

Pye, Lucian, and Sidney Verba, eds. *Political Culture and Political Development.* Princeton: Princeton University Press, 1965.

Scott, James C. *Political Ideology in Malaysia: Reality and the Beliefs of an Elite.* New Haven: Yale University Press, 1968.

Sigel, Roberta S., "Assumptions About the Learning of Political Values." *Annals* 361 (1965): pp. 1–9.

Sigel, Roberta S., ed. *Learning About Politics.* New York: Random House, 1970.

Soloman, Richard H. *Mao's Revolution and The Chinese Political Culture.* Berkeley: University of California Press, 1971.

Chapter IV: Group Politics

Almond, Gabriel A. "A Comparative Study of Interest Groups and the Political Process." *American Political Science Review* 52 (1958):270–82.

——— and G. Bingham Powell. *Comparative Politics: A Developmental Approach.* Boston and Toronto: Little, Brown, 1966, pp. 73–97.

Astiz, Carlos A. *Pressure Groups and Power Elites in Peruvian Politics.* Ithaca and London: Cornell University Press, 1969.

Beer, Samuel H. *British Politics in a Collectivist Age.* New York: Knopf, 1966.

Bentley, Arthur F. *The Process of Government.* Cambridge, Mass.: Belknap Press of Harvard University Press, 1967.

Bill, James A. *The Politics of Iran: Groups, Classes, and Modernization.* Columbus, Ohio: Merrill, 1972.

Blanksten, George I. "Political Groups in Latin America." *American Political Science Review* 53 (1959):106–27.

Blondel, Jean. *An Introduction to Comparative Government.* New York: Praeger, 1969, pp. 59–97.

Brown, Bernard E. "Pressure Groups in the Fifth Republic." *Journal of Politics* 25 (1963):509–25.

Dowling, R. E. "Pressure Group Theory: Its Methodological Range." *American Political Science Review* 54 (1960):944–54.

Eckstein, Harry. "Group Theory and the Comparative Study of Pressure Groups," in Harry Eckstein and David E. Apter, eds., *Comparative Politics: A Reader.* New York: Free Press of Glencoe, 1963, pp. 389–97.

Ehrmann, Henry W., ed. *Interest Groups on Four Continents.* Pittsburgh: University of Pittsburgh Press, 1958.

Eldersveld, Samuel J. "American Interest Groups: A Survey of Research and Some Implications for Theory and Method," in Henry W. Ehrmann, ed., *Interest Groups on Four Continents.* Pittsburgh: University of Pittsburgh Press, 1958, pp. 173–96.

Finer, Samuel E. *Anonymous Empire: A Study of the Lobby in Great Britain.* London: Pall Mall, 1966.

Frohlich, Norman, Joe A. Oppenheimer and Oran R. Young. *Political Leadership and Collective Goods.* Princeton: Princeton University Press, 1971.

Golembiewski, Robert T. " 'The Group Basis of Politics': Notes on Analysis and Development." *American Political Science Review* 54 (1960):962–71.

Golembiewski, Robert T., William A. Welsh and William J. Crotty. *A Methodological Primer for Political Scientists.* Chicago: Rand McNally, 1969, pp. 121–48.

Hagan, Charles B. "The Group in a Political Science," in Roland Young, ed., *Approaches to the Study of Politics.* Evanston, Ill.: Northwestern University Press, 1958, pp. 38–51.

Hale, Myron Q. "The Cosmology of Arthur F. Bentley." *American Political Science Review* 54 (1960):955–61.

Hare, A. Paul, Edgar F. Borgatta and Robert F. Bales, eds. *Small Groups: Studies in Social Interaction.* Rev. ed. New York: Knopf, 1965.

Kessel, John H., George F. Cole and Robert G. Seddig. *Micropolitics: Individual and Group Level Concepts.* New York: Holt, Rinehart and Winston, 1970, pp. 207–324.

LaPalombara, Joseph. *Interest Groups in Italian Politics.* Princeton: Princeton University Press, 1964.

———. "The Utility and Limitations of Interest Group Theory in Non-American Field Situations." *The Journal of Politics* 22 (1960):29–49.

Latham, Earl. *The Group Basis of Politics.* Ithaca, N.Y.: Cornell University Press, 1952.

MacKenzie, W. J. M. "Pressure Groups: The Conceptual Framework." *Political Studies* 3 (1955):247–55.

Macridis, Roy C. "Interest Groups in Comparative Analysis." *The Journal of Politics* 23 (1961):25–45.

Odegard, Peter H. "A Group Basis of Politics: A New Name for an Old Myth." *Western Political Quarterly* 11 (1958):689–702.

Olson, Mancur. *The Logic of Collective Action: Public Goods and the Theory of Groups.* New York: Schocken, 1968.

Riggs, Fred W. "The Theory of Developing Polities." *World Politics* 16 (1963):-147–71.

Rothman, Stanley. "Systematic Political Theory: Observations on the Group Approach." *American Political Science Review* 54 (1960):15–33.

Schmitter, Philippe C. *Interest Conflict and Political Change in Brazil.* Stanford, Calif.: Stanford University Press, 1971.

Swartz, Marc J., ed. *Local-Level Politics: Social and Cultural Perspectives.* Chicago: Aldine, 1968.

Truman, David B. *The Governmental Process.* New York: Knopf, 1951.

Verba, Sidney. *Small Groups and Political Behavior.* Princeton: Princeton University Press, 1961.

Wahlke, John C., William Buchanan, Heinz Eulau and LeRoy C. Ferguson. "American State Legislators' Role Orientations Toward Pressure Groups." *Journal of Politics* 22 (1960):203–27.

Weiner, Myron. *The Politics of Scarcity: Public Pressures and Political Response in India.* Chicago: University of Chicago Press, 1962.

Wooton, Graham. *Interest-Groups.* Englewood Cliffs, N.J.: Prentice-Hall, 1970.

Young, Oran R. *Systems of Political Science.* Englewood Cliffs, N.J.: Prentice-Hall, 1968, pp. 79–92.

Zeigler, Harmon. *Interest Groups in American Society.* Englewood Cliffs, N.J.: Prentice-Hall, 1964.

Chapter V: The Political Elite Approach

Bachrach, Peter. *The Theory of Democratic Elitism: A Critique.* Boston: Little, Brown, 1967.

Bachrach, Peter and Morton S. Baratz. "Decisions and Nondecisions: An Analytical Framework." *American Political Science Review* 57 (1963):632–42.

———. *Power and Poverty: Theory and Practice.* Oxford: Oxford University Press, 1970.

———. "Two Faces of Power." *American Political Science Review* 56 (1963): 947–52.

Beck, Carl and J. Thomas McKechnie. *Political Elites: A Select Computerized Bibliography.* Cambridge: M.I.T. Press, 1968.

Bennett, Gordon. "Chinese Elite Studies: Some Suggestions for the 1970s." Unpublished manuscript, December 1970.

Bottomore, T. B. *Elites and Society.* New York: Basic Books, 1964.

Dahl, Robert. "A Critique of the Ruling Elite Model." *American Political Science Review* 52 (1958):463–69.

———. *Who Governs?* New Haven: Yale University Press, 1961.

Domhoff, G. William. *Who Rules America?* Englewood Cliffs, N.J.: Prentice-Hall, 1967.

Domhoff, G. William and Hoyt B. Ballard, eds. *C. Wright Mills and The Power Elite.* Boston: Beacon Press, 1968.

Edinger, Lewis J. and Donald D. Searing. "Social Background in Elite Analysis: A Methodological Inquiry." *American Political Science Review* 61 (1967):428–45.

Frey, Frederick W. "Comment: On Issues and Nonissues in the Study of Power." *American Political Science Review* 65 (1971):1081–1101.

———. "The Determination and Location of Elites: A Critical Analysis." Paper prepared for delivery at the Sixty-sixth Annual Meeting of the American Political Science Association, Los Angeles, California, September 8–12, 1970.

———. *The Turkish Political Elite.* Cambridge: M.I.T. Press, 1965.

Golembiewski, Robert T., William A. Welsh and William J. Crotty. *A Methodological Primer for Political Scientists.* Chicago: Rand McNally, 1969, pp. 149–90.

Hunt, William H., Wilder W. Crane and John C. Wahlke. "Interviewing Political Elites in Cross-Cultural Comparative Research." *American Journal of Sociology* 70 (1964):59–68.

Hunter, Floyd. *Community Power Structure.* Chapel Hill: University of North Carolina Press, 1953.

Kautsky, John H. "Revolutionary and Managerial Elites in Modernizing Regimes." *Comparative Politics* 1 (1969):441–67.

Keller, Suzanne. *Beyond the Ruling Class: Strategic Elites in Modern Society.* New York: Random House, 1963.

Kornhauser, William. *The Politics of Mass Society.* New York: Free Press, 1959.

Lasswell, Harold D. *Politics: Who Gets What, When, How.* Cleveland and New York: Meridian Books, World Publishing Co., 1958.

———. *World Politics and Personal Insecurity.* 1st paperback ed. New York: Free Press, 1965.

Lasswell, Harold D. and Abraham Kaplan. *Power and Society: A Framework for Political Inquiry.* New Haven: Yale University Press, 1950.

Lasswell, Harold D. and Daniel Lerner, eds. *World Revolutionary Elites.* Cambridge: M.I.T. Press, 1965.

Lasswell, Harold D., Daniel Lerner and C. Easton Rothwell. *The Comparative Study of Elites.* Stanford: Stanford University Press, 1952.

Lipset, Seymour M. and Aldo Solari, eds. *Elites in Latin America.* New York: Oxford University Press, 1967.

Lopreato, Joseph. *Vilfredo Pareto.* New York: Crowell, 1965.

Meisel, James H. *The Myth of the Ruling Class.* Ann Arbor: University of Michigan Press, 1958.

Merritt, Richard L. *Systematic Approaches to Comparative Politics.* Chicago: Rand McNally, 1970, pp. 104–39.

Michels, Robert. *Political Parties.* Translated by Eden and Cedar Paul. Glencoe, Ill.: Free Press, 1949.

Miller, Delbert C. *International Community Power Structures.* Bloomington and London: Indiana University Press, 1970.

Mills, C. Wright. *The Power Elite.* New York: Oxford University Press, 1959.

Mosca, Gaetano. *The Ruling Class* [*Elementi di Scienza Politica*]. Translated by Hannah D. Kahn. New York: McGraw-Hill, 1939.

Nadel, S. F. "The Concept of Social Elites." *International Social Science Bulletin* 8 (1956):413–24.

Pareto, Vilfredo. *The Mind and Society* [*Trattato di Sociologia Generale*]. Translated by Andrew Bongiorno and Arthur Livingston. 4 vols. New York: Harcourt, Brace and Co., 1935.

Parry, Geraint. *Political Elites.* New York: Praeger, 1969.

Presthus, Robert. *Men at the Top.* New York: Oxford University Press, 1964.

Quandt, William B. *The Comparative Study of Political Elites.* Sage Professional Paper, Comparative Politics Series. Beverly Hills, Calif.: Sage, 1970.

Rose, Arnold M. *The Power Structure.* New York: Oxford University Press, 1967.

Rustow, Dankwart A. "The Study of Elites: Who's Who, When, and How." *World Politics* 18 (1966):690–717.

Searing, Donald D. "The Comparative Study of Elite Socialization." *Comparative Political Studies* 1 (1969):471–500.

Seligman, Lester G. *Leadership in a New Nation: Political Development in Israel.* New York: Atherton Press, 1964.

Sereno, Renzo. *The Rulers.* New York: Praeger, 1962.

Singer, Marshall R. *The Emerging Elite: A Study of Political Leadership in Ceylon.* Cambridge: M.I.T. Press, 1964.

Walker, Jack L. "A Critique of the Elitist Theory of Democracy." *American Political Science Review* 60 (1966):285–95.

Walton, John. "Discipline, Method, and Community Power: A Note on the Sociology of Knowledge." *American Sociological Review* 31 (1966):684–9.

Wilkinson, Rupert, ed. *Governing Elites: Studies in Training and Selection.* New York: Oxford University Press, 1969.

Wolfinger, Raymond E. "Nondecisions and the Study of Local Politics." *American Political Science Review* 65 (1971):1063–80.

Zonis, Marvin. *The Political Elite of Iran.* Princeton: Princeton University Press, 1971.

Chapter VI: Class Analysis

Abramson, Paul R. "Social Class and Political Change in Western Europe: A Cross-National Longitudinal Analysis." *Comparative Political Studies* 4 (1971): 131–55.

Adams, Richard Newbold. *The Second Sowing: Power and Secondary Development in Latin America.* San Francisco: Chandler, 1967.

Astiz, Carlos A. *Pressure Groups and Power Elites in Peruvian Politics.* Ithaca and London: Cornell University Press, 1969.

Bill, James A. "Class Analysis and the Challenge of Change." *Comparative Political Studies* 2 (1969):389–400.

———. "Class Analysis and the Dialectics of Modernization in the Middle East." *International Journal of Middle East Studies* 3 (1972): 417–34.

———. *The Politics of Iran: Groups, Classes, and Modernization.* Columbus, Ohio: Merrill, 1972.

Bendix, Reinhard and Seymour Martin Lipset, eds. *Class, Status, and Power.* 2nd ed. New York: Free Press, 1966.

Bottomore, T. B. *Classes in Modern Society.* New York: Pantheon Books, 1966.

———. *Elites and Society.* New York: Basic Books, 1964.

Dahrendorf, Ralf. *Class and Class Conflict in Industrial Society.* Rev. Eng. ed. Stanford: Stanford University Press, 1959.

———. "Recent Changes in the Class Structure of European Societies." *Daedalus* 93 (1964):225–70.

Eberhard, Wolfram. "Social Mobility and Stratification in China," in Reinhard Bendix and Seymour M. Lipset, eds. *Class, Status, and Power.* 2nd ed. New York: Free Press, 1966, pp. 171–82.

Fallers, Lloyd A. "Social Stratification and Economic Processes in Africa," in Reinhard Bendix and Seymour M. Lipset, eds., *Class Status, and Power.* 2nd ed. New York: Free Press, 1966, pp. 141–9.

Gordon, Milton M. *Social Class in American Sociology.* New York: McGraw-Hill, 1958.

Grundy, Kenneth W. "The 'Class Struggle' in Africa: An Examination of Conflicting Theories." *Journal of Modern African Studies* 2 (1964):379–93.

Halpern, Manfred. *The Politics of Social Change in the Middle East and North Africa.* Princeton: Princeton University Press, 1963.

Hardgrave, Robert L., Jr. "Caste: Fission and Fusion." *Economic and Political Weekly* (July 1968):1065–70.

Heath, Dwight B. and Richard N. Adams, eds. *Contemporary Cultures and Societies of Latin America.* New York: Random House, 1965, pp. 257–87, 379–404.

Heller, Celia S. *Structured Social Inequality: A Reader in Comparative Social Stratification.* London: Macmillan & Co., 1969, pp. 7–13, 51–62, 105–32, 479–87.

Kahl, Joseph A., ed. *Comparative Perspectives on Stratification.* Boston: Little, Brown, 1968.

Lasswell, Thomas E. *Class and Stratum.* Boston: Houghton Mifflin, 1965.

Leeds, Anthony. "Some Problems in the Analysis of Class and the Social Order," in Anthony Leeds, ed., *Social Structure, Stratification, and Mobility.* Washington, D.C.: Pan American Union, Secretariat of the OAS, 1967.

Lenski, Gerhard. *Power and Privilege: A Theory of Social Stratification.* New York: McGraw-Hill, 1966.

Lipset, Seymour M. and Reinhard Bendix. "Social Status and Social Structure—Parts I and II." *British Journal of Sociology* 2 (June and September, 1951): 150–68, 230–54.

Lipset, Seymour and Hans L. Zetterberg, "A Theory of Social Mobility," in Reinhard Bendix and Seymour M. Lipset, eds., *Class, Status, and Power.* 2nd ed. New York: Free Press, 1966, pp. 561–73.

Lopreato, Joseph. "Class Conflict and Images of Society." *The Journal of Conflict Resolution* 11 (1967) pp. 281–93.

Marshall, T. H., ed. *Class Conflict and Social Stratification.* London: Le Play House Press, 1938.

Mayer, Kurt. "The Theory of Social Classes," in *Transactions of the Third World Congress of Sociology.* London: International Sociological Association, 1956. Vol. II, pp. 321–35.

Moore, Barrington. *Social Origins of Dictatorship and Democracy: Lord and Peasant in the Making of the Modern World.* Boston: Beacon Press, 1966.

Myers, Frank E. "Social Class and Political Change in Western Industrial Systems." *Comparative Politics* 2 (1970):389–412.

Ossowski, Stanislaw. *Class Structure in the Social Consciousness.* Translated by Sheila Patterson. London: Routledge and Kegan Paul, 1963.

Petras, James F. "Class Structure and its Effects on Political Development." *Social Research* 36 (1969):206–30.

Reissman, Leonard. *Class in American Society.* Glencoe, Illinois: Free Press, 1959.

Schumpeter, Joseph. "The Problem of Classes," in Reinhard Bendix and Seymour M. Lipset, eds., *Class, Status, and Power.* 2nd ed. New York: Free Press, 1966, pp. 42–46.

Sklar, Richard L. *Nigerian Political Parties: Power in an Emergent African Nation.* Princeton: Princeton University Press, 1963.

———. "Political Science and National Integration—A Radical Approach." *Journal of Modern African Studies* 5 (1967):1–11.

Tumin, Melvin M. *Social Stratification: The Forms and Functions of Inequality.* Englewood Cliffs, N.J.: Prentice-Hall, 1967.

Warner, W. Lloyd and Paul S. Lunt. *The Social Life of a Modern Community.* New Haven: Yale University Press, 1941.

Wesolowski, W. "Some Notes on the Functional Theory of Stratification," in Reinhard Bendix and Seymour M. Lipset, eds., *Class, Status, and Power.* 2nd ed. New York: Free Press, 1966, pp. 64–69.

Chapter VII: Functionalism and Systems Analysis

Functionalism

Almond, Gabriel A., ed. *The Politics of Developing Areas.* Princeton: Princeton University Press, 1960.

Almond, Gabriel A., and G. Bingham Powell, Jr. *Comparative Politics: A Developmental Approach.* Boston: Little, Brown, 1966.

Cancian, Francesca M. "Varieties of Functional Analysis," in *The International Encyclopedia of the Social Sciences.* New York: Macmillan and Free Press, 1968. Vol. 6, pp. 29–43.

Coser, Lewis. *The Functions of Social Conflict.* New York: Free Press, 1956.

Dahrendorf, Ralf. "Out of Utopia: Toward a Reorientation of Sociological Analysis." *American Journal of Sociology* 64 (1958):115–27.

David, Kingsley. "The Myth of Functional Analysis as a Special Method in Sociology and Anthropology." *American Sociological Review* 24 (1959):757–72.

Deutsch, Karl. "Integration and the Social System: Implications of Functional Analysis," in Philip E. Jacob and James V. Toscano, eds., *The Integration of Political Communities.* New York: Lippincott, 1964, pp. 179–208.

Flanigan, William, and Edwin Fogelman, "Functional Analysis," in James C. Charlesworth, ed., *Contemporary Political Analysis.* New York: Free Press, 1967, pp. 72–85.

Gregor, A. James. "Political Science and the Uses of Functional Analysis." *American Political Science Review* 52 (1968):425–39.

Hempel, Carl G. "The Logic of Functional Analysis," in Llewellyn Gross, ed., *Symposium on Sociological Theory.* Evanston, Ill.: Row, Peterson, 1959, pp. 271–307.

Kaplan, Harold. "The Parsonian Image of Social Structure and Its Relevance for Political Science." *Journal of Politics* 30 (1968):883–909.

Levy, Marion J., Jr. "Functional Analysis," in *The International Encyclopedia of the Social Sciences.* New York: Macmillan and Free Press, 1968. Vol. 6, pp. 21–29.

———. *Modernization and the Structure of Societies.* Princeton: Princeton University Press, 1966.

———. "Some Aspects of 'Structural-Functional' Analysis and Political Science," in Roland Young, ed., *Approaches to the Study of Politics.* Evanston, Ill.: Northwestern University Press, 1958, pp. 52–66.

———. *The Structure of Society.* Princeton: Princeton University Press, 1952.

Merton, Robert K. *Social Theory and Social Structure.* Rev. ed. New York: Free Press, 1957, pp. 19–84.

Mandelbaum, Maurice, "Functionalism in Social Anthropology," in Sidney Morgenbesser et al., eds., *Philosophy, Science, and Method.* New York: St. Martin's Press, 1969, pp. 306–32.

Parsons, Talcott. *The Social System,* New York: Free Press, 1951.

Rothman, Stanley. "Functionalism and Its Critics: An Analysis of the Writings of Gabriel Almond." *Political Science Reviewer* 1 (1971):236–76.

Van den Berghe, Pierre L. "Dialectic and Functionalism: Toward a Theoretical Synthesis." *American Sociological Review* 28 (1963):695–705.

Young, Oran. *Systems of Political Science,* Englewood Cliffs, N.J.: Prentice-Hall, 1968, pp. 27–37.

Systems Analysis

Bertalanffy, Ludwig von. *General System Theory.* New York: Braziller, 1968.

Deutsch, Karl. *The Nerves of Government: Models of Political Communication and Control.* New York: Free Press, 1963.

Easton, David. *A Framework for Political Analysis.* Englewood Cliffs, N.J.: Prentice-Hall, 1965.

———. *The Political System,* New York: Knopf, 1953.

———. *A Systems Analysis of Political Life,* New York: John Wiley and Sons, 1965.

Kaplan, Morton A. *System and Process in International Relations.* New York: John Wiley and Sons, 1957.

———. "Systems Theory," in James C. Charlesworth, ed., *Contemporary Political Analysis.* New York: Free Press, 1967, pp. 150–63.

Miller, Eugene F. "David Easton's Political Theory." *Political Science Reviewer* 1 (1971):184–235.

Rosecrance, Richard. *Action and Reaction in World Politics.* Boston: Little, Brown, 1963.

Spiro, Herbert. "An Evaluation of Systems Theory," in James C. Charlesworth, ed., *Contemporary Political Analysis.* New York: Free Press, 1967, pp. 164–74.

Young, Oran. *Systems of Political Science,* Englewood Cliffs, N.J.: Prentice-Hall, 1968, pp. 13–26; 37–48.

Index

Abduction, 26
Adams, Henry, 49
Adams, Richard N., 191
Adult socialization, 107, 113, 115
Aeschylus, 47
Africa, 6, 13, 20, 22, 43, 55, 81, 87, 169
  class concept, 177
  elite approach, 171
  group structures, 125
  modernity, 63
  new nations, 110-13
  power in class analysis, 191
Almond, Gabriel, 15, 40, 52, 54, 68, 71-73, 87-93 *passim,* 96, 97, 103, 106, 114, 118, 121, 139, 208, 209, 212-14, 217-18, 228, 230, 231, 238
  comparative political systems, 85-86
  group scheme, 122-125 *passim*
  The Politics of the Developing Areas, 99
American Political Science Association, 4, 8, 17
Ancient Regime, The, 146
Anomie, 49
Anomic interest groups, 123
Anthropology, 18, 85, 86, 129, 170, 204, 205
Apathy, 209-210
Appalachian region, political socialization, 105, 108-9
Application of theory, 34, 37
Approach and theory, 23, 24, 25
Apter, David E., 15, 40, 53, 238
Area studies, 19
Aristotle, 7, 45, 150
Asia, 5, 6, 13, 20, 43, 55, 81, 169
  class analysis, 177, 191
  elite approach, 171
  formal and informal group politics, 125-26
  Marx's views, 184-85
  modernity, 63
Asia, (continued)
  new nations, 110-12
  power, 191
Associational interest groups, 121-25 *passim*
Attitudes, 86, 92, 93, 95, 99, 104, 170, 173
Authority, 51, 88, 111, 138, 139, 171, 178, 179, 222
  class analysis, 187-90
  elites, 160, 162

Bachrach, Peter, 166
Bancroft, W. D., 236
Banfield, Edward, 102
Baratz, Morton S., 166
Beck, Carl, 159
Beer, Samuel, 92
Behavior
  and orientation, 92-96
  political, 164
Behavioralism, 15-18, 21, 30, 232, 236
Behavioral movement, and class analysis, 176
Bendix, Reinhard, 54
Bentley, Arthur F., 117-21 *passim,* 130, 134, 137, 139
Beveridge, W.I.B., 236
Binder, Leonard, 15, 57, 125, 139, 238
Biology, 19, 21, 36, 202, 216
Black, C. E., 63, 65
Bleibtreu, John N., 19
Blondel, Jean, 118, 139
Bottomore, T. B., 159, 163, 172, 194
Brazil, 126, 127, 128
Bridgman, P. W., 232
Bruner, Edward M., 111
Bullitt, William C., 103
Burgess, John, 5
Burma, 101, 102

Capabilities, in system performance, 71-73

Capacity
and demands, 79, 81
as a variable in political development, 69-75 *passim*
Calhoun, John C., 117
Cassinelli, C. W., 153
Catlin, George E. G., 12, 13
Caws, Peter, 136
Chance, in scientific investigation, 34, 35
Change
and class analysis, 195
dynamic equilibrium, 80, 82
in elite anlaysis, 171-73
and functionalism, 216
in group politics, 138
and mass media, 108-10
and political development, 57-62
in social evolution, 46-47
in society, 44, 45
and stability, 225-26
Child rearing, political socialization, 101-104, 105, 114-15
China, 12, 77, 127, 185
Civic culture, 90-91
Civic Culture, The, 94, 103, 114, 208
Class analysis
and authority, 187-90
and elite, 193-95
evaluation of, 195-99
and group, 191, 192
means of production, 183-85
and power, 190-91
and status, 186-87
Class and Class Conflict in Industrial Society, 188
Classes, and elite approach, 156-59, 172, 173
Classification, and theory building, 136, 230, 231
Classificatory scheme, 23-29 *passim,* 35
Class structures, 179-83
diagram of basic four, 181
Coleman, James, S., 68, 69, 121
Collective goods, and group approach, 129-34
Communication (*see* Mass media)
Communism, 176, 199
Community Power Structure, 167
Community study, and class analysis, 186-87
Comparative Politics: A Developmental Approach, 123, 213
Comparative politics course, in universities, *Table 1,* 14
Comte, Auguste, 8, 46
Conant, James B., 35
Concepts
and behavioralism, 15
of class, 198
theory, 22-23
Conceptual framework, 23-27 *passim,* 36
and elite analysis, 158, 162-64
in structural-functional approach, 202-8
Conceptualization
in group approach, 136
and theory building, 230, 231, 235, 238
Configurative description, 3, 9, 12
Confirmation, 34
Conflict
in class analysis, 178, 196
groups, 188-89
in system analysis, 222, 227
Conservatism, 6, 141, 155, 207, 227
Constructs concepts, 26
Contradictions, external and internal, 56
Control, in elite analysis, 171
Control relationships, 12
Converse, Phillip, 93, 100
Cooperation and communication
academic, 20
interdisciplinary, 18
scientific, 237
Cooperation and comprehension, intersocietal, 19-20
Coser, Lewis, 227
Crises, in political development, 69-71
Crotty, William J., 170
Cuba, 111
Cultural mix, 208-9
Culture, and political socialization, 98
Cutright, Phillips, 58

Dahl, Robert, 163, 167, 168
Dahrendorf, Ralf, 183, 188-90, 196, 215
Darwin, Charles, *Origin of Species,* 46
Davis, Kingsley, 211
Dawson, Richard E., 98, 109
Decisional technique in elite analysis, 165-69 *passim*
Deductive reasoning, 22, 36, 233, 236
Definitional system, 23, 25
Demands, in developmental process, 79, 81
Demands and supports, in systems analysis, 222-25
Democracy, 6, 49, 57, 208-10
Democratic systems and civic culture, 91
Dennis, Jack, 104
Depeux, George, 100
Deutsch, Karl W., 76, 238
Developmental approach, 72

Development, political
  compared with political modernization, 66-67
  defined, 57
  dialectics of, 75-83
  four stages of, 61
  historical and typological views, 68-69
  national index, 58
  problems, 69-71
  ratio between capacity and demands, 79, 81
  ten definitions of, 66
Dexter, Lewis A., 9
Dialectical analysis, 56-57, 83
Diamant, Alfred, 74, 238
Dichotomous schemes, 50-57
Differentiation, a variable in political development, 69-74 *passim*
Domhoff, G. William, 159, 163
Duhem, Pierre, 233
Durkheim, Emile, 46, 49, 51, 204
Dysfunctions, 206

Easton, David, 16, 17, 18, 23, 92, 93, 102, 104, 105, 111, 218-28 *passim*
Eckstein, Harry, 40, 118, 136, 138, 139, 238
Economic growth, stages of, 60
Economics
  and class concept, 176
  and Marx, 184, 185
Edinger, Lewis J., 159, 167
Einstein, Albert, 22, 33, 232
Eisenstadt, S. N., 74, 190
Eldersveld, Samuel J., 117
Elite analysis
  and class analysis, 191, 193-95
  classical, summary comparison of, 157
  class struggle, 146-47
  and group analysis, 160-61
  pyramid, 145
  road to theory, 161-67
  ruling class, 146
  two strata, 144
Elite culture, 88-89
Elite identification, categories of, 165
Elites, definitions of, 163
Elitist vs. pluralist, 167-70
Empirical theory, 30-33
Enlightenment, 45, 48
Environment, in systems analysis, 219, 222
Equality
  political, 76, 77, 182, 192
  as a variable in political development, 69-74 *passim*
Equilibrium, 82, 140-41, 160-61, 196, 216, 217, 226
Erikson, Erik, 101
Ethics, 7, 8
Ethology, 19
Eulau, Heinz, 36
Evolution, social, 48-50
  six premises, 46-47
Experimentation and adaptation, 21
Explanations, 39, 40, 114, 135, 138, 236
  and behavioralism, 15
  in political science, 12

Factional politics, 126-29
Fagen, Richard, 111, 115
Feedback, in systems analysis, 219, 224, 225
Feynman, Richard, 31, 32, 234
Flanigan, William, 211, 214
Fleron, Frederic J., Jr., 105
Fogelman, Edwin, 211, 214
Formal-legal approach, 3-5, 9, 12
Formal-positional technique of elite, 165-66
France, 5, 100, 101, 102, 105
Frank, A. G., 61-62
Freud, Sigmund, 103
Frey, Frederick, 159, 165
Frolich, Norman, 133-34
Function, as a word, 202
Functional analysis
  Almond's seven functional requisites, 212
  four functional imperatives, 211
  three postulates
    functional unity, 205-6
    indispensability, 207
    universal functionals, 206-7
Functionalism
  in comparative political analysis, 212-13
  conceptual framework, 202-8
  explanation and change, 215-17
  functional indispensability, 208-12
Functions
  Almond's three levels, 213-14

Generalization, 22, 23, 24, 26, 29-33, 34, 36, 37, 39, 136, 137, 164, 236
Germany, 5, 58, 103
Golembiewski, Robert T., 118, 119, 170
Governmental Process, The, 117
Great Britain, 5, 6, 90, 91, 126, 208-9
Greek philosophy, 43, 44-45
Greenstein, Fred, 99-100, 104, 105, 111
Group, definitions of, 120-121

Group analysis, 134-41
  and class approach, 191, 192
  modernization, 138-41
  relationship to elite analysis, 160-61
  and collectivities, 130-34
  formal and informal, 126-27
  four conditions of organization, 125
Group typologies, 128-29
  four kinds, 121-23
Growth, metaphor of, 44-45
Gumplowicz. Ludwig, 145, 146, 147, 156

Hagan, Charles B., 117, 136
Hagen, Everett, 101
Halpern, Manfred, 15, 74-75, 191
Hanson, Norwood, R., 34
Hawley, Claud E., 9
Heckscher, August, 17
Hegel, Georg Wilhelm Friedrich, 46
Heller, Celia S., 194, 198
Hempel, Carl G., 27, 30, 36, 204, 215, 216, 217
Heraclitus, 44, 47
Hesiod, 48
Hess, Robert D., 100, 102, 104, 105, 111
Hierarchical class structure, 180
Hill, Norman L., 6
Hirsch, Herbert, 98, 105, 108, 109, 115
Hirschman, Albert, 79
Hobbes, Thomas, 227
Horowitz, Irving Louis, 60-61
Hume, David, 48
Hunter, Floyd, 159, 167
Huntington, Samuel P., 15, 40, 66, 67, 73, 77, 78-79, 238
Hutchins, Robert M., 234
Huxley, Thomas H., 22
Hyman, Herbert, *Political Socialization,* 99, 110
Hypotheses, 15, 16, 21, 23, 24, 25, 35, 38, 40, 129, 136, 138, 178, 211, 228, 231, 238

Ideology, 81, 112, 141, 169
  latent, 92-93, 94, 96, 97
India, 88-89, 95, 97, 111, 124-25, 185
Individual, in group studies, 119
Individual concepts, 26
Inductive-deductive interaction, 36
Inductive reasoning, 22, 236
Inductive theory building in physical sciences, 232
Inequality, 61, 106, 160, 189-90, 192, 193, 196
Influence, in elite analysis, 158-63 *passim,* 167
Informal group politics, 126-29
Integration
  in functionalism, 205, 216
  in group approach, 139, 140
  horizontal and vertical, 80
Institutional interest groups, 122, 124, 125
Institutionalization, political, 75-80 *passim*
Interest groups, 120, 189
  four kinds, 121-23
Intuition, in scientific investigation, 34, 35, 236
Iran, 125, 126, 127, 128
Italy, 5, 90, 96, 102, 105, 126

Japan, 105, 126, 127, 128
Jargon, in political science, 201
Jaros, Dean, 105
Johnson, Chalmers, 204
Juridical defense, 148, 149
Jurisprudence, 8

Kant, Immanuel, 46, 47
Kaplan, Harold, 211
Kaplan, Morton, 226
Keller, Suzanne, 159, 163
Kelvin, Lord, 234
Khaldun, Ibn, 117
Klonoski, James R., 228
Kornhauser, William, 159, 163
Kahn, Thomas, 28

Lane, Robert, 92, 93
LaPalombara, Joseph, 118
Lasswell, Harold, 12, 17-18, 20, 100, 159, 162-63, 230
Latent functions, 206-207
Latham, Earl, 117, 130
Latin America, 13, 55
  class analysis, 177, 191
  elite approach, 171
  formal and informal group politics, 125-26
  power in class analysis, 191
Leibniz, Gottfried Wilhelm von, 45, 46
Leighton, Alexander, 96, 97
Lenin, Nickolai, 57
Lenski, Gerhard, 180, 182, 191, 231
Lerner, Daniel, 109, 110
LeVine, Robert, 110, 112
Levy, Marion, 63, 203, 207, 210, 214
Lewin, Kurt, 40
Lipset, Seymour Martin, 57, 159, 190
Litt, Edward, 106
Loewenstein, Karl, 13
Logic of Collective Action, The, 130, 132
Lorenz, Konrad, 19
Lucretius, 47
Lynd, Robert and Helen, 186

Machiavelli, 7, 150
MacIntyre, Alasdair, 95
McLuhan, Marshall, 109
Madison, James, 7, 117
Maine, Sir Henry, 46, 49, 51, 54
Malinowski, Bronislaw, 204, 205, 206, 207, 216
Manifest functions, 206
Marshall, T. H., 175
Marx, Karl, 46, 47, 60, 145, 146-47, 156, 175, 176, 183-84, 188, 197, 198, 199
Mass culture, 88-89
Masses, the, 78, 155, 160, 172-3, 194
Mass media, 108, 109-10, 114
Matthews, Donald, 107
Meehan, Eugene, 31
Merriam, Charles E., 12
Merton, Robert, 202, 203, 205, 206, 210, 214
Methodological insensitivity, 8-9
Mexico, 90, 94, 95, 127
Michels, Robert, 144-48 *passim,* 157, 158, 159
  the oligarchy, 153-156
Middle East, 6, 13, 20, 21
  class concept, 177, 185
  elite approach, 171
  formal and informal group politics, 125-26
  process of change, 110
Military elite, 149, 150
Mill, John Stuart, 8
Miller, Eugene, 226
Mills, C. Wright, 159, 163, 168, 186, 187
Mind and Society, The, 148
Models, 23, 24, 27-29, 35, 36
Modernity of Tradition, The, 50
Modernization
  definitions of, 63
  in elite analysis, 170-73
  image, 64
  phases of, 65
  social change, 15
  three dimensions of
    attitudinal, 63, 67
    organizational, 63, 67
    technological, 63, 64, 67
  types of changing group patterns, 139
Modern polity, characteristics of, 68
Modification, type of change, 75, 81-82, 115, 138-41, 170-72
Montesquieu, 7, 150
Moore, Barrington, 34
Moral philosophy, 7, 8
Morgenthau, Hans J., 17
Mosca, Gaetana, 7, 144-48 *passim,* 151-59 *passim,* 165, 168
Mosca, Gaetana, (continued)
    political class, 148-51, 153, 158

Nation building, process of, 89
Neubauer, Deane, 59
New Left movement, 103
New nations, 43, 110-13
Newton, Sir Isaac, 232
Nicolle, Charles, 236
Nisbet, Robert, *Social Change and History,* 44, 46, 47, 48
Nkrumah, Kwame, 75
Nonassociational interest groups, 122, 123-24, 125, 128-29
Nondecision-making process, 166
Nonstratified universe, in group approach, 160
Nontheoretical emphasis on study, 7-8
Non-Western societies, 5, 9, 15, 49, 52, 56, 62, 82, 125, 135, 166, 169, 179
Normative political theory, 7, 9, 30

Observable concepts, 26
Observational technique of elite analysis, 165
Observations, 30, 34, 36
Oligarchy, 153-56
Olson, Mancur, Jr., 118, 119, 130-134, 137
Oppenheimer, J. Robert, 236
Oppenheimer, Joe A., 133-34
Organization
  of groups, 124-25
  and oligarchy, 153-54, 156
Organski, F. K., 61
Orientation
  affective, cognitive, and evaluative, 86-87, 88, 96-97
  and behavior, 92-96, 99
    cross-cultural methodology, 94-96
  to culture, 86-91 *passim*
  in elite analysis, 154, 170, 173
  political socialization, 98
Ossowski, Stanislaw, 183

Paley, William, 7
Paradigm, 23, 24, 28, 202
Pareto, Vilfredo, 7, 144-48 *passim,* 155-59 *passim,* 165, 168
  the governing elite, 151-53
Parmenides, 44
Parochialism, 5-6, 9, 87-91 *passim*
Parry, Geraint, 159, 163, 168
Parsons, Talcott, 52, 54, 86, 210-11, 214, 216, 231

Participant political culture, 88, 89, 90, 91
Participation, in the political system, 76-80, 171
Philosophy of science, 24
Physical sciences, 232-33
Physics, 44-45, 46, 136, 232, 233, 234
Physis, 44-47
Plato, 44, 48
Pluralism, 209-10
Pluralist vs. elitist, 167-70
  and group approach, 140
Poincare, Henri, 236
Polarities in society (*see* Societies)
Political behavior, 115
Political class, 148-51
Political science courses, comparative growth, *Figure 1,* 11
Political community, 89
Political culture
  descriptions of, 85
  evaluation, 113-16
  nesting system, 97
  three types, 87-88
Political Culture and Political Development, 113
Political decay, 73, 78, 80
Political elites, 164
  definition, 144
Political formula, 148, 151, 155, 158-59
Political identity, 96-98
Political objects, three classes of, 87
Political Parties, 148, 153, 154, 155, 156
Political party systems, 58, 68, 95
Political philosophy, 7
Political Systems, The, 218
Political systems, four characteristics, 212
Politics of Developing Areas, 99, 212
Pollock, Sir Frederick, 8
Positional techniques, 169
Popper, Karl, 26, 233
Powell, G. Bingham, Jr., 71-73, 121, 123, 213
Power, 12, 135, 138-39, 148, 153, 178-79, 182
  and class analysis, 189-91
  and community, 170
  and elite analysis, 158-69 *passim*
Prewitt, Kenneth, 98, 109
Probabilistic generalizations, 31-33
Problemation, 33-34, 136
Process, input and output, 87-88
Process of Government, The, 117
Prometheus, 48
Psychological condition, 47, 48
Pye, Lucian W., 15, 51, 56, 66, 69, 71, 86, 92, 101, 113, 139
Pyramidal class structure, 179
Radcliffe-Brown, A. R., 204, 205
Reciprocal class structure, 182
Reflections of a Physicist, 232
Reform, and change, in elite approach, 172
Reissman, Leonard, 190-91
Religious elite, 149
Reputational technique in elite analysis, 165-69 *passim*
Research
  and class analysis, 199
  cross cultural, 94-96, 105
  and elite analysis, 164
  empirical methods of, 15
  political, 8-9
  and socialization, 114-15
Revolution, 76, 77, 82, 152, 184, 195, 197, 198
Riggs, Fred W., 15, 40, 53, 118, 125
Role socialization, 107
Rose, Arnold M., 159
Rose, Richard, 106
Rostow, W. W., 60-61
Rousseau, Jean Jacques, 46, 48
Rudner, Richard, 27
Rudolph, Lloyd and Suzanne, 50, 56
Ruling Class, The, 147, 150
Ruling elites, 164
Russia, 5, 185
Rustow, Dankwart A., 15, 19, 62-68 *passim,* 165

St. Augustine, 47, 48
Saint-Simon, Henri Comte de, 145, 147, 156
Sartori, Giovanni, 230, 232, 234, 235
Schools, in political socialization, 104-107
Schumpeter, Joseph, 175
Science of politics, 7, 8
Scientific method (theory building), 33
Searing, Donald D., 159, 167
Secularization, 73
Sentiments, 98
  primordial, 111, 112
  three elements of, 96-97
Sereno, Renzo, 156
Sherrill, Kenneth, 208, 209
Shils, Edward, 86
Sigel, Roberta, 108
Simmel, Georg, 227
Singer, David, 18
Smith, Adam, 46, 175
Social force, 148
Socialism, 199
Socialization, political, 98
  adult, 107
  family, 100-104

Socialization, (continued)
  the school, 104-107
Social mobilization, 76, 78
Social Science Research Council (SSRC), Committee on Comparative Politics, 68, 69, 73
Social sciences, 12, 13, 18
Social type, 148, 149
Societies, types of polarities
  agricultural and industrial, 53-54
  folk and urban, 50
  Gemainschaft and Gesellschaft, 51
  mechanical & organic, 51
  pattern variable, 52
  primitive and civilized, 51
  rural and urban, 55
  sacred and secular, 53
  static and dynamic, 51
  traditional and modern, 50, 54, 55
  traditional and rational, 51
Society, and coercion theory, 178-79
Sociology, 18, 186, 211
Somit, Albert, 10
Sorokin, Pitrim, 175
Spencer, Henry Russell, 3
Spencer, Herbert, 8, 46, 47
Spiro, Herbert, 226, 227
Stability, in systems analysis, 225-26, 227
Status, 158, 163, 186-87
Stinchcombe, Arthur, 26
Stratification
  in class approach, 178, 188, 192, 193
  and power, 190
  from society, 145, 146-47
  vertical, 160
Structural-functional approach, 201-17
Subject political culture, 87-91 *passim*
Support, three levels in systems analysis, 223
Sutton, F. X., 53
Systems analysis
  in comparative political study, 218-22
    four premises, 218-19
  demands and supports, 222-25
  stability and change, 225-26
System performance, capabilities, 71-72

Taine, Hippolyte, 145, 146, 147, 156
Tanenhaus, Joseph, 10
Taxonomy, 23, 24, 27-29, 36, 129, 136, 230
Technology, relationship to man, 63
Tendency statements, 31, 32
Theory, definition of, 24, 30
Theory-building
  eight roles of, 37-40
  process of, 33-37
Third World systems, 13, 43, 55-62 *passim*, 71, 177, 179
Tocqueville, Alexis de, 7, 49, 207
Tönnies, Ferdinand, 49, 51
Torney, Judith V., 100
Toward a General Theory of Action, 86
Traditional approach to comparative politics, six characteristics, 2-10
Traditional modern societies, 50-57
Transformation, type of change, 74-75, 81-82, 115, 141, 170-172, 197-98, 230
Truman, David B., 117, 119, 120, 121, 130, 139
Typology, 23, 24, 27-29, 35, 36, 230

Underdevelopment, 61-62
Unilinear development, 59-60, 61
United States, 5, 20 21, 49, 90, 91, 95, 100, 112, 113, 124, 126, 175-77, 208, 209
United States Senate and political culture, 107
Universal concepts, 26
Urbanization, 112

Values, 93, 104, 108, 113, 221
Variables, in systems analysis, 225
Veblen, Thorstein, 175
Verba, Sidney, 71, 86-92 *passim*, 96, 97, 103, 106, 113, 114, 208, 209, 231

Ward, Robert, 67, 68
Warner, W. Lloyd, "Yankee City," 186-87
Weber, Max, 7, 51, 54, 175, 190
Weiner, Myron, 88, 118, 125
Welsh, William A., 170
Wesolowski, W., 188
Whitehead, Alfred North, 21
Who Governs, 167-68
Wilson, Woodrow, 4, 103
Wittfogel, Karl, 185
Wolin, Sheldon, 17
Women, political roles in new nations, 111-12
World Politics and Personal Insecurity, 159
Wylie, Lawrence, 102

Young, Oran R., 118, 133-34, 136, 137, 227

Zetterberg, Hans L., 190